Black Mexico

Other titles in the Diálogos series available from the University of New Mexico Press:

Independence in Spanish America: Civil Wars, Revolutions, and Underdevelopment (revised edition)
—Jay Kinsbruner

Heroes on Horseback: A Life and Times of the Last Gaucho Caudillos
—John Charles Chasteen

The Life and Death of Carolina Maria de Jesus
—Robert M. Levine and José Carlos Sebe Bom Meihy

¡Que vivan los tamales! Food and the Making of Mexican Identity
—Jeffrey M. Pilcher

The Faces of Honor: Sex, Shame, and Violence in Colonial Latin America
—Edited by Lyman L. Johnson and Sonya Lipsett-Rivera

The Century of U.S. Capitalism in Latin America—Thomas F. O'Brien

Tangled Destinies: Latin America and the United States
—Don Coerver and Linda Hall

Everyday Life and Politics in Nineteenth Century Mexico: Men, Women, and War
—Mark Wasserman

Lives of the Bigamists: Marriage, Family, and Community in Colonial Mexico
—Richard Boyer

Andean Worlds: Indigenous History, Culture, and Consciousness Under Spanish Rule, 1532–1825
—Kenneth J. Andrien

The Mexican Revolution, 1910–1940—Michael J. Gonzales

Quito 1599: City and Colony in Transition—Kris Lane

A Pest in the Land: New World Epidemics in a Global Perspective
—Suzanne Austin Alchon

The Silver King: The Remarkable Life of the Count of Regla in Colonial Mexico
—Edith Boorstein Couturier

National Rhythms, African Roots: The Deep History of Latin American Popular Dance
—John Charles Chasteen

The Great Festivals of Colonial Mexico City: Performing Power and Identity
—Linda A. Curcio-Nagy

The Souls of Purgatory: The Spiritual Diary of a Seventeenth-Century Afro-Peruvian Mystic, Ursula de Jesús
—Nancy E. van Deusen

Dutra's World: Wealth and Family in Nineteenth-Century Rio de Janeiro
—Zephyr L. Frank

Death, Dismemberment, and Memory: Body Politics in Latin America
—Edited by Lyman L. Johnson

Plaza of Sacrifices: Gender, Power, and Terror in 1968 Mexico
—Elaine Carey

*Women in the Crucible of Conquest:
The Gendered Genesis of Spanish American Society, 1500–1600*
—Karen Vieira Powers

Beyond Black and Red: African-Native Relations in Colonial Latin America
—Edited by Matthew Restall

Mexico OtherWise: Modern Mexico in the Eyes of Foreign Observers
—Edited and translated by Jürgen Buchenau

Local Religion in Colonial Mexico
—Edited by Martin Austin Nesvig

Malintzin's Choices: An Indian Woman in the Conquest of Mexico
—Camilla Townsend

From Slavery to Freedom in Brazil: Bahia, 1835–1900
—Dale Torston Graden

Slaves, Subjects, and Subversives: Blacks in Colonial Latin America
—Edited by Jane G. Landers and Barry M. Robinson

Private Passions and Public Sins: Men and Women in Seventeenth-Century Lima
—María Emma Mannarelli

*Making the Americas: The United States and Latin America
from the Age of Revolutions to the Era of Globalization*
—Thomas F. O'Brien

*Remembering a Massacre in El Salvador: The Insurrection of 1932,
Roque Dalton, and the Politics of Historical Memory*
—Héctor Lindo-Fuentes, Erik Ching, and Rafael A. Lara-Martínez

Raising an Empire: Children in Early Modern Iberia and Colonial Latin America
—Ondina E. González and Bianca Premo

*Christians, Blasphemers, and Witches:
Afro-Mexican Rituals in the Seventeenth Century*
—Joan Cameron Bristol

Art and Architecture of Viceregal Latin America, 1521–1821
—Kelly Donahue-Wallace

Rethinking Jewish-Latin Americans
—Edited by Jeffrey Lesser and Raanan Rein

True Stories of Crime in Modern Mexico
—Edited by Robert Buffington and Pablo Piccato

Aftershocks: Earthquakes and Popular Politics in Latin America
—Edited by Jürgen Buchenau and Lyman L. Johnson

SERIES ADVISORY EDITOR:
LYMAN L. JOHNSON,
UNIVERSITY OF NORTH CAROLINA AT CHARLOTTE

Black Mexico

Race and Society from Colonial to Modern Times

Edited by
BEN VINSON III
and
MATTHEW RESTALL

University of New Mexico Press ✢ Albuquerque

© 2009 by the University of New Mexico Press
All rights reserved. Published 2009
Printed in the United States of America
14 13 12 11 10 09   1 2 3 4 5 6

LIBRARY OF CONGRESS CATALOGING-IN-PUBLICATION DATA

Black Mexico : race and society from colonial to modern times /
edited by Ben Vinson III and Matthew Restall.
p. cm. — (Diálogos)
Includes bibliographical references and index.
ISBN 978-0-8263-4701-5 (pbk. : alk. paper)
1. Blacks—Mexico—History. 2. Blacks—Mexico—Social conditions.
3. Blacks—Race identity—Mexico. 4. Mexico—Race relations.
5. Mexico—History—Spanish colony, 1540–1810.
6. Mexico—History—1810– I. Vinson, Ben, III. II. Restall, Matthew, 1964–
F1392.B55B55 2009
972'.00496—dc22
2009020457

DESIGN AND LAYOUT: MELISSA TANDYSH
Composed in 10/13.5 Janson Text Lt Std
Display type is Bernhard Modern Std

For Allyson and Yolanda, Lucy and Helen

Contents

Illustrations
xi

Acknowledgments
xiii

Introduction: Black Mexico and the Historical Discipline
BEN VINSON III
1

Section I: Entering the Colonial World

Slave Rebellion and Liberty in Colonial Mexico
FRANK "TREY" PROCTOR III
21

Negotiating Two Worlds: The Free-Black Experience
in Guerrero's Tierra Caliente
ANDREW B. FISHER
51

Black Aliens and Black Natives in
New Spain's Indigenous Communities
PAT CARROLL
72

From Dawn 'til Dusk: Black Labor in Late Colonial Mexico
BEN VINSON III
96

Colonial Middle Men?
Mulatto Identity in New Spain's Confraternities
NICOLE VON GERMETEN
136

Potions and Perils: Love-Magic in Seventeenth-Century
Afro-Mexico and Afro-Yucatan
JOAN BRISTOL AND MATTHEW RESTALL
155

Section II: Engaging Modernity

"Afro" Mexico in Black, White, and Indian:
An Anthropologist Reflects on Fieldwork
LAURA A. LEWIS
183

My Blackness and Theirs: Viewing Mexican Blackness Up Close
BOBBY VAUGHN
209

The Thorntons: Saga of an Afro-Mexican Family
ALVA MOORE STEVENSON
220

The Need to Recognize Afro-Mexicans as an Ethnic Group
JEAN-PHILIBERT MOBWA MOBWA N'DJOLI
224

Glossary
233

Bibliography
241

Contributors
266

Index
269

Illustrations

MAPS

General Map of New Spain Sites.		xvi–xvii
Map 5.1	Mexico's provinces.	104
Map 5.2	Mexico's cities.	104
Map 5.3	Mexico City and *cuarteles* 1, 20, and 23.	109

FIGURES

Figure 2.1	Mexico City's Plaza Mayor.	22
Figure 2.2	Plan of Nuestra Señora de Guadalupe de los Negros de Amapa.	32
Figure 6.1	Eighteenth-century expression of Mexican religious piety.	151
Figure 7.1	A black slave or domestic servant preparing chocolate in the kitchen of a Spanish household.	164
Figure 7.2	A Spanish-American salamander, likely from South America, similar to that allegedly used by Leonor de Isla to bewitch her lover.	165
Figure 8.1	San Nicolás, central plaza.	185

Figure 8.2	Many migrant San Nicoladenses live in this apartment complex in Winston-Salem.	185
Figure 8.3	La América and Los Apaches.	189
Figure 8.4	Young extended (joint) "Indian-moreno" family from San Nicolás in Winston-Salem.	191
Figure 9.1	Replica of traditional Costa Chica *redondo* dwelling.	211
Figure 9.2	Mother and youngest child, Costa Chica region, Oaxaca.	213
Figure 9.3	Teenager, Costa Chica region, Oaxaca.	214
Figure 9.4	Child relaxing, Costa Chica region, Oaxaca.	216
Figure 9.5	Woman and a neighborhood child, Costa Chica region, Oaxaca.	217

TABLES

Table 5.1	Free-Colored Labor in Late Colonial Mexico, 1780–1794	102
Table 5.2	Free-Colored Workforce in Three *Cuarteles* of Mexico City, 1790	112
Table 5.3	Free-Colored Workforce in Puebla, 1794	116
Table 5.4	Free-Colored Workforce in Guanajuato, 1792	122
Table 5.5	Free-Colored Workforce in Querétaro, 1790	122
Table 7.1	The Protagonists in the Casanova-Maldonado Love-Magic Case (Mérida, Yucatan, 1670s)	157
Table 7.2	Love-Potion Ingredients Used in Seventeenth-Century Mexico and Yucatan	162

ACKNOWLEDGMENTS

This book has been a long time in the making and the editors would like to thank the community of scholars, activists, and intellectuals who have made the study of Black Mexico their lives' work. All of the authors in this volume would also like to collectively acknowledge the modern Afro-Mexican communities that continue to thrive in various regions of Mexico and, more recently, the United States.

A book such as this could not have been possible without substantial support from many institutions and individuals. The Africana Research Center at Penn State University provided the funding that made the "New Directions in North American Scholarship on Afro-Mexico" conference possible in 2004. The marvelous presentations that were first presented there have formed the nucleus of this book. Several papers from the conference have not been included in this volume, but have since appeared (or are in preparation) as manuscripts and articles. We certainly hope that the intellectual work of synthesis that began at that event will continue to shape and inform future work in the field.

Financial support for the preparation of this manuscript was also provided by a National Endowment for the Humanities Fellowship at the National Humanities Center in North Carolina. The leave time offered by the fellowship proved crucial in the editorial process. Indeed, the book could not have been completed in a timely fashion without it. Additionally, the tireless efforts of our wonderful editorial assistant, Andrew Devereux (a graduate student in the History Department at Johns Hopkins University), was instrumental in ensuring the manuscript was properly prepared for final submission to the press. We thank him tremendously for the time he spent working with us (as a break from his dissertation!). Of course, this book would not have been possible without the support and editorial acumen of the Diálogos series editor, Lyman Johnson. A very special thanks to him.

General Map of New Spain Sites. Map drawn by Séverine Rebourcet.

Introduction

Black Mexico and the Historical Discipline

BEN VINSON III

❦

⁜ EXAMINING ISSUES OF RACE IN LATIN AMERICA HAS ALWAYS BEEN a rather slippery enterprise given the multiplicity of racial categories that have existed in the region, the ways racial identities have been historically embraced and denied over the past few centuries, and the political stakes involved in claiming them. The premium placed upon racial mixture has only added to the task, making race so malleable that its very utility and meaning has been subject to question. Throughout the nineteenth, twentieth, and early twenty-first centuries, and even during moments in the colonial period, some questions arise: To what extent has blackness or even mulatto identities really mattered when one considers that racial mixture can distort the boundaries of these identities? How can whiteness or indigenous identities be meaningfully mobilized when the preponderance of the region's populations can claim these heritages through hybrid ancestries? And finally, because race is so ideologically contested, should concerns over nationalism, national identity, class consciousness, and even ethnic identity be deemed more important toward understanding the social relations of the region?

In various forms, these have been many of the classic questions that have faced students and scholars of Latin American race relations for decades.[1] Given differing racial landscapes and demographics, some countries have tackled them more pointedly than others. Regional differences have also allowed blackness to matter more in certain places. It is no surprise that Brazil and Cuba, with larger modern black populations, have been centerpieces of research into the Afro–Latin American condition, in contrast to Chile and Uruguay.

It is not that black populations were merely incidental to the development of nations where they have not been as deeply discussed (although in some cases they were). Rather, their contributions have often been considered more historical, relegated to the colonial era or the early national period. In numerous cases, the independence era of Latin America was supposed to represent a racial watershed, signaling a time when the lingering remnants of the caste-like hierarchies of the colonial world were eliminated in the heat of war and in the efforts to construct a national peace. In this context, concentrating too heavily upon issues of race, discrimination, and race-based claims to citizenship could be interpreted as antithetical to the health of the body politic. By the same token, invocations of blackness received particular ire in some circles as debates brewed in the press, in intellectual forums, and in policy arenas as to the true worth of blacks in the evolution of successful nations. Nineteenth-century pseudoscientific racist theories, steeped in positivist philosophies, deemed some races naturally "inferior," and therefore detrimental to national ambitions of economic and political stability, health, and well-being. As scores of emergent Latin American nations anxiously sought these goals, one can see why black populations, among others, have not always received sustained, focused attention. In fact, the very complexities involved in talking about race have led to difficulties in openly and frankly acknowledging blackness.

Over the past several decades, however, important hemispheric-wide conversations have taken place surrounding the role of blacks in both contemporary and historical contexts, accompanied by a surge in publications and conferences on related themes. The impetus has come from a number of quarters. A rise in identity politics has been enabled by a score of global incidents, including the decolonization movement in Africa, the U.S. Civil Rights movement, escalating indigenous social movements within Latin America, international forums on racism, discrimination, and xenophobia (such as the 2001 Durban conference), and the evolution of neoliberal politics that has created distinct opportunities for racial and ethnic interest groups. Additionally, new and increasingly accessible technologies have produced more prospects for transnational networking that have in turn generated collaborations between race-based interest groups within Latin America. Meanwhile, on the scholarly front, historians have reached deeper into exploring questions of social and cultural history, with a penchant for examining systems of slavery, social structures, and race relations. Even Latin American nations that have been traditionally less preoccupied with race-based inquiries have generated ever-richer, empirical social histories that have included blacks in the broader historical narrative.[2]

Black Mexico comes at a particular historical juncture in which Mexico and Mexicanists are caught midstream in these discussions. This book is a contribution to a growing historiography that, until very recently, could not be categorized as forming a particular school of thought or intellectual inquiry. Looking back on the growth of the field, we discover that, in many ways, the discussion of blacks in Mexico has tended to follow the trajectory of the political development of the nation. Writings on Afro-Mexicans can be largely grouped into three periods: (1) Mexico's colonial and independence era (1521–1821); (2) the prerevolutionary period (1822–1910); and (3) the postrevolutionary period (1921–present).

In the colonial period, outside of the abundant documentation that can still be found in the archives, very few published works were written that concentrated directly upon blacks. What survives comes mainly from travelers' accounts, narrative renditions of the conquest of Mexico, and political treatises.[3] Although many of these writings depict blacks and mulattos negatively, what is interesting is that, nonetheless, Afro-Mexicans appear as embedded figures in colonial life. Especially in political treatises, a tight association can be made between blacks and the colony's more amorphous "plebeian" class.[4]

During the prerevolutionary period, as assessments were being made regarding the value of blacks to the emerging nation, Afro-Mexicans began appearing in historical writings in more central ways. Some intellectuals discovered a certain freedom in being able to appropriate the black image to advance their specific political agendas. The writings of Vicente Riva Palacio provide a good example. One of the central figures behind the popularization of a literary genre known as the "historical novel," Riva Palacio's archival research brought to life the struggles of black runaway slaves, as well as free blacks that pushed for rights in colonial society. Through stories such as those found in *El libro rojo* and *Los trienta y tres negros*, the plight of these blacks served as a didactic tool, helping the Mexican readership of the mid-nineteenth century confront issues of their own oppression at the hands of foreign powers (France and the United States).[5] These stories also helped Mexicans better understand the intricacies of homegrown class inequity. Embedded distantly and comfortably in the early colonial period, the experience of blacks, as recounted by Riva Palacio, offered poignant social commentary in ways that felt safe to a divided nation. Moreover, because blacks were viewed ambivalently, both as a part and not a part of the nation, their experiences possessed an added voyeuristic effect.

The prerevolutionary era also produced a very different type of writing. Sprawled across the pages of Mexico's newspapers and journals were articles inspired by social Darwinist theories debating the merit of blacks to the nation. Some upheld the view that blacks were a stain on progress, but others heralded blacks as a possible solution to some of Mexico's nagging economic woes. Especially in backwater regions where the climate was deemed too inhospitable to attract coveted white immigrants, foreign blacks were encouraged to settle as colonists. Some believed that through their labor they might be able to perform the same economic miracles they did for the U.S. South, or for Cuba's sugar plantations. As intellectuals argued over black "worth," they substantiated some of their claims with historical evidence.[6]

Debates about the worth of blacks took a slightly different course in the context of the Mexican Revolution. Indeed, the cultural landscape produced by this seminal event had a lasting effect on Afro-Mexican historiography. After the revolution, Mexico placed a heightened emphasis on the hybrid nature of its population to demonstrate the strength of its national character. But a certain type of hybrid phenotype was praised—the *mestizo*, or mixture of white and Indian.[7] Blacks were literally written out of the national narrative. Excluding blacks from the national image was a process that was long in the making but, arguably, it was in the 1920s that the process had some of its strongest influences.

Regardless, a number of key historical works appeared that continued to valorize or at least mention blacks. Alfonso Toro was among those who postulated that, in order to better understand the temperament of the Mexican citizenry, one needed a better grasp of the long-term contributions of Afro-Mexicans. Citing the writings of colonial missionaries, as well as episodes of slave rebellion and resistance, Toro recounted that the black population had been extremely bellicose in New Spain. As blacks became assimilated into the general population, he believed that they slowly transmitted their belligerent behavioral qualities into the character of the broader citizen body. As a result, the Mexican people's propensity for revolt, which had been witnessed during the Mexican Revolution, the struggle for independence, and the tumultuous nineteenth century, could be partly attributed to the nation's Afro-Mexican heritage.[8]

While a string of books and articles were written in the 1920s and 1930s on Afro-Mexicans, it was in the 1940s that the so-called birth of Afro-Mexican historical studies began. The credit is usually given to the work of Gonzalo Aguirre Beltrán, whose *La población negra de México* (1946) has become the cornerstone of the field.[9] Having been trained by Melville Herskovits at Northwestern University, Aguirre Beltrán's book was the first to systematically employ a methodology for examining the African roots of Mexico's population. His book also offered a sweeping demographic analysis of the colonial black population, stressing the extent to which blacks could be found throughout New Spain. One of the book's main arguments took its cue from the Mexican Revolution. As revisionist as it was in giving space to Afro-Mexicans in the nation's history, *La población negra* emphasized assimilation and hybridity, noting that the colonial Mexican caste system and its abolition during the independence era created superb circumstances for racial mixture. Apart from a few isolated regional pockets, Aguirre Beltrán wrote that Afro-Mexicans had eagerly and spontaneously blended into the broader national population by the early years of independence.

It is important to stress that Aguirre Beltrán's work, while pioneering, was not written in isolation. German Latorre (1920) had already started the demographic work that proved foundational to the writings of Aguirre Beltrán. Carlos Basauri's (1943) ethnographic study of Mexico's black populations proved influential to Aguirre Beltrán's later writings. Lastly, Aguirre Beltrán's decision to study Afro-Mexicans was not an idea he conceived of wholly himself. Rather, he appears to have been prodded into the project upon the suggestion of Manuel Gamio, one of the leading intellectual figures of Mexico's revolutionary period.[10]

The era of scholarship on Afro-Mexicans that stretched through the 1940s, 1950s, and early 1960s can be categorized as one of gradual internationalization, as more scholars from outside of Mexico began paying closer attention to the Mexican case. Aguirre Beltrán's study came at a particularly opportune time in this regard. It was published almost at the same time as Frank Tannenbaum's *Slave and Citizen* (1946), which opened a series of debates that launched the comparative slavery school.[11] Through an increasingly internationalized understanding of slave systems, scholars began trying to uncover the roots of the "negro problem" that had so beleaguered the United States, but which seemed largely resolved in Latin American societies. Tannenbaum's thesis, that Latin American slavery was qualitatively different than that practiced in North America and the British colonies, sent scores of scholars scurrying to prove (or disprove) his points. Aguirre Beltrán's book, although engaged in conversation with a different historiography, emerged in the context of the Tannenbaum debate as an important tome on Mexican slavery and Latin American race relations, offering some support to the idealized, benign portrait of Latin American slave systems. The book was positioned alongside other important classics that were written by nationalistically oriented scholars who sought to affirm Latin American race mixture, such as Gilberto Freyre in Brazil and, to a lesser extent, Fernando Ortiz in Cuba.[12] The ramifications of these early investigations into the condition of race within individual Latin American countries have been wide reaching, particularly in the past few decades, as the African Diaspora research paradigm has been affecting worldwide scholarship on the black presence.

The late 1950s and early 1960s witnessed another important development in Latin American historiography that affected Mexico. Inquiries into the hierarchical structure of colonial society generated great interest in the Mexican caste system. A new generation of scholars began to wonder if the importance of class differences in the colonial period outweighed the power of race/caste and estate structures in the articulation of social relations. The questions generated the caste vs. class debate, whose rich historiography has contributed greatly to our understanding of black colonial life.[13] Meanwhile, Phillip Curtin's *The Slave Trade, A Census* (1969) reinvigorated the field of comparative slavery studies by offering a panoramic overview of slave demography.[14] To test his numbers, scholars began the hard work of advancing case studies, of which Mexico became a part.[15]

The internationalization of scholarship on Afro-Mexico after the 1950s essentially helped establish a three-track research system. On one track, scholars have pursued the research path initially set forth by

Aguirre Beltrán in seeking to understand how blackness fits into the larger, postrevolutionary national discourse of *mestizaje* (racial mixture). These studies have become quite sophisticated in their analysis, postulating new visions of hybridity that push and test mestizaje. In making use of the literature on transculturation and syncretism, and by carefully periodizing the influences of black populations from the colonial period into modern times, this work is showing the spaces for the survival and transformation of African cultures. On another track, scholars have examined the Mexican case to better understand processes of slavery, freedom, and blackness, but within a broader global context. The third track has seen scholars working toward understanding the intricacies of Mexican colonial and nation-state hierarchies and determining how blackness fits within such social organizational schemes. New trends are seeing these questions pushed into the transnational realm.

The past decade has witnessed a flurry of new research on all three tracks, with some important shifts in the methodological and conceptual approaches taken to these issues. Among the most notable shifts have been the cultural and linguistic turns in historical analysis, prodding scholars to make deeper and richer use of records, such as Inquisition cases. As the foray into discourse analysis has ensued, new appreciations have emerged for the symbolic workings of power. Moreover, the themes of individual and collective agency, which have always been apparent in works on slave resistance, have reached new levels of sophistication. Scholars are paying closer attention to more everyday forms of agency, located not just in the struggle between masters and slaves, but between freedmen and bureaucrats, slaves and ecclesiastical authorities, men and women, and between the races themselves. Furthermore, recent public debates on race held in Mexico during the spring and summer of 2005, surrounding the international controversies raised by the comments of President Vicente Fox,[16] as well as Mexico's decision to release a stamp in the image of the comic book character Memín Penguin,[17] have shown new Mexican sensitivities to the topic of black identity. Within Mexico, there have even been movements by a limited number of Afro-Mexicans and politicians to press for the formal recognition of blacks as an ethnic group, so as to facilitate their acquisition of important communal rights.[18] In this sense, a small segment of the Afro-Mexican community is engaging in the project of multicultural politics that has been sweeping Latin America since the 1980s.[19] Meanwhile, in the academic realm, a number of Mexican scholars are mapping out research trajectories that include subaltern approaches and the history of "mentalities," along the lines of the French school of historical analysis. Additionally, Mexican scholars, who have always been seemingly more committed to fusing anthropological and sociological techniques into their historical research than have U.S. scholars, are developing and expanding the interdisciplinary nature of their work.[20]

Current historical work on the Afro-Mexican experience appears to be headed in several directions. First, while slavery remains an important lens through which to study the black experience, scholars are becoming increasingly interested in the lives of free-black populations.[21] Others are exploring the conceptual meaning of freedom, both for slaves and freedmen.[22] A few have made inquiries into black political participation in the nineteenth century.[23] However, black life in the nineteenth and twentieth centuries remains an understudied topic in need of more research. On the other hand, religion and magic are themes of great importance to current and emerging studies, since these arenas offered power to Afro-Mexicans, especially in the colonial period.[24] Historians are also beginning to triangulate studies of blacks with greater precision, studying the interrelationships between Indians, Afro-Mexicans, and Spaniards.[25] Matthew Restall, for example, argues in a new study that Afro-Yucatecans were integrated into colonial society in intermediate roles that he summarizes as "the black middle."[26] Studies of caste relationships remain important, although some of the newer inquiries are starting to examine the origins of the system and its relationship to Spanish concepts of blood purity (*limpieza de sangre*) and citizenry (*vecindad*).[27] Work on regional history continues to increase both in sophistication, coverage, and thematic complexity.

The essays in this collection touch upon nearly all of the areas cited above and are the product of a series of conversations and conference papers that came about as a result of a symposium held at Pennsylvania State University in 2004 entitled: "New Directions in North American Scholarship on Afro-Mexico." The intention of this event was to coordinate a range of scholars from several disciplines, working on a variety of topics, in order to take the beginning steps toward building a necessary North American research consensus that will prove valuable in the future as greater collaboration and interconnectivity takes place between U.S.- and Mexico-based scholars. In fact, it is our hope that these essays will not only prove valuable to students and scholars in North America, but will serve to inspire dialogue across the border toward generating a more holistic understanding of the black presence in Mexico.

This book is composed of a core set of chapters (Section I) examining the colonial period and a shorter Section II that addresses the modern era. This format allows the reader to trace some of the ideas of racial representation in the sixteenth, seventeenth, and eighteenth centuries, into the twenty-first century, and to ponder the legacy of such concepts. The colonial essays are all historical in nature (written by historians), providing us with an updated understanding of slavery and resistance, caste identity, native/black relations, free-colored labor, religiosity, magic, and spirituality. Among the dominant themes crosscutting these essays is the issue of black integration into colonial Mexican society.

In studying four distinct episodes of slave rebellion in the seventeenth and eighteenth centuries, Frank Proctor's chapter underscores how black resistance to slavery was both a means of bucking the colonial order (and thereby marginalizing blacks from the mainstream), as much as it was a manifestation of black desires to play a more significant part in the broader society. Free-colored townships, particularly those created by runaway slaves through treaties with the government, were representative of slave integration as much as they were symbols of successful resistance on the former slaves' own terms. In what is a decidedly revisionist historical interpretation, Proctor also reminds us that the Spanish colonial system provided tremendous prospects for negotiating personal and corporate status and that these opportunities were available, albeit limitedly, to the enslaved. In his view, this had distinct and understudied ramifications. Slave acts of flight, mutiny, riot, and unrest, rather than championing "universal" notions of liberty (akin to the "natural rights of man" championed by the Enlightenment), may have actually been steps along a continuum of negotiation wherein slaves reworked their status in the colonial world. In other words, the freedom that black rebel slaves sought within colonial Mexico may have been of a less lofty grade than previously imagined and more rooted in the daily machinations for survival on local estates. But once slaves became runaways, he argues, they were qualitatively different individuals with distinct worldviews, desires, and abilities to exercise and envision a broader freedom.

The chapters by Andrew Fisher and Patrick Carroll implore us to ponder the relationship between blacks and natives in the quest for social inclusion. In studying nearly three centuries of colonial rule, Andrew Fisher demonstrates how blacks found both solace and feud in the stream of native villages dotting the Pacific basin. The small number of Spaniards who populated the region of the Tierra Caliente in the sixteenth and seventeenth centuries proved a boon to black migration as they settled comfortably in townships where they felt liberated from the surveillance and onerous presence of colonial institutions. But as the native populations in these villages grew in the eighteenth century, and as new economic pressures pinched the region, blacks who were once welcomed into the Tierra Caliente were now seen as rivals for scarce resources. Fisher writes that it was in the eighteenth century that these blacks realized the extent to which their freedom was conditional and circumscribed. With reduced access to landownership and with weak ties to influential colonial institutions, politicians, and economic magnates, the Tierra Caliente's blacks lived turbulently through the end of the eighteenth century, gradually losing their independent access to the basic means of sustenance.

In studying the role of blacks in indigenous communities, Patrick Carroll argues that free coloreds did not simply find themselves incorporated into a Hispanic social order, but that they also found themselves being swept into an indigenous world that operated according to different rules. Within native communities, he argues, ethnicity mattered more than race and caste, which were the prevailing forces of social design in New Spain's townships and cities. Consequently, blacks who assimilated fully into native communities enjoyed refashioned identities, coexisting as natives themselves. Even colonial census documents failed to record these individuals as blacks, given their high level of acceptance within Indian townships and villages. On the other hand, blacks who only partially assimilated into these communities (if at all), were construed as foreigners and had a more conflict-ridden history with native settlements.

Ben Vinson's chapter studies how free-colored occupational status in the late colonial period served as a barometer to measure the "success" by which blacks became a part of the broader colonial economy. In a sweeping survey of professions, encompassing Mexico's largest colonial cities, as well as the Pacific coast (home to large numbers of contemporary Afro-Mexicans), he demonstrates how, on the surface, free-black laborers were inextricably linked to the major anchors of Mexican industrial life. At the same time, there were certain spaces, especially in the service sector, but also in the type of artisan opportunities that were open to blacks, that revealed some limitations to free black economic life. Even in the late eighteenth century, despite certain relaxations in the colony's socioracial hierarchies and definite advances in black occupational status, several aspects of the economy were not as open as they might initially seem.

By studying religious confraternities, Nicole von Germeten's chapter looks at the institutional mechanisms by which blacks (mainly free coloreds) maneuvered in a largely urban world. She argues that many may have conceived of themselves as middle men—not necessarily free from the restraints that race and caste placed on their social ascension, but certainly occupying a position from which to broker their lives between the more successful Spaniards and the more marginal groups, including natives and slaves. The sometimes fragile intermediary position brought a host of tensions, revealing that free blacks were far from homogenous. But the confraternity, as an institution, also helped inculcate a sense of caste identity for some black members. In this way, mulattos and others found themselves both assimilating and demarcating a unique identity within the colonial landscape.

In Joan Bristol and Matthew Restall's essay, we see how the world of love-magic became a practical instrument in the everyday negotiations between blacks and nonblacks. Through the leverage that blacks were able to acquire over masters and their "social betters," they were able to partially re-create the colonial system in their favor, albeit temporarily and in a limited arena. Through their spells and potions, blacks also entered into the innermost personal fantasies of their clients, thereby becoming active participants in the psychological and emotional worlds of members of all walks of colonial life. But even as their expertise in the supernatural arts served to integrate them into the societies of places like Mexico City and Mérida, at the same time, they were marginalized by their roles. As we see in von Germeten's and Proctor's articles, there was ambivalence about blacks and their place in the social order.

In contrast to the core chapters in Section I, Section II is written with a different style and a more suggestive purpose. Featuring the writings of two anthropologists, an African living currently in Mexico and an oral historian, these essays, in part, interrogate how North American scholars have navigated their own identities in the task of trying to understand contemporary Afro-Mexicans. In particular, Laura Lewis's chapter wrestles with her identification as a "gringa" (white American woman) and what this has meant to her informants and her relationship with her research. She also informs her analysis with a sensitive interpretation of the dynamics of racial identity in the Costa Chica (on the Pacific coast), demonstrating how native ethnicity and nationalism have been central to understanding blackness. Bobby Vaughn's chapter, meanwhile, reveals how his status as an African-American has aroused a number of curiosities in the field and has impacted his understandings of the México Negro movement in the Costa Chica. As with Lewis, he also takes up the task of examining how blacks in Mexico refer to themselves. While both chapters indirectly address the topic of discrimination and racism, the chapter by Jean Philibert Mobwa Mobwa (a Congolese-born, Mexican resident) deals most pointedly with the issue, in light of the recent antidiscrimination campaigns that have been launched in Mexico. Finally, the chapters by Alva Moore Stevenson and Laura Lewis both tackle the effects of migration and transnationalism, seeking to understand how the international border has complicated black Mexican identities, even within the United States.

✣ NOTES ✣

Portions of this article were previously published. See Ben Vinson III, "Afro-Mexican History: Trends and Directions in Scholarship," *History Compass* 3, LA 156 (September 2005): 1–14. The authors would like to thank the *History Compass Journal* for allowing these sections to be reprinted.

1. The list of texts examining these issues is extensive, but some good introductory texts include: Peter Wade, *Race and Ethnicity in Latin America* (London: Pluto Press, 1997); George Reid Andrews, *Afro–Latin America, 1800–2000* (Oxford and New York: Oxford University Press, 2004); Darén J. Davis, ed., *Beyond Slavery: The Multilayered Legacy of Africans in Latin America and the Caribbean* (New York: Rowman and Littlefield, 2007); and Nancy Priscilla Naro, ed., *Blacks, Coloureds and National Identity in 19th Century Latin America* (London: London Institute of Latin American Studies, University of London, 2003).

2. While falling outside the scope of this article, it is important to note that alongside the slow creation of the Afro-Mexican historical subfield, parallel developments took place in areas such as Nicaragua, Colombia, Ecuador, Panama, Venezuela, Peru, Costa Rica, and Guatemala, among others. Although each of these historiographies on Afro–Latin Americans enjoys an independent track, they are interdependently related, and scholars working in

one area feed off the research advances of the others. International conferences and events, such as annual workshops held by the Association for the Study of the Worldwide African Diaspora (ASWAD), UNESCO's Tracking the Slave Route Project, and Harvard's Atlantic History Seminar have provided active forums for maintaining fertile scholarly dialogue. Recent panels at the Latin American Studies Association (LASA) conference have also revealed intense interest in topics of blackness, and a number of NGOs have been actively promoting the topic. The next step that this emerging, nationally bounded literature may take is to embark upon grand synthesis, as signaled by the late Frederick Bowser. The literature on these regions is vast. A few examples include: Kim D. Butler, *Freedoms Given, Freedoms Won: Afro-Brazilians in Post-Abolition São Paulo and Salvador* (New Brunswick: Rutgers University Press, 1998); Alejandro de la Fuente, *A Nation For All: Race, Inequality, and Politics in Twentieth-Century Cuba* (Chapel Hill: University of North Carolina Press, 2001); Matthew Restall, ed., *Beyond Black and Red: African-Native Relations in Colonial Latin America* (Albuquerque: University of New Mexico Press, 2005); Ben Vinson III and Stewart R. King, "Introducing the 'New' African Diasporic Military History in Latin America," *Journal of Colonialism and Colonial History* 5, no. 2 (special issue, 2004); Edmund T. Gordon, *Disparate Diasporas: Identity and Politics in an African Nicaraguan Community* (Austin: University of Texas Press, 1998); James H. Sweet, *Recreating Africa: Culture, Kinship, and Religion in the African-Portuguese World, 1441–1770* (Chapel Hill: University of North Carolina Press, 2003); Robinson A. Herrera, *Natives, Europeans, and Africans in Sixteenth-Century Santiago de Guatemala* (Austin: University of Texas Press, 2003); Christine Hünefeldt, *Paying the Price of Freedom: Family and Labor Among Lima's Slaves, 1800–1854* (Berkeley: University of California Press, 1994); Jane Landers, *Black Society in Spanish Florida* (Urbana: University of Illinois Press, 1999); Peter Blanchard, *Slavery and Abolition in Early Republican Peru* (Wilmington, DE: Scholarly Resources, 1992); Peter Blanchard, *Under the Flags of Freedom: Slave Soldiers and the Wars of Independence in Spanish South America* (Pittsburgh: University of Pittsburgh Press, 2008); David Howard, *Coloring the Nation: Race and Ethnicity in the Dominican Republic* (Boulder: Lynne Rienner, 2001); Robin E. Sheriff, *Dreaming Equality: Color, Race, and Racism in Urban Brazil* (New Brunswick: Rutgers University Press, 2001); Winthrop R. Wright, *Café con Leche: Race, Class, and National Image in Venezuela* (Austin: University of Texas Press, 1990); Ernesto Sagás, *Race and Politics in the Dominican Republic* (Gainesville: University of Florida Press, 2001); Kris Lane, *Quito 1599: City and Colony in Transition* (Albuquerque: University of New Mexico Press, 2002); Berta Ares Queija and Alessandro Stella, eds., *Negros, mulatos, zambaigos: derroteros africanos en los mundos ibéricos* (Seville: EEHA/CSIC, 2000); Rina Cáceres, *Negros, mulatos, esclavos y libertos en la Costa Rica del siglo XVII* (Mexico City: Instituto Panamericano de Geografía e Historia, 2000); María Eugenia Chaves, *María Chiquinquirá Díaz: Una esclava del siglo XVIII: acerca de las identidades de amo y esclavo en el puerto colonial de Guayaquil* (Guayaquil: Archivo Histórico del Guayas, 1998); Carlos Aguirre, *Agentes de su propia libertad: Los esclavos de Lima y la desintegración de la esclavitud: 1821–1854* (Lima: Pontificia Universidad Católica del Perú, Fondo Editorial, 1993); Juan Manuel de la Serna Herrera, *Pautas de convivencia étnica en la América Latina colonial (indios, negros, mulatos, pardos y esclavos)* (Mexico City: Universidad Autónoma de México, 2005). As noted above, nongovernmental organizations (NGOs) and multilateral organizations such as the Inter-American Development Bank (IDB), Afroamérica XXI, and the Inter-American Dialogue's Inter-Agency Consultation on Race have been instrumental as well in lending voice to black Latin American activists. See: Inter-American Dialogue, Inter-American Development Bank, and the World Bank, "Race and Poverty: Interagency Consultation on Afro-Latin Americans," LCR Sustainable Development Working Paper Number 9 (Washington, D.C., November, 2000).

3. Francisco de Ajofrín, *Diario del viaje que hizo a la América en el siglo XVIII el padre fray Francisco de Ajofrín* (Mexico City: Instituto Cultural Hispano Mexicano, 1965); Juan F. Gemelli Carreri, *Viaje a la Nueva España, México a fines del siglo XVII* (Mexico City: Ediciones Libro-Mex, 1995); Thomas Gage, *Nuevo reconocimiento de las Indias Occidentales* (Mexico City: Fondo de Cultura Económica, 1982); Alexander von Humboldt, *Ensayo Político sobre el reino de la Nueva España*, trans. Vicente González Arnao, 4 vols. (Paris: Rosa, 1822); Bernal Díaz del Castillo, *Historia verdadera de la conquista de la Nueva España, introducción y notas de Joaquín Ramírez Cabañas* (Mexico City: Editorial Porrúa, 1983), 421; Baltasar Fra Molinero, "Ser mulato en España y América: discursos legales y otros discursos literarios," in *Negros, mulatos, zambaigos, derroteros africanos en los mundos ibéricos*, ed. Berta Ares Queija and Alessandro Stella, 135 (Seville, Spain: Escuela de Estudios Hispano-Americanos, 2001); Fray Diego Durán, *The History of the Indies of New Spain*, ed. Doris Heyden (Norman: University of Oklahoma Press, 1994), 510, 563; Francisco López de Gómara, *Cortés, the Life of the Conqueror by His Secretary* (Berkeley: University of California Press, 1964), 204–5, 238, 397; Alvar Núñez Cabeza de Vaca, *La relación; o Naufragios* (Potomac, MD: Scripta Humanistica, 1986); Peter Gerhard, "A Black Conquistador in Mexico," *The Hispanic American Historical Review (HAHR)* 58, no. 3(1978): 451–59; Matthew Restall, "Black Conquistadors: Armed Africans in Early Spanish America," *The Americas (TAM)* 57, no. 2(2000): 167–205; Francisco Seijas y Lobera, *Gobierno militar y político del reino imperial de la Nueva España*, ed. Pablo Emilio Pérez-Mallaína

Bueno (Mexico City: Universidad Nacional Autónoma de México, 1986); and Carlos Sigüenza y Gongora, *Alboroto y motín de México del 8 de junio de 1692* (Mexico City: Talleres Gráficos del Museo Nacional de Arqueologóa, Historia y Etnografía, 1932).

4. For more on the "plebeian" nature of Afro-Mexicans, see: R. Douglas Cope, *The Limits of Racial Domination: Plebeian society in Colonial Mexico City, 1660–1720* (Madison: University of Wisconsin Press, 1994).

5. Vicente Riva Palacio, Manuel Payno, Juan A. Mateos, y Rafael Martínez de la Torre, *El libro rojo* (Mexico City: Editorial Leyenda, 1946); Vicente Riva Palacio, *Los treinta y tres negros* (Mexico City: SEP-Conasupo, 1981). Note that good discussion on Riva Palacio can be found in Theodore G. Vincent, *The Legacy of Vicente Guerrero: Mexico's First Black Indian President* (Gainesville: University of Florida Press, 2001).

6. Good summary treatment of these points can be found in Moisés González Navarro, *Los Extranjeros en México y los Mexicanos en el extranjero, 1821–1970*, 3 vols. (Mexico City: COLMEX, 1994). For African-Americans crossing into Mexico, see Ben Vinson III, *Flight: The Story of Virgil Richardson, A Tuskegee Airman in Mexico* (New York: Palgrave-Macmillan, 2004); Gerald Horne, *Black and Brown: African-Americans and the Mexican Revolution* (New York: New York University Press, 2005); and Rosalie Schwartz, *Across the Rio to Freedom: U.S. Negroes in Mexico*, Southwestern Studies Monograph 44 (El Paso: Texas Western Press, 1975).

7. José Vasconcelos, *La raza cósmica: Misión de la raza Iberoamericana* (Barcelona: Agencia Mundial de Librería, 1958).

8. Alfonso Toro, "Influencia de la raza negra en la formación del pueblo mexicano," *Ethnos. Revista para la vulgarización de Estudios Antropológicos sobre México y Centro América* 1, no. 8–12 (1920–21): 215–18.

9. Gonzalo Aguirre Beltrán, *La población negra de México: Estudio etnohistórico*, 3rd ed. (Mexico City: Fondo de Cultura Económica, 1989).

10. Germán LaTorre, *Relaciones geográficas de Indias (contenidas en el Archivo General de Indias de Sevilla. La Hispanoamérica del siglo XVI). Virreinato de Nueva España (México. Censos de población)* 4, no. 4 (1920); Carlos Basauri, *Breves notas etnográficas sobre la población negra del distrito de Jamiltepec, Oaxaca* (Mexico City: Consejo Editorial del Primer Congreso Demográfico, 1943); Guillermo de la Peña, "Gonzalo Aguirre Beltrán: Historia y Mestizaje," in *Historiadores de Mexico en el Siglo XX.* ed. Enrique Florescano and Ricardo Pérez Montfort, 192 93 (Mexico City: Fondo de Cultura Económica, 1995).

11. Frank Tannenbaum, *Slave and Citizen: The Negro in the Americas* (New York: Vintage Books, 1946).

12. Gilberto Freyre, *Casa grande y senzala* (Rio de Janeiro: José Olympio, 1933); Fernando Ortiz, *Hampa afrocubana. Los negros brujos (apuntes para un estudio de etnología criminal)* (Madrid: Editorial América, 1917).
13. Some important works among the extensive bibliography on the caste vs. class debate include: Woodrow Borah and Sherburne F. Cook, "Sobre las posibilidades de hacer el estudio histórico del mestizaje sobre una base demografica," *Revista de historia de América* 53/54 (1962): 181–90; Patricia Seed, "The Social Dimensions of Race: Mexico City 1753," *HAHR* LXII, no. 4 (1982): 569–606; Cope, *Limits of Racial Domination*; John K. Chance and William B. Taylor, "Estate and Class in a Colonial City, Oaxaca in 1792," *Comparative Studies in Society and History* 19 (1977): 454–87.
14. Phillip D. Curtin, *The Atlantic Slave Trade, A Census* (Madison: University of Wisconsin Press, 1969).
15. Among the better known works that came as a result of the early internationalization of Afro-Mexican history are the books and articles written by Patrick Carroll, Colin Palmer, Peter Boyd-Bowman, Edgar Love, David Davidson, Robert Brady, and William H. Dusenberry. While their works largely investigated the intricacies of Mexican slavery, their research questions were in dialogue with some of the issues of the comparative slavery school. A number of Mexico-based scholars were drawn into this arena of research as well, however, the strong tradition of regional history, which has continued to be a prevalent feature of the Mexican academy today, generated a score of studies from the 1970s–1990s that sought to examine the local contributions of blacks to regional society. For a sample of works see: Patrick J. Carroll, "Estudio sociodemográfico de personas de sangre negra en Jalapa, 1791," *Historia Mexicana* 23, no. 1 (1973): 111–25; Patrick Carroll, "Mandinga: The Evolution of a Mexican Runaway Slave Community, 1735–1827," *Comparative Studies in Society and History* 19, no. 4 (1977): 488–505; Patrick Carroll and Aurelio de los Reyes, "Amapa, Oaxaca. Pueblo de cimarrones," *Boletín del Instituto Nacional de Antropología e Historia* 4 (1973): 43–50; Colin A. Palmer, *Slaves of the White God: Blacks in Mexico, 1570–1650* (Cambridge: Harvard University Press, 1976); Peter Boyd-Bowman, "Negro Slaves in Early Colonial México," *TAM* 26, no. 2 (1969): 134–51; Edgar F. Love, "Legal Restrictions on Afro-Indian Relations in Colonial Mexico," *The Journal of Negro History* IV, no. 2 (1970): 131–39; Edgar F. Love, "Marriage Patterns of Persons of Africans Descent in a Colonial Mexico City Parish," *HAHR* LI, no. 1 (1971): 79–91; Edgar F. Love, "Negro Resistance to Spanish Rule in Colonial Mexico," *The Journal of Negro History* LII, no. 2 (1967): 89–103; David M. Davidson, "Negro Slave Control and Resistance in Colonial Mexico: 1519–1650," *HAHR* XLVI, no. 3 (1966): 235–53; Robert LaDon Brady, "The Domestic Slave Trade

in Sixteenth Century México," *TAM* 24, no. 3 (1968): 281–89; William H. Dusenberry, "Discriminatory Aspects of Legislation in Colonial Mexico," *The Journal of Negro History* XXXIII, no. 3 (1948): 284–302; Francisco Fernández Repetto and Genny Negroe Sierra, *Una población perdida en la memoria: Los negros de Yucatán* (Mérida: Universidad Autónoma de Yucatán, 1995); Juan Andrade Torres, *El comercio de esclavos en la provincia de Tabasco (siglos XVI–XIX)* (Villahermosa: Universidad Juárez Autónoma de Tabasco, 1994); Maria Guadalupe Chávez Carbajal, *Propietarios y esclavos negros en Michoacán (1600–1650)* (Morelia: Universidad Michoacana de San Nicolás de Hidalgo, 1994); Rafael Valdez Aguilar, *Sinaola: Negritud y Olvido* (Culiacán: Talleres Gráficos El Diario de Sinaloa, 1993); Mónica Leticia Gálvez Jiménez, *Celaya: sus raíces africanas* (Guanajuato: Ediciones la Rana, 1995). See also several regional articles in *Memoria del III Encuentro Nacional de Afromexicanistas*, ed. Luz María Martínez Montiel and Juan Carlos Reyes G. (Colima: Gobierno del Estado de Colima y Consejo Nacional para la Cultura y las Artes, 1993); *Pardos, mulatos y libertos, Sexto encuentro de afromexicanistas*, ed. Adriana Naveda Chávez-Hita (Xalapa: Universidad Veracruzana, 2001); and *Presencia africana en México*, ed. Luz María Martínez Montiel (Mexico City: Consejo Nacional para la Cultura y las Artes, 1994).

16. President Fox was widely criticized when he made a public statement to the effect that Mexican immigrants to the United States take jobs "that not even blacks want to do." See: "Mexican Leader Criticized for Comment on Blacks," CNN.com, May 15, 2005 available at www.cnn.com/2005/US/05/14/fox.jackson/.

17. Memín Penguin, a traditional Mexican comic book character originally produced in the 1940s, has been compared in international circles to offensive stereotyped caricatures such as "little black Sambo," among others. In Mexico, the comic book character represents a positive national icon for many. Although much has been written on this in newspapers and on the Internet, see: Ben Vinson III, "How Memín Sparks Race-Relation Talks Between U.S., Mexico," *Centre Daily Times (State College)*, July 25, 2005, A6, and Ben Vinson III and Bobby Vaughn, "Unfinished Migrations: From the Mexican South to the American South—Impressions on Afro-Mexican Migration to North Carolina," in Davis, *Beyond Slavery*, 223–45.

18. Laura Castellanos, "Buscan volver etnia a los afromexicanos," *Reforma* (Mexico City), June 8, 2005, 3C.

19. Juliet Hooker, "Indigenous Inclusion/Black Exclusion. Race, Ethnicity and Multicultural Citizenship in Latin America," *Journal of Latin American Studies (JLAS)* 37, no. 2 (2005): 285–310.

20. See the historiographical essays in the edited volume compiled by María Elisa Velázquez and Ethel Correa, *Poblaciones y culturas de origin africano en México* (Mexico City: Instituto Nacional de Antropología e Historia, 2005), especially the essays in pages 65–141. There still remain those in Mexico who cling to the idea that care must be exercised when reifying blacks within scholarly and public discourse, since invoking "race" is analogous to inculcating racism. However, their opinions are being heavily challenged from within, as well as from without. See: Quince Duncan, "Existen las razas?" in *Poblaciones y culturas de origin africano en México*, ed. María Elisa Velázquez and Ethel Correa, 217–25 (Mexico City: Instituto Nacional de Antropología e Historia, 2005).

21. Some have taken an institutional approach, examining free-black participation in military and religious institutions. See Ben Vinson III, *Bearing Arms for His Majesty: The Free-Colored Militia in Colonial Mexico* (Stanford: Stanford University Press, 2001); and Nicole von Germeten, *Black Blood Brothers: Confraternities and Social Mobility for Afro-Mexicans* (Gainesville: University of Florida Press, 2006). Note that Juan Manuel de la Serna is also increasingly dedicating himself to the study of free-black soldiers in the militia units of Veracruz (los Lanceros de Veracruz).

22. Frank Proctor III, "Slavery, Identity, and Culture: An Afro-Mexican Counterpoint, 1640–1763," Ph.D. diss., Emory University, 2003. Herman L. Bennett is also working on the theme of freedom as a complementary work to his *Africans in Colonial Mexico. Absolutism, Christianity, and Afro-creole Consciousness, 1570–1640* (Bloomington: Indiana University Press, 2003).

23. Vincent, *Legacy of Vicente Guerrero*.

24. Joan Cameron Bristol, *Christians, Blasphemers, and Witches: Afro-Mexican Ritual Practice in the Seventeenth Century* (Albuquerque: University of New Mexico Press, 2007); Javier Villa-Flores, "'To Lose One's Soul': Blasphemy and Slavery in New Spain, 1596–1669," *HAHR* LXXXII, no. 3 (2002): 435–69; and Laura A. Lewis, *Hall of Mirrors: Power, Witchcraft and Caste in Colonial Mexico* (Durham and London: Duke University Press, 2003).

25. Herrera, *Natives, Europeans, and Africans*; Lane, *Quito, 1599*; Lewis, *Hall of Mirrors*; Restall, *Beyond Black and Red*; de la Serna Herrera, *Pautas de convivencia étnica*.

26. Matthew Restall, *The Black Middle: Africans, Mayas, and Spaniards in Colonial Yucatan* (Stanford: Stanford University Press, 2009).

27. María Elena Martínez, *Geneological Fictions: Limpieza de Sangre, Religion, and Gender in Colonial Mexico* (Stanford: Stanford University Press, 2008).

Section I

Entering the Colonial World

Slave Rebellion and Liberty in Colonial Mexico

FRANK "TREY" PROCTOR III

❧

❦ ON MAY 2, 1612, BETWEEN 9:00 A.M. AND 2:00 P.M., HUNDREDS AND perhaps thousands of people filled Mexico City's central plaza to witness the hangings of thirty-five Afro-Mexicans, including at least seven women, condemned as the leaders of a slave rebellion that had sent shockwaves through the city. The goals of the rebellion, according to an anonymous description, were the liberation of the city's slaves and the murder of all Spaniards. The bodies were left hanging from the gallows overnight to be drawn and quartered the following day.[1] Only six were thus desecrated, the body parts placed on pikes throughout the city, while the remaining twenty-nine bodies were decapitated, their heads displayed on top of the gallows to serve as a stark message to Afro-Mexicans about the consequences for rebelliousness.

Ironically, perhaps, on August 12, 1763, over a century and a half later, the viceroy awoke to find nearly fifty slaves encamped in the very same plaza demanding an audience with him. These slaves had fled, armed and en masse, from a sugar plantation where they labored near Cuernavaca, Morelos, and walked two days to Mexico City to lodge a complaint

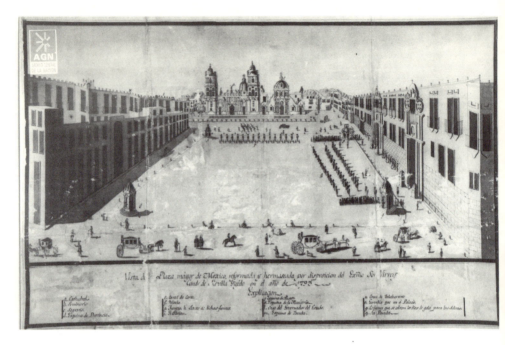

FIGURE 2.1. Mexico City's Plaza Mayor.
Courtesy of the Archivo General de la Nación, Mexico City.

with colonial authorities regarding the living and working conditions on their hacienda.[2] They were quickly arrested, jailed, and the leaders eventually beaten.

The two moments of collective slave rebelliousness discussed above occurred nearly simultaneously with the establishment of two *palenques* (runaway slave communities) in New Spain (colonial Mexico). Perhaps most compelling about these two palenques is that in both cases colonial authorities negotiated with the runaways, after failing to destroy them militarily, and eventually granted these particular runaways their freedom and the right to establish free towns—San Lorenzo de los Negros (1630s?) and Nuestra Señora de Guadalupe de los Negros de Amapa (1769). By comparing these four seemingly disparate yet interconnected stories of collective slave resistance we are poised to learn much about the texture of slavery and the meanings and processes of slave resistance in New Spain, in a setting where slavery played a lesser social role than in places like Cuba and Brazil.

The height of the Mexican experience with African slavery can be viewed as delimited by these two sets of unrelated yet nearly concurrent slave uprisings. Slavery in New Spain followed a fairly novel historical trajectory when compared with much of the Atlantic world. Demand for slaves spiked between 1580 and 1640 due to the expansion of the mining and sugar industries. As a result, New Spain was, by the end of the regular slave trade in 1640, home to the second largest slave population in the New World, surpassed only by Brazil.[3] The first two rebellions under consideration here occurred during that expansion.

After the end of the slave trade, the primary demand for slave labor did not come from the colony's dominant export sector (silver), but rather from two industries aimed at internal markets that required large, stable workforces—woolen textiles and sugar.[4] Sugar production was centered in and around the modern states of Veracruz and Morelos shortly after conquest and spread to the Córdoba and Orizaba regions near the Veracruz/Oaxaca border in the seventeenth century (see map of New Spain on pp. xvi–xvii). Woolen textile production, on the other hand, became heavily concentrated in the environs of Mexico City and Querétaro in the seventeenth century.

Most historians suggest that the highpoint of slavery coincided with the end of the regular slave trade and that it slowly withered away in the face of the increasing availability of wage labor.[5] Despite expectations to the contrary, demand from these industries remained steady until the last half of the eighteenth century. The final two rebellions under consideration here broke out in the context of this shift, but in regions where slavery remained dominant, suggesting that we may have underestimated its importance to the eighteenth-century economy.

Slavery was also very important in Mexico's urban centers, particularly Mexico City, through the second half of the eighteenth century. While historians generally treat urban slaves in New Spain as domestic servants and "status symbols . . . used by elites . . . to advertise their social standing,"[6] they filled important roles in the urban economies as master craftsmen, street vendors, day laborers, and shop keepers for their owners, among others, throughout the colonial period.

This chapter uses the four rebellions introduced above to situate New Spain within hemispheric understandings of collective slave resistance. As we move through the discussion of these rebellions there are at least three questions to consider. First, what motivated slaves to rebel?

In light of Spanish testimony that a goal of the 1612 rebellion was to free the city's slaves and the negotiations undertaken by the runaways of San Lorenzo and Amapa to secure their free status, we might be tempted to assume that a general and universal desire for liberty among slaves provides the answer to that question, but we need to interrogate that assumption. Second, while the creation of runaway communities was clearly an act of slave resistance, do attempts by runaways to secure their permanent freedom speak, at all, to the motivations of slaves to resist their enslavement? Third, what are the dangers of trying to answer such questions with available sources?

Seventeenth-Century Rebellions: The Foundation of San Lorenzo de los Negros

By the end of the sixteenth century, levels of slave flight and rebellion in the sugar-producing regions of Veracruz and Córdoba had become alarming to local planters and Spanish authorities, particularly when a group of runaways began attacking local towns, plantations, and caravans on the Royal Road between Mexico City and the port of Veracruz as early as 1606.[7] Colonial authorities were unsure of the best course of action because early attempts to subdue the runaways proved unsuccessful. As a result, in 1608 Viceroy Luis de Velasco decided, remarkably, to negotiate with the *cimarrones* (runaway slaves), sending Padre Alonso de Benavides, a Franciscan friar, and Capitán Manuel Carrillo, a *regidor* of Veracruz, to negotiate a treaty with Yanga, the palenque's leader.[8] Padre Benavides and Capitán Carrillo successfully established a truce by the end of 1608 with Yanga, a Bran from the Senegambia region of Northwestern Africa, who had been a runaway for nearly thirty years and claimed to be a descendant of African royalty.[9]

Carrillo subsequently delivered a set of demands from Yanga to the viceroy stipulating the conditions under which he and his followers would stop raiding and lay down their arms.[10] Yanga requested that everyone in his community who had fled slavery before September of 1608 be freed. In exchange, the community would become slave catchers, returning all those who had escaped after that date to their masters, and assist in repelling foreign attacks on the colony. He asked that his palenque be recognized as a free town, complete with its own *cabildo* (town council) and *justicia mayor* (appeals judge). In addition, Spaniards were not to be allowed to live in the town but could visit on market days, as was standard practice in native villages. Yanga insisted that he be named the pueblo's governor and that his descendants succeed him in office. Lastly, he asked that a Franciscan friar be sent to minister to his followers and that the Crown pay for the ornamentation of a Church.[11] Despite a sense that these demands were too high, Velasco believed that meeting them, "within limits," offered the best solution to the cimarrón problem.[12]

Meanwhile, Padre Benavides stayed in the runaway camp to assure Yanga that the negotiations were proceeding well. Conditions remained peaceful until May of 1609 when the situation took a turn for the worse. The Yanguicos (Yanga's followers) cast Padre Benavides out of their encampment, alleging him to be a spy. Shortly thereafter, the cimarrones began to foray into neighboring ranches and towns, "robbing" them of slaves and women, both black and Indian in order to increase their numbers. Velasco attributed the renewed violence to the death of Capitán Carrillo, the chief intermediary between the government and Yanga but reiterated that negotiations for peace were the only viable solution.[13]

Belief in the power of negotiation still did not preclude Velasco from attempting a military resolution. In 1609, he ordered Capitán Pedro González de Herrera to begin military preparations to destroy the palenque. Yet, just in case diplomacy remained an option, Velasco sent two Jesuits with González in the hope that they might be able to secure a last-minute truce. Padre Juan Laurencio, a Jesuit selected to accompany González, wrote a detailed description of the assault on the runaway encampment.[14]

Capitán González arrived in the region in October of 1609. When Yanga learned of his presence, he dispatched reconnaissance parties to gather information about the Spanish forces. During one such mission a group of cimarrones captured two Spaniards and some Indian women on a livestock ranch. When the Spaniards refused to answer questions about González's army, the leader of the band crushed one Spaniard's skull with a club. Padre Laurencio wrote that the cimarrón then licked the blood off his club while his compatriots drank the dead man's blood before scalping him. It is difficult to know if this description is accurate or was sensationalized in order to justify the efforts to destroy the runaway community. In either case, such an accusation would have resonated with local planters and Mexico City's political elite due to their fear that black rebelliousness represented the "greatest threat" to colonial stability.[15]

The raiders then took the surviving Spaniard and six Indian women to their palenque as captives. Yanga spared the unnamed Spaniard's life and ordered him to draft a letter to González celebrating Yanguico victories over the Spaniards, denouncing Spanish cruelty and faithlessness, and calling Capitán González a coward, boldly challenging him to meet Yanga in battle.

Once the surviving Spaniard delivered the letter to González, informing him of Yanga's exact whereabouts, the assault began in early 1610. Too old to fight, Yanga delegated military command to Francisco de la Matiza, an Angolan runaway. During the battle Yanga remained with the women and children in the camp's rustic church leading them in prayer. Despite careful planning to defend the encampment and initial reports of success, the runaways were eventually forced to abandon their stronghold.

When the Spaniards entered the palenque they found it completely deserted. The camp consisted of nearly seventy houses and a church. Before being evacuated, the camp's population had approximately eighty warriors, twenty-four black women and an unspecified number of Indian men, women, and Afro-Mexican children. Outside the palenque the Spanish found a well and fields planted with corn, squash, and cotton, in addition to fruit trees, sweet potatoes, beans, sugar cane, and various other vegetables. Inside the compound additional cotton, corn, and squash were raised. The Spanish also found an abundance of chickens, along with spades, axes, firearms, some coins, salt, and butter. Capitán González ultimately decided to attempt negotiations with Yanga, but the cimarrón leader retreated before the two could meet.[16]

What transpired next is not clear; while historians agree that Yanga, or his descendants, successfully negotiated a truce with colonial authorities resulting in the establishment of San Lorenzo de los Negros, no one is sure when. Pérez de Ribas argues that the viceroy accepted terms similar to those in Yanga's initial demands to establish peace in the region, freeing it of marauding highwaymen, but he failed to record the name of the pueblo or when it was founded.[17] Other chroniclers report that the Yanguico pueblo was named San Lorenzo but do not indicate when it was established.[18]

Over the following decades the region remained troublesome for the Spanish due to activities associated with the Yanguico cimarrones. In 1618, Viceroy don Rodrigo Fernández de Córdoba, Marqués de Guadalacar, founded the town of Córdoba, named in his honor, where he established a presidio to prevent the attacks on cargo trains between Veracruz and Mexico City, which he attributed to the Yanguicos.[19] Adriana Naveda argues that San Lorenzo was founded in 1635 based on a criminal trial of Gaspar Ñanga, capitán of the blacks of San Lorenzo (who may have been either Yanga or one of his descendants), for aiding and abetting runaway slaves.[20] From this information, it is safe to assume that the Yanguicos probably received their freedom and the right to establish San Lorenzo sometime between 1619 and 1641 as the result of protracted negotiations with colonial authorities.

Rebellion in the Capital

On the heels of the attempt to destroy Yanga's palenque, Mexico City faced the specter of a large slave rebellion that culminated with the macabre execution of the thirty-five Afro-Mexicans described above. As with establishing the exact date of the founding of San Lorenzo, discussing the Mexico City slave rebellion of 1611–12 is complicated. Colonial historians remain undecided on whether Spanish paranoia or a real plan on the part of the city's slaves to rebel best explains the violent crackdown against Afro-Mexicans.[21] A wide variety of contemporary sources describe the executions, leaving little doubt about their veracity or that a general fear of slave rebellion pervaded the city.[22] More difficult to ascertain, however, is whether slaves were actually planning a rebellion, what they believed to be the cause of that rebellion, and what their goals might have been.

The following account is based on a combination of the account of the rebellion in an anonymous letter written in 1612 and interpretations of the tumult and repression by historian María Elena Martínez, based on new materials, including a contemporaneous description of the uprising by the indigenous historian Chimalpahín and colonial correspondence housed in Spain, which complicate and corroborate the anonymous description.[23] These sources are problematic because none contain any slave testimony regarding the rebellion and its causes. We will proceed under the assumption that such a rebellion was possible and try to ascertain what we can about slavery in Mexico City from the sources in question.

The letter associated the origins of the uprising with the repression of the Afro-Mexican community following a slave funeral. It began with a general warning of the insolence of Mexico City's Afro-Mexican population despite the good treatment they received from their masters, including access to expensive clothing and the rights to have dances, marry, bury their dead, and to form and join confraternities. The problems began when more than fifteen hundred members of the Cofradía de Nuestra Señora de la Merced—a black and mulatto religious confraternity—gathered to bury one of their members in 1611, an unnamed black slave woman. Apparently, they believed she had been killed by her abusive owner, Luís Moreno de Monroy. In their increasing fury, the mourning crowd took up her corpse and marched it through the streets, parading past the palaces of the viceroy, the archbishop, and the offices of the Inquisition before ending up at Monroy's home where they began shouting threats and throwing stones.

The authorities responded quickly by arresting and publicly whipping the suspected leaders of the demonstration. Among the most important figures to be punished was Diego, a member of the confraternity and an old African slave. According to the anonymous account, Diego's punishment, and that of the other confraternity leaders, was very disconcerting to the city's Afro-Mexican population. This crackdown precipitated the decision to rebel, kill the Spaniards, and loot their homes. The leaders decided to name Pablo and Maria, married Angolan slaves, as the king and queen of their movement and planned their rebellion for Christmas of 1611. The positions of king and queen appear to have been more ceremonial than effectual roles within the rebellion.[24] The insurrection was postponed, however, due to the arrival of numerous companies of infantry in Mexico City on their way to the Philippines.

In the spring of 1612, "King" Pablo fell ill and died. According to the letter, the ceremonies surrounding his burial marked the intention of the city's slaves and free coloreds to rebel against their Spanish oppressors. Again, a large number of blacks and mulattos convened for Pablo's funeral, marked by dancing, singing, and "barbarous rites and ceremonies [from Africa]." They anointed his body with wine and oil, which were also poured into his open grave. Then the mourners threw one of their members into the grave, showering him with wine and dirt. When that mourner leapt from the grave with weapon in hand it supposedly signaled the call to arms for the city's Afro-Mexican population.[25]

Following the scene at the graveyard, a large crowd returned to Pablo's house to plan the logistics of their insurrection, now set for Holy Thursday during Easter Week, a time when Spaniards would be preoccupied with religious activities. Subsequent planning sessions were held in the home of

Andrés Garcia, a free mulatto, suggesting that participation in the rebellion was not limited to slaves. The leaders of the rebellion offered the title of king to Diego, one of the slaves punished in the unrest of 1611. Because of his advanced age, he declined the title but insisted that "King" Pablo's brother Pedro, also from Angola, be named. He also recommended that Pedro marry María, Pablo's widow, so that she might remain queen.

The insurrection began falling apart during the Lenten season when two Portuguese merchants who spoke "the language of Angola" overheard an unidentified slave woman complaining about the abuse suffered by another slave. They reported having overheard her say that a plan was afoot for the blacks and mulattos to take control of the city and massacre the Spanish during Holy Week. This testimony was corroborated by two more witnesses who overheard similar discussions by slaves about the uprising.

The Audiencia responded to these reports by suspending Holy Week processions and closing churches in Mexico City and its environs on Holy Thursday.[26] Colonial authorities also imposed a series of measures they hoped would thwart the rebellion. On April 2, 1612, all black and mulatto confraternities were suppressed. On April 14, authorities issued prohibitions against blacks and mulattos carrying arms or congregating in groups larger than four for any reason including funerals, dances, or parties (under penalty of two hundred lashes). That order also admonished masters not to leave their slaves unmonitored at night. Finally, on April 17, the Audiencia imposed an 8:00 p.m. to 5:00 a.m. curfew for slaves in the city (under penalty of one hundred lashes).[27]

In late April or early May the accused leaders of the rebellion were arrested, jailed, and tortured to confess. According to the letter, authorities found caches of arms and strongboxes of valuables while searching their homes. Upon discovering the weapons, the authorities condemned the leaders to be hung, drawn, and quartered. The sentence was carried out on May 2, 1612, as described above. In the end, the enslaved and free blacks and mulattos of Mexico City never did rise up in rebellion.

Examining the insurrectionary activities of the Yanguicos alongside the reported conspiracy in Mexico City speaks volumes about slavery in early New Spain, while illuminating the limitations faced by historians interested in the motivations for and causes of slave rebellion. First, the reactions of colonial authorities to these rebellions underscore the general fear among the Spanish of the growing Afro-Mexican population.

Although highly unreliable, population figures suggest that blacks and mulattos made up a substantial portion of Mexico City's population in the first half of the seventeenth century, perhaps outnumbering Spaniards. For example, Antonio Vázquez de Espinosa, a visitor to Mexico City in 1612, estimated that the population of the capital included 50,000 blacks and mulattos, 15,000 Spaniards, and 80,000 Indians.[28] Similarly, historian Gonzalo Aguirre Beltrán estimated that the Archbishopric of Mexico, which includes Mexico City, was home to an Afro-Mexican population of approximately 62,800 and that the total non-Indian population was approximately 208,500 in 1646.[29] Faced with a large indigenous majority in the colony, the specter of a mobilized and unified Afro-Mexican population must have been frightening to the Spanish.

A second interesting component of these rebellions was the participation by African-born slaves. Many scholars are coming to understand slave rebellions prior to the Age of Revolution in the Atlantic world as ethnic revolts "dominated by a specific African ethnic group possessed of a clear sense of common identity and a set of goals that excluded other groups of slaves."[30] In the case of the Yanguicos, we know that Yanga was a Bran, while Francisco de la Matiza, the military captain, was an Angolan, meaning that these two leaders came from very different regions in Africa. African participation, however, is not surprising, as the majority of slaves in New Spain prior to 1640 were Africa-born. However, the ethnic configuration of the remaining cimarrones is not found in the sources, making it difficult to test the importance of African ethnicities, or contemporaneous political events in Africa, for these rebellions.[31]

Conversely, while a number of the leaders of the 1612 Mexico City rebellion were Africa-born, what is most striking about this movement is its apparent heterogeneity. The close collaboration of free and enslaved Africans, Creole blacks, and mulattos defies expectations, perhaps throwing doubt on descriptions of the rebellion. Marriage patterns from Mexico City prior to 1650 suggest that Africans and Creoles did not identify with each other strongly enough to intermarry in significant numbers, seemingly undercutting the possibility of unity across the lines of race, ethnicity, and status (free vs. enslaved).[32]

Yet, Ben Vinson argues that although Afro-Mexican militiamen often played the "race card" by making clear distinctions between black and mulatto members, reflecting the hierarchical structure of the *sistema de castas* in the eighteenth century, in internal struggles over access to privileges within the colored militia of New Spain, those differences were subsumed to a broader racial identity in order to confront the threats from outside.[33] Perhaps, then, this apparent willingness to unite against the Spanish despite differences in status, ethnicity, race, and perhaps even class, affirms Spanish fears of the Afro-Mexican population. Therefore, although Nicole von Germeten's chapter in this volume discusses how confraternities served to regulate ethnic boundaries, the apparent unity of blacks in the 1612 insurrectionary activities *might* speak to the potential power of *cofradías* in overcoming the racial and ethnic barriers that were so significant in other slave contexts.

Third and lastly, in the case of both rebellions we are faced with a lamentable lack of slave voices as to the causes for and expectations of these movements. Clearly, Yanguico resistance to being returned to slavery, combined with the tantalizing assertion from the anonymous letter on the 1612 rebellion that slaves hoped to secure their liberty and planned to kill all the Spaniards, resonate with our expectations of slave actions. But at the same time, we must remember that it was perceived abuses—the murder of an unnamed slave woman and the subsequent public beatings of significant cofradía leaders following her funeral—that drove Afro-Mexicans in Mexico City to the point of armed rebellion in the first place. Did these abuses provide slaves the opportunity to galvanize support for a movement that expressed their desire for freedom? Or did it represent the conclusion on their part that conditions under slavery had become too oppressive, causing them to sense that they were losing what little power they had in their own lives to protect themselves from the violence and exploitation inherent in slavery? These are much more difficult questions to answer.

Eighteenth-Century Rebellion: The Foundation of Nuestra Señora de Guadalupe de los Negros de Amapa

Following the suppression of the Yanguico cimarrones and the 1612 slave rebellion there is little evidence to suggest that the colony faced other instances of significant slave rebelliousness until the mid-eighteenth century. At that point, however, new hot spots of slave rebellion began to pop up throughout the colony's sugar producing regions. Another group of runaways, a large majority of whom fled during a slave rebellion around Córdoba in 1735, established six palenques in the eastern mountains of Oaxaca. The residents of one such stronghold, Palacios de Mandinga,

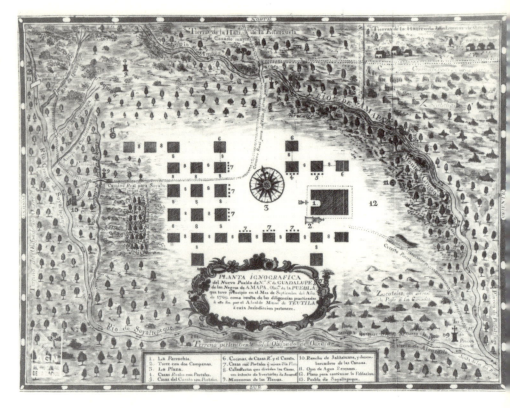

FIGURE 2.2. Plan of Nuestra Señora de Guadalupe de los Negros de Amapa. Courtesy of the Archivo General de la Nación, Mexico City.

eventually received their freedom and the right to establish a free pueblo, Nuestra Señora de Guadalupe de los Negros de Amapa (hereinafter Amapa; see Figure 2.2) in 1769 following a long series of armed clashes and subsequent negotiations with Spanish authorities.[34]

Their saga began in 1725, when a group of slaves who had fled their masters in the context of a general slave rebellion in Córdoba joined forces with other cimarrones and established the palenque called Mandinga. Similar to the case of the Yanguicos, the Spanish first sent numerous expeditions against the runaways but proved unable to subdue them due to rough terrain, their expertise at avoiding capture, and the network of free informants that kept them abreast of Spanish plans.[35]

In 1734, the group of twenty-three runaways promised to lay down their arms in return for the right to establish a free pueblo, an offer rejected by the government. Following this failed attempt, the Córdoba region was once again enveloped by a major slave rebellion due, apparently, to a rumor that the King had freed all slaves around Córdoba. Local planters vehemently blamed the rumor on the cimarrones who, they claimed, were "pouring their damned ideas about liberty" into the slave quarters.[36] In June 1735, as many as five hundred slaves, representing nearly one-third of all slaves in the region, gathered in San Juan de la Punta, near Córdoba, and demanded that the local authorities obey the king's rumored wishes.[37]

The Spanish response was swift and forceful, sending six hundred militiamen to the region. In a letter dated July 7, 1735, viceregal authorities impressed upon local leaders in Córdoba the need for a rapid resolution of the problem. They recommended that the slaves who had fled their masters be given ten days to return. Once that amnesty period had passed, however, punishment for those implicated in the rebellion was to be swift, severe, and public. In addition, the viceroy pressed local priests to do all that they could to convince the rebels that the liberty supposedly granted by the king was a hoax.

Although planters contended that it took nearly five months, the Spanish forces eventually crushed the rebellion. Many of the rebels were captured, including two mulatto slaves named José Pérez and José Tadeo (aka "the Carpenter"), who were publicly executed in 1737 as the principal leaders of the uprising. Yet, a significant number of the rebels remained at large and joined existing palenques such as Mandinga, or founded new ones.

The rebellion of 1735 clearly unsettled the Spanish population in the region of Córdoba for quite some time. Over thirty years later, *hacendados* (plantation owners) described it as totally crippling to regional sugar and tobacco production.[38] Perhaps most frightening to the local planters was what they perceived to be the clear and close contact between the rebels and the slaves that remained on the *ingenios* (sugar plantations). Without close collaboration between the two, planters asserted, the 1735 rebellion would not have attained such magnitude.

Following the violence of 1735, the Spanish authorities in Córdoba launched numerous unsuccessful expeditions to subdue the growing number of palenques in the region. Conditions remained unsettled—with outbreaks of rebellion in 1741 and 1749—until 1762, when a group of cimarrones once again petitioned for legal recognition of their freedom.

This time they appealed directly to the viceroy, responding to his colony-wide call for men to assist in defending the coast against an imminent British naval attack following the successful English invasion of Havana. The runaways offered their militia service in return for their freedom. The viceroy agreed to their terms but, once the emergency had passed, planters stubbornly refused to recognize this agreement and tried to reimpose their former slave status.[39]

As time passed the cimarrones began to experience internal discord due, in part, to the fact that their numbers were growing larger thanks to a steady influx of new runaways. In 1767, when the cimarrones began their final round of negotiations with Spanish authorities, the total population of Mandinga numbered sixty-nine persons, three times the number three decades earlier.[40] At some point, a power struggle developed among the cimarrones as they debated over the future course of their settlement.

Many of the older and battle-weary runaways favored negotiating a truce with the Spaniards, but a small segment of newcomers resisted peace negotiations. In 1767, the former group, led by Fernando Manuel, renewed their petition for freedom. The move led to tensions within the group and resulted in armed conflict between Manuel's followers and the more radical group led by a runaway named Macute. Manuel's group eventually defeated Macute's, taking seventeen prisoners who were returned to their masters by Manuel.[41]

However you read it, the internal unrest in the Mandinga community presents us with a striking turn of events. Runaways regularly agreed to become slave catchers in the wake of negotiations to secure their own personal freedom, but in this instance the cimarrones led by Manuel actually returned some of their compatriots *during* such negotiations, perhaps as a show of good faith and/or to simply remove internal rivals.

In 1769, the cimarrones were granted their freedom and given permission to build a town on a site along the Amapa River. The recently freed ex-slaves swore allegiance to the king, vowed to obey local authorities, pledged to serve in the colonial militia, agreed to capture and return future runaways for a fee, and promised to pay the tribute that the Crown imposed upon free blacks.[42] Fernando Manuel named his town in honor of Our Lady of Guadalupe for her assistance in defeating the upstart Macute and his supporters.[43] As was the case with the Yanguicos, however, the documents provide little clue as to what caused slaves in Córdoba to run away and rebel in the first place.

The "Great Escape" from Santa Bárbara de Calderón

During the same decade that Amapa was founded, a novel form of collective slave resistance rocked another major sugar-producing region in Mexico, this time in the modern state of Morelos. On August 9, 1763, nearly fifty panicked slaves frantically descended the stairs from the main house of Santa Bárbara de Calderón, a sugar plantation, and fled the hacienda wielding their weapons, or tools, depending on whose testimony you read.

Founded in the first decade of the seventeenth century, Calderón was one of the oldest and largest sugar plantations in the Amilpas region near Cuautla, maintaining a slave population of over one hundred slaves throughout the eighteenth century, when it came into the possession of don Ascencio González in 1758.[44] On the morning of August 9, on orders from the *mayordomo* (overseer), the entire slave population, totaling 104 men, women, and children, left the fields where they were working in order to be appraised and evaluated in the course of settling the last will and testament of the recently deceased don Ascencio. The assessors testified that the slaves "insolently" refused to lay down their "weapons" prior to being appraised and thus remained armed throughout the process. The slaves testified that they refused to lay down their "tools" because they feared they might be stolen.[45]

Once the evaluation was completed, the slaves, still armed, demanded to know who, exactly, would become their owner in light of don Ascencio's death. When they were told that don Manuel Ruiz de Castañeda, the husband of don Ascencio's daughter, was to be their new owner, the slaves cried out "in a single voice" that they refused to recognize him as their master. Rather, the slaves preferred that don Juan Díaz Cano, a friend of don Ascencio, take control of the hacienda.

Powerless to intervene, don Manuel and the assessors watched as the armed slaves then left the house and fled the hacienda. Two of these slaves returned to the hacienda and informed don Manuel that the runaways planned to make their way to Mexico City to appeal to colonial officials to improve living conditions on the hacienda. The group who fled the plantation—including at least forty-nine slaves (thirty males over eight years of age and nineteen women) and seven free workers—arrived in Mexico City two days later and set up camp in front of the viceregal palace. On their journey, they had sold their tools/weapons to buy food. On August 12, 1763, they were taken into custody and moved to the royal jail. The six slaves identified as the leaders of the rebellion, five men and one woman, were separated from their compatriots and interrogated. The transcripts of the interrogations provide rare and invaluable access to slave testimony regarding the causes and goals for their rebellious actions.

The actions taken by the Calderón slaves were quite novel compared to the other instances of collective resistive action taken by slaves we have seen so far. Rather than fleeing into the countryside and establishing a runaway community, or dispersing and trying to integrate themselves into the sizeable free population of African descent in the colony (which was actually larger than the slave population at this point), these slaves made their way to Mexico City in the hopes of appearing before the highest-ranking colonial officials to complain about the unbearable conditions on their plantation.[46]

The principal complaint of this group of slaves was that life had become insufferable since the death of their owner don Ascencio in April 1763, so bad, they argued, that they felt compelled to run away despite a real fear of being executed for doing so. Specifically, they complained that their workloads had been increased to unbearable levels, that the intensity of physical coercion had reached abusive proportions, and that their new owners ignored their frequent complaints to that effect.

Under the new regime, the daily workload for field slaves had been increased such that it was twice the labor assigned to paid, free field hands. Completing the new quotas required working from before daybreak until after nightfall without taking a rest, even for food or water. In addition, the slaves complained that they were being forced to work on Sundays and festival days, which were as a rule set aside for rest and prayer. Lastly, skilled slaves, who normally only worked in the crushing mill/boiling house complex, were now expected to labor in the fields as well. These new demands were, the slaves suggested, significantly higher than those faced by slaves on any other plantation in the region and much greater than those they had experienced under don Ascencio.

If deteriorating labor conditions represented the principal complaint of the slaves and a primary justification for their flight, it was rivaled by their concerns about their sadistic mayordomo, Pedro de Luna. The slaves testified that de Luna increasingly resorted to violence to compel the completion of the augmented daily workload, punishing slaves for the slightest mistakes, if they stopped for rest, or if they asked to eat. In addition, they accused Luna of beating them with whips and sticks dipped in burning embers and/or lye with the expressed intent of significantly increasing the level of pain. In fact, "in his cruelty" he had recently beaten three slaves so severely that two had subsequently died of their wounds while the third lay on his deathbed when they fled the hacienda.[47]

Making matters worse, the slaves argued that despite their frequent complaints their new masters, don Manuel and his wife doña Ignacia, had refused to intervene on their behalf. Ana María Chiquita, the only woman to be interrogated, testified to her dashed hopes that her masters would treat her and her fellow slaves as *criados*—which translates as servant but implies a level of concern, care, and protection provided by the master— and protect them. However, in response to such complaints their new owners simply "put [their] hands in [their] belt[s]" and did nothing to protect them from the abuses of the mayordomo.[48] In the eyes of the slaves, this lack of action by their new owners, who appear to have been resident at the ingenio, suggested that they were complicit in the abuses they suffered.

Importantly, their visions of acceptable master-slave relations were grounded squarely in their experiences under don Ascencio who they clearly viewed as kind and fair when compared to don Manuel. To drive this point home Ana María testified that when it rained don Ascencio would send blankets to the fieldworkers to protect them from the downpour. Additionally, in instances of torrential rainfall and fierce storms, he would bring all the workers in from the fields. Since his death, however, the slaves were required to work in the fields even in the most violent of rainstorms and were still expected to complete the increased daily workload.[49] Under don Ascencio's benign mastership, they argued, the Calderón slaves were the envy of the other ingenios of the region due to their reputation as good and faithful workers. Moreover, they intimated that if conditions were restored to levels experienced during his administration they would gladly return to the hacienda, their labors, and, by extension, their enslavement.

Don Manuel painted a completely different picture in his description of the breakdown of order at Calderón. The slaves, he argued, were a lazy and unruly bunch, unwilling to submit to his demands and those of the mayordomo. The slaves worked only at their own whim, with little or no respect for those who ran the plantation because they were more concerned with dancing and getting drunk than working. Their insolence was so great, he suggested, that they openly discussed their plans to murder anyone other than don Juan Díaz Cano who might be placed in charge of the hacienda.

Don Manuel defended his administration of the plantation by arguing that he was dealing with slaves, a "rude and simple" people who are predisposed to being troublesome and violently resisting their subjugation. Therefore, he argued, to excuse them from their servitude would result, and had resulted, in serious damage to the interests of the hacienda. Moreover, their very nature made it necessary, he wrote, to commit grave excesses in order to subjugate them to their normal and customary labors. To subdue his slaves, who he felt were united against him, it was necessary to intimidate and dominate three or four them as examples for the rest.[50] Don Manuel tacitly implies that he had ratcheted up the workload and the level of physical coercion on the hacienda in order to re-subject the slaves to their servitude.

Importantly, the mass flight and the slaves' belief that the colonial authorities would intervene on their behalf if they could prove mistreatment were not aberrations, but rather the most recent in a series of ongoing conflicts between masters and slaves at Calderón. Following don Ascencio's death, six unidentified slaves had fled the hacienda at different times carrying complaints regarding their treatment to the Audiencia, which responded by sending at least two dispatches admonishing the managers of Calderón to treat their slaves better. The slaves testified that the severity of mistreatment and overwork, save being forced to work on festival days, had subsided since then but, based on their decision to flee in August 1763, conditions remained unbearable.

From don Manuel's perspective, however, these intrusions by colonial authorities into hacienda discipline made the slaves recalcitrant and unwilling to submit to his authority. He complained that the slaves could not be forced to complete any more work than what they believed to be acceptable. Any attempt on his part to extract additional labor was met with a threat to once again appeal to colonial authorities. Additionally, don Manuel wrote that the confrontation on August 9 was not the only time in the recent past that the slaves, as an armed mass, had threatened their owners and overseers. Following the receipt of one of the dispatches from the Audiencia reprimanding the overseers, the slaves had entered the main house en masse, and brandished their weapons and tools, threatening that someone would pay for the recent deaths of their compatriots.

The Calderón slaves were obviously emboldened by the apparent support of the Audiencia. Equally significant, an incident in their collective past might have led them to believe that outside assistance was available and that they could get away with trying to intimidate their owners with the threat of violence. On May 26, 1728, following another appraisal related to the apparent bankruptcy of the ingenio, the Calderón slaves—armed with knives and machetes—imposed themselves on colonial authorities in an attempt to influence the transfer of control of the hacienda. They threatened to burn it to the ground "sending [all those who lived there] to the Devil" if it fell under the control of the neighboring Hospital and Casasano ingenios. Their actions, in this instance, were driven by a real fear that the owners of the aforementioned haciendas would break up their slave community in retribution for the alleged theft of some cattle.[51] In the end, the colonial officials convinced the slaves to lay down their arms with assurances that they would not be placed under the control of either ingenio.

Whether or not the actions and threats by the slaves actually affected who subsequently took control of Calderón is not really important, because the slaves certainly believed they influenced the outcome. Perhaps some of the slaves living on Calderón in 1763 had actually lived through the tumult in 1728. If not, it is highly likely that stories of that incident were passed from generation to generation of slaves and served as a blueprint for collective action in 1763.

The nature of this action by slaves has significant implications for our understanding of the other slave rebellions discussed herein. Unlike sources on the previously discussed uprisings, those for Calderón provide both the slaves' and masters' perspectives on the ongoing conflict between the two. Master-slave relations were clearly conflictual and slave rebellion and flight could be seen as a last resort when slaves became convinced that they were losing what little agency they had in those daily conflicts to affect their living and working conditions.

A larger, and at this point unanswerable, question is whether or not slaves at Calderón and on neighboring haciendas had any knowledge of the ongoing conflict and negotiations between the cimarrones and the state in Córdoba that would eventually result in the foundation of Amapa or the Yanguicos' successful establishment of San Lorenzo in the seventeenth century. Whether they did or not the Calderón slaves chose negotiation over *cimarronaje* (flight) to address their concerns. Their actions do not appear to have been in pursuit of liberty but rather aimed at improving the conditions of their servitude.

Measuring the success of the mass flight from the slaves' perspective is a difficult task. On August 19, all of the identified leaders of the mutiny, save Ana María, were brought before the rest of the runaways in Mexico City, tied to a post, and given six lashes apiece. At that point, the remaining slaves requested that they be returned to the hacienda where they promised to live obediently. More devastating to the Calderón slave community, however, was the fact that the six leaders of the mutiny were not allowed to return with their compatriots, but were sent to an *obraje* (woolen textile mill) in Mexico City to be sold in accordance with don Manuel's wishes. The loss of these six slaves not only as community leaders but also potentially as spouses, lovers, parents, relatives, and friends of the remaining slaves must have been a severe blow.

Yet, in the same court order that prescribed the punishment discussed above, the members of the Audiencia also admonished Calderón's administrators, again, to treat their slaves better, beginning immediately. In fact, the Audiencia demanded that the slaves not be punished in any excessive manner and that they not be forced to complete any more work than was the customary expectation on all the haciendas throughout the Amilpas. And finally, the judges recommended that the mayordomo, Pedro de Luna, be replaced with someone who would treat the slaves better, and thereby secure the smooth operation of the hacienda. This might appear to be a victory of sorts for the slaves, but it was not uncommon for the Audiencia and ecclesiastical or inquisitorial courts to caution slave owners to treat their chattel better in instances of apparent abuse. The unanswerable question becomes: did the colonial authorities enforce those orders?

These instances of slave rebelliousness in the eighteenth century underscore the continued importance of slavery to the colonial economy, particularly to sugar production, despite expectations of decline after 1640. The nature of the eighteenth-century rebellions discussed above does not suggest that the ideological strength of slavery was slipping and that the rebels from Calderón and Córdoba were emboldened by their sense that slavery was slowly dying.[52] The Calderón slaves attempted to negotiate improvements in their servitude to levels they had experienced under their previous master but did not question the basic legitimacy of their status as chattel. Similarly, despite the continued presence of runaways in Córdoba the sugar and tobacco economies there recovered from the effects of the 1735, 1741, and 1749 rebellions and continued to rely on a predominantly slave-labor force for over half a century. In fact, as late as 1788 the 1,265 slaves laboring on the sixteen sugar plantations in the province of Córdoba represented a third of the total rural population and nearly 67 percent of total resident laborers.⁵³ If sufficient free wage laborers, Indians, or *castas*, were available in Morelos and Córdoba, as is suggested by historiographical convention, why then would sugar producers in these regions continue to rely upon such a volatile labor force as chattel slavery?

Conclusion: Slaves, Masters, and the State

Another interesting theme that emerges from our discussions of these four rebellions is the willingness of the Spanish colonial state to interject itself into these disputes, to serve as mediator between masters and slaves, planters and runaway slaves. Historians have long treated Latin American slavery as distinctive because of the limited legal protections extended to the enslaved and the fact that slaves could appear in legal proceedings as plaintiffs and witnesses (even against their masters), both of which were largely denied slaves in British North America.⁵⁴ A key component of Spanish colonial rule was the deployment of civil, ecclesiastical, and even inquisitorial courts that literally and figuratively represented the state's authority to mediate disputes, resolve conflicts, and impose decisions and punishments in the name of colonial stability. By allowing all colonials—regardless of their race, class, gender, or status (free vs. enslaved)—access to these institutions, the Spanish defused dissent, thereby weakening the ability of colonial subjects to mount a radical challenge to the colonial structure.⁵⁵ Herman Bennett asserts, correctly in my mind, that the state's goal in extending such protections to the enslaved was not to ameliorate slavery, as Frank Tannenbaum argued in *Slave and Citizen*, but to empower the state at the expense of the absolute authority that slaveholders theoretically enjoyed over their chattel.⁵⁶

Moreover, it was the politically expedient thing to do. The inability of colonial authorities to subdue the Yanguico and Mandinga runaways, the constant threat of slave rebellion in Córdoba after 1725, the destruction wrought by the 1735 rebellion, and the potential for violence inherent in the mass flight of the armed Calderón slaves all suggest that colonial stability and maintenance of slavery as an institution was precarious. Thus, the state was defusing potentially destructive situations in the best way possible. But violent repression, as seen in the response to the 1612 rebellion and the numerous attempts to destroy the Yanguico and Mandinga palenques, was always the preferred method of controlling the slave population.

The ability of the Calderón slaves to engage the state, to press their demands and expectations for how slavery should operate in colonial courts, and the fact that runaway slaves could successfully petition the colonial state for their freedom (inherently divesting their masters of their right of ownership) and citizenship, provide clear evidence of the negotiated nature of power relations in the colony. Each of these cases is extraordinary, but the negotiations within them, I would suggest, are not. Negotiation between masters and slaves was not limited only to those instances of state mediation.[57] Rather, such interventions, although exceptional, produced historical documents (much to the delight of historians) that bring into view the ongoing contestations, the normal social dynamics, of master-slave relations.[58] In other words, master-slave relations cannot be characterized simply by compliance, on one hand, and rebellion on the other, but rather by continual negotiation that had the potential to become violent.

But how do we interpret these rebellions? Are they evidence of a popular slave ideology, a universal desire for freedom, which created the constant potential for revolt, even before the rhetoric of the Atlantic revolutions provided a fully developed "lexicon of liberty" with which to express those desires?[59] Certainly planters and colonial authorities feared they were. But are there distinctions to be made between suggesting that slaves resisted slavery in pursuit of liberty and that they resisted in order to escape or alleviate elements of their particular oppression? Indeed, in cases of flight, was "personal liberty" in the abstract sense, mainly an outcome or a fundamental cause of resistance? In other words, did a slave ideology exist that truly asserted an inert desire for liberty or, if such an ideology existed, was it more predicated upon simply searching for enough freedom for slaves to make "a life of their own in the circumstances [i.e. slavery] in which they found themselves"?[60]

These are difficult and challenging questions to answer. Perhaps part of the confusion in trying to address them comes from the tendency to treat slave rebellion (which might include the creation of runaway communities) and the actions of runaways as a single phenomenon. But, there is a real danger in reading the actions taken by runaway communities to preserve, and at times legalize, their newfound liberty as representative of, or evidence for, a universal desire for liberty among slaves. For example, both of the palenques discussed in this chapter were clear manifestations of slave resistance. They were created by slaves who made the decision to flee, individually or in groups, the particular conditions of their enslavement. However, for our purposes, it is important to keep in mind that the residents of the palenques entered into a series of successful negotiations with colonial officials to secure and make permanent their personal status as freed persons. Negotiations such as these could be used as evidence of the universal desire for liberty among slaves. But in reality, the negotiations do not necessarily address the issues that prompted the slaves to flee in the first place.

Put plainly, slaves who had successfully escaped slavery and become cimarrones had undergone a change in their subject position. Their actions were no longer representative of slaves, but of *runaway* slaves. Thus, while the creation of runaway communities serves as clear evidence of slave resistance, it is not necessarily true that the actions of successful runaways speaks to worldviews, opinions, and actions of slaves who were still in captivity. If we are to achieve a deeper understanding of their perspectives, then we need to focus our attention on the motivations for *initial* slave flight. Unfortunately, given the nature of archival evidence, this is not always possible.

These rebellions highlight the difficulty in assessing the motivations for collective slave resistance in the absence of actual rebel testimony to that effect. In most cases, we are left to infer causes for flight and rebellion from elite descriptions of such movements. It is for that reason that the sources on the Calderón mass flight are so extraordinary. Based on the testimony from slaves in that instance, it is clear that their rebellious energies might be better described as aimed at improving the conditions of their servitude, rather than escaping or destroying it. Rebellion and flight might be seen as evidence of an understanding on the part of slaves that normal master-slave relations, based in conflict but allowing for slight improvements in the social position of slaves, had broken down. Or, that the particular circumstances of their servitude had become untenable from the perspective of slaves. Perhaps then, slave resistance should be treated as a continuum in which flight and rebellion, while lying at one pole, were often motivated by the very same issues that prompted day-to-day resistance that would lie at the other pole. In the continuum of slave resistance, then, rebellion and flight were more often than not actions of last resort.

In closing, there are two important points that need to be made. First, we cannot universalize slave motivations for rebellion from the Calderón example because it is the only source that provides slave voices discussed herein. But their actions and testimonies do call into question the possibility that slaves across all chronological and geographical contexts shared a popular slave ideology or a universal desire for liberty. Second, and equally important, in no way should that fact be used to support the assertion that slaves accepted their social position. Clearly, each instance of rebellion discussed herein highlights the extremes to which slaves were willing to go to fight back against the near total oppression inherent in slavery. Their actions alone are enough to validate their constant struggle against its dehumanizing effects. As such, it behooves us as students of history to better understand how they comprehended that struggle and *their* motivations for violent resistance.

✢ NOTES ✢

This essay is explicitly focused on collective resistance, primarily armed rebellion and the formation of palenques; day-to-day forms of resistance that are equally important to understanding the operation and experiences of slavery are not explored here.

1. Luís Querol y Ruso, *Negros y mulatos de Nueva España, historia de su alzamiento de 1612* (Valencia: Imprenta Hijo F. Vives Mora, 1935), 25–32. He includes a transcription of an anonymous description of the rebellion, ms. 2010, fol. 236, no. 168 from the *Sección de Manuscritos de la Biblioteca Nacional de Madrid*.

2. Archivo General de la Nación (AGN), Criminal, vol. 135, exp. 56, fols. 183–214.

3. Herman L. Bennett, *Africans in Colonial Mexico: Absolutism, Christianity, and Afro-Creole Consciousness, 1570–1640* (Bloomington: University of Indiana Press, 2003), 14. Regular imports to New Spain ended in 1640; after that point the delivery of slaves was sporadic at best.

4. Frank "Trey" Proctor III, "Afro-Mexican Slave Labor in the Obrajes de Paños of New Spain, Seventeenth and Eighteenth Centuries," *The Americas* 60, no. 1 (2003): 33–58.

5. Patrick J. Carroll, *Blacks in Colonial Veracruz: Race, Ethnicity, and Regional Development* (Austin: University of Texas Press, 2001), 30–34; and Russell R. Menard and Stuart B. Schwartz, "Why African Slavery? Labor Force Transitions in Brazil, Mexico, and the Carolina Lowcountry," in *Slavery in the Americas*, ed. Wolfgang Binder, 96–101 (Würzburg, Germany:

Königshausen and Neumann, 1993); Colin A. Palmer, *Slaves of the White God: Blacks in Mexico, 1570–1650* (Cambridge: Harvard University Press, 1976), 1–4; and Dennis N. Valdés, "The Decline of Slavery in Mexico," *The Americas* 44, no. 2 (1987): 167–94.

6. R. Douglas Cope, *The Limits of Racial Domination: Plebian Society in Colonial Mexico City, 1660–1720* (Madison: University of Wisconsin Press, 1994), 95–96.

7. Andrés Pérez de Ribas, *Corónica y historia religiosa de la provincia de la Compañía de Jesús de México en Nueva España*, 2 vols. (México, 1896), I:282–84; Virrey Montesclaros a Pedro de Bahena, August 23, 1606, quoted in Octaviano Corro, *Los Cimarrones y la fundación de Amapa* (México, 1951), 17.

8. Archivo General de Indias (AGI), México, Carta de Virrey Luís de Velasco a S.M., 9 de Marzo, 1608, sección 6. For a discussion of typical responses to runaway communities by colonial authorities, see Patrick J. Carroll, "Mandinga: The Evolution of a Mexican Runaway Slave Community," *Comparative Studies in Society and History* 19, no. 4 (1977): 488–93; and João José Reis, "Quilombos e revoltas escravas no Brasil," *Revista USP, São Paulo* 28 (1995–96): 21.

9. AGN, Tierras, vol. 2959, exp. 66, fol. 1.

10. AGI, México, Carta de Virrey Luís de Velasco a S.M., 9 de Marzo, 1608, sección 6.

11. AGN, Inquisición, vol. 283, exp. 26, fol. 186.

12. AGI, México, Carta de Virrey Velasco a S.M., 17 de Diciembre, 1608, sección 7.

13. Ibid., 13 de Febrero, 1609, sección 12; and Ibid., 24 de Mayo, 1609, secciones 13 and 14.

14. Excerpts of this account are included in Pérez de Ribas, *Corónica y historia religiosa*, I:282.

15. Bennett, *Africans in Colonial Mexico*, 52.

16. At this point in the saga, Padre Laurencio's first-hand narration of the assault ends, but Pérez de Ribas continued with the account, *Corónica y historia religiosa*, I:282–85; 288–89.

17. Pérez de Ribas, *Corónica y historia religiosa*, I:292–93.

18. Francisco Javier Alegre, *Historia de la Compañía de Jesús en Nueva España*, 2 vols. (México, 1842), II:16; and Enrique Herrera Moreno, *El Cantón de Córdoba*, 2 vols. (Tacubaya, México: Editorial Citlaltépetl, 1959), I:96–97.

Viceregal correspondence detailing Gonzalez's expedition did not mention a settlement between Yanga and the Spaniards; see AGI, México, Carta de Virrey Velasco a S.M., 12 de Octubre, 1610, sección 10. William Taylor asserts that two separate communities were founded in the jurisdiction of Veracruz—San Lorenzo de los Negros in 1612 and San Lorenzo de Cerralvo in 1630—both as the result of negotiations between cimarrones and the viceroyalty; see William B. Taylor, "The Foundation of Nuestra Señora de Guadalupe de los Morenos de Amapa," *The Americas* 26, no. 4 (1970): 440. But he based his conclusions on those of David Davidson who argued that the list of demands from 1608 was actually a misdated treaty written after the assault, an assertion that now seems unlikely; see David M. Davidson, "Negro Slave Control and Resistance in Colonial Mexico, 1519–1650," *HAHR* 46, no. 3 (1966): 250.

19. AGI, México, Virrey Don Rodrigo Fernández de Córdoba al Consejo de Indies, 25 de Mayo, 1618, sección 5.

20. Adriana Naveda Chávez-Hita argues that the town was founded in 1635 as San Lorenzo de los Negros or San Lorenzo de Cerralvo; see *Esclavos negros en las haciendas azucareras de Córdoba, Veracruz, 1690–1830* (Xalapa: Universidad Veracruzana, Centro de Investigaciones Históricas, 1987), 126–28.

21. María Elena Martínez, "The Black Blood of New Spain: *Limpieza de Sangre*, Racial Violence, and Gendered Power in Early Colonial Mexico," *William and Mary Quarterly, Third Series* 61, no. 3 (2004): 480.

22. Juan de Torquemada, *Monarquía Indiana*, 3 vols. (México: Editorial Porrúa, 1969), 719; and Augustín Vetancourt, *Teatro Mexicano* (México: Editorial Porrúa, 1971), 217. These fears were only amplified in light of the repression of another group of free and enslaved Afro-Mexicans in 1608. Viceroy Velasco reported that the *alcalde del crimen* was pursuing a case against a group of Afro-Mexicans that had joined together to "spend their money [stolen from their masters] in excessive drinking, eating and gaming. And that the last time they got together they elected a King and Queen, as well as some other titles and offices with too much liberty." See AGI, México, Carta de Viceroy Velasco a S.M., 13 de Febrero, 1609, sección 9. For a fuller discussion of the rebellion see, Palmer, *Slaves of the White God*, 135–38.

23. Martínez, "The Black Blood of New Spain"; and Querol y Ruso, *Negros y mulatos*, 25–37.

24. For a discussion of the ceremonial roles of the king and queen and their importance within black and mulatto confraternities, see Joan Cameron Bristol, "Negotiating Authority in New Spain: Blacks, Mulattos, and Religious

Practice in the Seventeenth Century," Ph.D. diss., University of Pennsylvania, 2001, 94.

25. Querol y Ruso, *Negros y mulatos*, 30. Joan Bristol suggests that the ceremony may have had Central African origins, see "Negotiating Authority in New Spain," 94.

26. Vetancourt, *Teatro Mexicano*, 217.

27. AGN, Ordenanzas, vol. 1, exp. 164, fol. 146; exp. 167, fol. 147; and, exp. 172, fols. 149–50.

28. Antonio Vázquez de Espinosa, *Compendio y descripción de la Indias Occidentales*, ed. Charles Clark (Washington, D.C.: Smithsonian Institute, 1948), 146.

29. Gonzalo Aguirre Beltrán, *La población negra de México. Estudio etnohistórico*, 3rd ed. (Mexico City: Fondo de Cultura Económica, 1989), 219.

30. Monica Schuler, "Akan Slave Rebellions in the British Caribbean," *Savacou* 1, no. 1 (June 1970): 373–86; and Monica Schuler, "Ethnic Slave Rebellions in the Caribbean and the Guianas," *Journal of Social History* 3 (1970): 274–85.

31. For studies that do try to make direct connections between political change in Africa and slave rebellion in the Americas see, Paul E. Lovejoy, "Background to Rebellion: The Origins of Muslim Slaves in Bahia," *Slavery and Abolition* 15 (1995): 151–80; and John K. Thornton, "African Dimensions of the Stono Rebellion," *American Historical Review* 96, no. 4 (1991): 1101–13.

32. In the 1640s less than 10 percent of African slaves who married in Mexico City selected Mexico-born blacks or mulattos to be their spouse; see Frank "Trey" Proctor III, "African Diasporic Ethnicity and Slave Community Formation in Mexico City to 1650," in *Expanding the Diaspora: Africans in Colonial Latin America*, ed. Sherwin Bryant, Rachel O'Toole, and Ben Vinson III (Champaign: University of Illinois Press, forthcoming); and Frank "Trey" Proctor III, "Slavery, Identity, and Culture: An Afro-Mexican Counterpoint, 1640–1763," Ph.D. diss., Emory University, 2003, particularly Chapter 4, "Marriage Patterns and Community Formation," 135–98.

33. Ben Vinson III, *Bearing Arms for His Majesty: The Free-Colored Militia in Colonial Mexico* (Stanford: Stanford University Press, 2001), 205–7.

34. Carroll, "Mandinga," 494. Also see, AGN Tierras, vol. 3543, exp. 1–3; Patrick J. Carroll and Aurelio de los Reyes, "Amapa, Oaxaca: Pueblos de Cimarrones (Noticias Históricas)," *Boletín del Instituto Nacional de Antropología e Historia de México, época II, num. 4* (1973): 43–50; and Taylor, "Foundation of Amapa," 439–46. Taylor includes a translated copy of the introduction to the baptismal book of Amapa recounting the founding of

the pueblo, which is housed in the manuscript collection of the Zimmerman Library, University of New Mexico.

35. Taylor, "Foundation of Amapa," 443; and Carroll, "Mandinga," 497.
36. AGN, Tierras, vol. 3543, exp. 1, fols. 67 and 78v.
37. Archivo Municipal de Córdoba (AMC), vol. 21, año 1735, fols. 3–5, as quoted in Naveda Chávez-Hita, *Esclavos negros en Córdoba*, 133. See also Carroll, *Blacks in Colonial Veracruz*, 97.
38. AGN, Tierras, vol. 3543, exp. 1, fols. 77–78.
39. Taylor, "Foundation of Amapa," 444.
40. This number included the fifty-two listed in Mandinga and seventeen others who had been turned over to local authorities to be returned to their masters. See AGN, Tierras, vol. 3543, exp. 1, fols. 7 and 111.
41. AGN, Tierras, vol. 3543, exp. 1, fol. 111.
42. Manuel proved true to his promise, capturing twenty-seven runaways, and actively pursuing some eight others near Orizaba in 1771 (AGN, Tierras, vol. 3543, exp. 2, fol. 126).
43. Taylor, "Foundation of Amapa," 443.
44. Brígida von Mentz, *Trabajo, sujeción y libertad en el centro de la Nueva España. Esclavos, aprendices, campesinos y operarios manufactureros, siglos XVI a XVIII* (Mexico City: CIESAS, 1999), 381.

    In 1708, the slave population totaled 130 slaves, in 1728 the total was 101 slaves, and in 1763 there were 104 slaves. See, AGN Bienes Nacionales leg. 908 exp. 11 fols. 70–82 (1708); AGN Bienes Nacionales leg. 98 exp. 2 (1728); and, AGN Tierras vol. 1935 fols. 48–50 (1763). The average slave holding in region during the eighteenth century was approximately seventy-one slaves; see Proctor III, "Slavery, Identity, and Culture," 35.
45. AGN, Criminal, vol. 135, exp. 56, fols. 1–21.
46. According to one estimate, the free population of African descent outnumbered slaves by a ratio of three-to-one by 1646. See Gonzalo Aguirre Beltrán, *La población negra de México: Estudio etnohistórico* (Mexico City: Fondo de Cultura Económica, 1946, 1989): 214–19.
47. For a discussion of slave reactions to physical coercion in New Spain, see Proctor, "Slavery, Identity and Culture," esp. chap. 6, "The Negotiation of Mastery and Slavery in New Spain," 235–80.
48. AGN, Criminal, vol. 135, exp. 56, fols. 183–214. The list of complaints was compiled from the six slave testimonies.
49. AGN, Criminal, vol. 135, exp. 56, fol. 213.

50. Don Manuel's letter reads both as a call for the Audiencia to show no leniency to the runaways in order to reestablish his authority as well as an explanation for the reported slave deaths and general defense of his administration of the hacienda. See AGN, Criminal, vol. 135, exp. 56, fols. 187–91.

51. AGN, Bienes Nacionales, vol. 131, exp. 10, fol. 2.

52. For examples of studies of nineteenth-century contexts where slave agency was affected by a general sense that slavery was coming to an end, see Carlos Aguirre, *Agentes de su propia libertad: Los esclavos de Lima y la desintegración de la esclavitud, 1821–1854* (Lima: Fondo Editorial de Pontificia Universidad Católica del Perú, 1993); and Ronaldo Vainfas, *Visões da liberdade: uma história das últimas décadas da escravidão na corte* (São Paulo: Companhia das Letras, 1990).

53. Fernando Winfield Capitaine, "Población rural en Córdoba, 1788," *La Palabra y el Hombre* 30, no. 2 (1979): 64–72. Slaves represented over 35 percent of the total rural population of the jurisdiction of Córdoba in 1788.

54. For example, see Frank Tannenbaum, *Slave and Citizen: The Negro in the Americas* (New York: Vintage Books, 1946; reprint, Boston: Beacon Press, 1992); and Herbert S. Klein, *Slavery in the Americas: A Comparative Study of Virginia and Cuba* (Chicago: University of Chicago Press, 1967).

55. For some of the best examples from the voluminous literature on the role of courts in imposing and maintaining colonial rule over indigenous peoples, see Susan Kellogg, *Law and the Transformation of Aztec Culture, 1500–1700* (Norman: University of Oklahoma Press, 1995); and Steve J. Stern, *Peru's Indian Peoples and the Challenge of Spanish Conquest: Huamanga to 1640*, 2nd ed. (Madison: University of Wisconsin Press, 1993). For discussions of the role of the colonial judicial institutions in mediating patriarchy, see Patricia Seed, *To Love, Honor, and Obey in Colonial Mexico: Conflicts over Marriage Choice, 1574–1821* (Stanford: Stanford University Press, 1988); and Steve J. Stern, *The Secret History of Gender: Women, Men, and Power in Late Colonial Mexico* (Chapel Hill: University of North Carolina Press, 1995).

56. Bennett, *Africans in Colonial Mexico*, 54.

57. For a similar understanding of criminal cases, see Stern, *Secret History of Gender*, 66.

58. Also see Lowell Gudmundson, "Negotiating Rights Under Slavery: The Slaves of San Geronimo (Baja Verapaz, Guatemala) Confront Their Dominican Masters in 1810," *The Americas* 60, no. 1 (2003): 109–14; and Stuart B. Schwartz, "Resistance and Accommodation in Eighteenth-century Brazil: The Slaves' View of Slavery," *HAHR* 57, no. 1 (1977): 69–81.

59. David Barry Gaspar, *Bondmen and Rebels: A Study of Master-Slave Relations in Antigua with Implications for Colonial British America* (Baltimore: Johns Hopkins University Press, 1985), 172, 256; Hilary McD. Beckles, *Black Rebellion in Barbados: The Struggle Against Slavery, 1627–1838* (Bridgetown, Barbados: Antilles Publications, 1984), 3. For a discussion of the "lexicon of liberation," see Peter Blanchard, "The Language of Liberation: Slave Voices in the Wars of Independence," *HAHR* 82, no. 3 (2002): 499–523.

60. Michael Craton, *Testing the Chains: Resistance to Slavery in the British West Indies* (Ithaca: Cornell University Press, 1982), 14.

Negotiating Two Worlds
The Free-Black Experience in Guerrero's Tierra Caliente

ANDREW B. FISHER

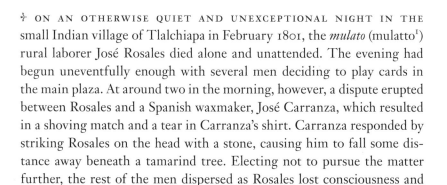

✣ ON AN OTHERWISE QUIET AND UNEXCEPTIONAL NIGHT IN THE small Indian village of Tlalchiapa in February 1801, the *mulato* (mulatto[1]) rural laborer José Rosales died alone and unattended. The evening had begun uneventfully enough with several men deciding to play cards in the main plaza. At around two in the morning, however, a dispute erupted between Rosales and a Spanish waxmaker, José Carranza, which resulted in a shoving match and a tear in Carranza's shirt. Carranza responded by striking Rosales on the head with a stone, causing him to fall some distance away beneath a tamarind tree. Electing not to pursue the matter further, the rest of the men dispersed as Rosales lost consciousness and eventually expired.

While Rosales was obviously unable to share his side of the story, the subsequent investigation into his apparent homicide did bring to light some of the factors that precipitated the night's violence. Most importantly, several witnesses and the defendant alluded to a series of exchanges involving contested notions of honor and racial identity. Carranza had allegedly told Rosales during their tussle, "go on, *negro*, tomorrow you will have to pay for my shirt," to which Rosales retorted, "yes, because of your gossipy mouth." Carranza claimed he struck Rosales with the stone because the deceased had slapped him, "which caused him much pain... as Rosales was a *mulato*." That Rosales might have taken similar umbrage to Carranza's behavior went unnoted. Instead, Spanish witnesses supported the actions of the waxmaker and vouched for Carranza's good character, despite his penchant for gambling. In contrast, Rosales, they claimed, had received his comeuppance as he "was a very quarrelsome provoker and braggart." To his peers, and probably to much of colonial Mexican society, José Carranza had justly defended his reputation and standing by not bowing down to someone he deemed his social and racial inferior. José Rosales, on the other hand, had paid the ultimate price by responding in kind with his own outburst of angry words and physical force. Thus it was the victim, not his attacker, whose character came away defamed.[2]

The last night of José Rosales's life underscores some of New Spain's most enduring sources of tension and conflict. Long associated with the stain of slavery, people of African descent faced racial prejudice and hostility well after most were no longer held in bondage.[3] To be born free, in other words, was hardly a marker of social acceptance nor did it provide blacks a secure position in a society so often characterized in outdated sixteenth-century terms: that is, one divided between privileged Spanish colonizers and a mass of indigenous peasants. Not well accommodated within this ideological schema, blacks like José Rosales faced ostracism and suspicion from those who saw them as a volatile and violent people who (ironically) did not accept their "place" in society. This sentiment extended beyond New Spain's white population. Indigenous people, too, were known to voice hostility, repugnance, and fear when it came to dealing with their fellow colonized subjects.

Of these two sets of relationships, historians have focused more on how enslaved and free blacks interacted with Hispanic colonists and institutions than with the indigenous world.[4] Recent studies have addressed this imbalance and in the process challenged previous assumptions about Indian-black relations. In particular, and as Patrick Carroll demonstrates in his chapter in this volume, the relationship could be relatively harmonious given the right set of circumstances.[5] This chapter seeks to demonstrate the benefits of uniting these two analytical threads through an examination of the region José Morales called his home, the *tierra caliente* (or hot lands) of the mid-Balsas River Depression, which comprises the northwest corner of the modern-day state of Guerrero and adjacent areas of Michoacán. The options open to blacks in the tierra caliente changed profoundly over the span of two centuries and were shaped by concurrent changes taking place in the region's indigenous peasant communities, its Hispanic ranches and mining camps, and the larger colony. After all, although his death came at the hands of a Spaniard, José Rosales lived in an Indian village, suggesting that both social spheres informed his life and that the boundary between the two could be quite porous.

Examining how the Hispanic and indigenous worlds impacted the choices available to blacks, we will see that the tierra caliente first proved attractive because of its thin Spanish presence and the absence of slavery as a dominant institution. For much of the early colonial period blacks found refuge, and at times relative autonomy, in a region marginal to Spanish interests. As they eschewed a racist Hispanic culture, blacks looked to establish a niche in the region's Indian peasant communities (*pueblos de indios*), then wracked by Old World disease and colonial dislocations. In the process, these newcomers and their descendants helped rebuild village society and reshape its culture.

Despite this history of collaboration, late eighteenth-century black residents and migrants to the tierra caliente received a decidedly hostile response from the indigenous peasantry. The last decades of the colonial period brought great duress to the region's peasant communities as a new generation of aggressive Hispanic estate owners and the Bourbon state seized scarce village land, municipal treasuries, and other collective resources.[6] Peasants responded by lashing out against unwelcome outsiders. Blacks proved to be particularly vulnerable to this hostility. While many Spaniards enjoyed the privileges and political clout their wealth and position in society afforded them, blacks generally lacked such resources and thus suffered the brunt of native ire with little protection.

Residing in a region undergoing mounting agrarian stress and social tensions, individuals like José Rosales found few opportunities and little tolerance. Facing the hostilities and suspicions of both whites and the indigenous population, they responded as best they could. Many continued to foster ties with their Indian neighbors, who still controlled much of the region's arable land. Others, however, found this established strategy of survival increasingly ineffective and sought other ways to protect their precarious social position between ambivalent Spanish ranchers and Indian villagers. As did Rosales, some responded to aggression and violence in kind, occasionally winning short-term relief. In the long run, however, these actions confirmed the stereotypical view of black people as violent, untrustworthy, and of low moral character, which Indians and Spaniards alike used to further their own interests.

Black Settlement in the Tierra Caliente

The presence of people of African descent in the tierra caliente dates to the earliest years of the Spanish colonial regime in Mexico. The first such individual was the famed "black conquistador" Juan Garrido, who participated in Antonio de Carvajal's expedition through much of what now comprises the state of Michoacán. Garrido and the rest of the group entered the far western end of the mid-Balsas Valley sometime around 1523–1524 to establish Spanish dominion over the region, but they did not linger for more than a few days. Erecting a Christian cross in the town of Zirándaro, the party secured additional supplies and Indian porters before continuing their journey to the coast.[7]

The economic order that coalesced over the following decades brought about the conditions that shaped the subsequent growth of the region's black population. The early colonial elite sought to enrich themselves through their access to local Indian labor and tribute. These men (*encomenderos*) also brokered business contracts with other colonists to exploit the region's mines. Through these profit-sharing arrangements, one partner purchased and brought to the tierra caliente enslaved Indians captured in the campaigns to extend the colony's northern frontier. Extant notarial records reveal that hundreds of Indians were shipped to the region from the north for this purpose. Encomenderos then arranged for their local tributary communities to construct shelters for the slaves and to supply food, clothing, and various tools.[8] This arrangement was not long lasting, however. Epidemic diseases brought on the catastrophic decline of the region's indigenous population and consequently limited how many resources encomenderos could extract from the peasantry. Combined with the exhaustion of easily worked mines and the gradual abolition of Indian slavery, Spanish interest in the tierra caliente declined appreciably after the mid-sixteenth century. Colonists thereafter abandoned the region in droves.[9]

In similar ecological zones of the colony, the indigenous demographic crisis often spurred the development of commercial estates and the introduction of large numbers of African slaves.¹⁰ Some encomenderos did traffic in the burgeoning African slave trade from the early 1520s, but this new form of slavery did not take hold in the tierra caliente. Quite simply, the unappealing prospects for commercial agriculture in the region and its plummeting mining economy made African slavery prohibitively expensive. In 1528, for instance, when the encomendero Juan de Burgos purchased a single black slave for 157 *pesos de oro de minas*, his compatriot Pedro Bazán was able to procure a total of fifty Indian slaves for just seven pesos less.¹¹ Given this price differential and the dismal prospects for commercial profit, African slavery could not replace the diminishing Indian labor supply. Paradoxically, then, the precipitous decline of the region's indigenous population, and the subsequent collapse of its dependent economy, prevented African slavery from proliferating as it did in areas of the colony with greater economic promise.

The crisis did, however, stimulate the migration of other blacks who were attracted by the region's thinly populated lands and weak government presence. Runaway slaves sought refuge in the tierra caliente's isolated and difficult terrain. In 1582, a Spanish rancher alerted colonial authorities to the activities of a group of fugitive blacks in the Cutzio vicinity, who rustled livestock, abused Indians and travelers, and seized women for their consorts. The rancher complained that the runaways were difficult to apprehend, since they made use of horses to move from one jurisdiction to another through rough roads and country.¹² Free people of African descent were also beginning to enter the region by around this time, although their presence, too, was not always welcomed. In 1592 colonial authorities promulgated an order of expulsion against mestizo and *mulato* bachelors residing in the Indian community of Pungarabato, citing complaints concerning their alleged abuse of the villagers.¹³

Official mandates and rancher complaints aside, free individuals of African descent continued to settle in this colonial backwater. Over time many of these people integrated into village society, although given legal restrictions against non-Indians residing in native communities such a presence was often overlooked and left unrecorded unless a particular grievance (such as in Pungarabato in 1592) was registered with authorities.¹⁴ Nevertheless, demographic data from the early 1680s reveal the presence of a significant number of free-born blacks in indigenous communities. Parish priests registered in these years 213 *negros* and *mulatos* living in the area, of whom only four were enslaved. They represented just 7.5 percent of the total population, but they played a particularly important role in pueblo society. The vast majority (157) resided on Indian land; what is more, eighty-eight of these individuals resided in some of the region's smallest villages and hamlets where they constituted a significant share of the population. Racial nomenclature also reflected clear residential patterns. While forty-five of the reported fifty *negros* resided in the Hispanic world of haciendas and mines, 152 of the 163 *mulatos* lived in Indian villages. This difference suggests that "*mulato*" may have shifted in local parlance from a term designating black-white intermixture to black-Indian ancestry.[15] From a colonial perspective, both terms were no doubt still viewed as blunt instruments that did not capture the growing racial heterogeneity of the rural poor after decades of interaction. Thus, in 1716, one crown official wrote nervously of the government's tenuous hold on "such remote lands," populated entirely by "Indians and people of 'broken color' [*gente de color quebrado*] and many delinquents [who were] favored by its harshness."[16]

A second magnet for black migration emerged by the late seventeenth century when livestock ranches overtook mining as the principal motor of commercial growth in the tierra caliente. These private estates offered employment opportunity for native-born blacks and migrants alike. A report filed in 1743, for instance, notes the seasonal influx of 218 "*mulato* vagabonds" from outlying jurisdictions in Michoacán, many of whom sought work collecting honey, planting corn, or driving cattle back to their home provinces.[17] As the eighteenth century progressed, land pressures in more heavily commercialized and densely populated zones of the viceroyalty served as a further incentive for black migration to the tierra caliente. Both the shift from ranching to farming in the nearby Iguala Valley of central Guerrero and the growing job insecurity and landlessness in the viceroyalty's breadbasket, the Bajío, contributed to the movement of cattle enterprises and laborers to the tierra caliente.[18]

Census reports reveal the long-term consequences of these economic developments. Approximately 1,856 *mulatos* (the most common term by then for local blacks) resided in the mid-Balsas Valley by the 1740s, representing 16.2 percent of the population, more than double their share sixty years earlier.[19] The following sixty years witnessed even greater growth. Most tellingly, blacks outpaced the indigenous population, which was rebounding from its previous demographic malaise. The Indian tributary count totaled 4,969 by the years 1800–1801, while the black tributary population registered a total of 1,976.[20] Stated differently, the proportion of

Indians to blacks declined over this sixty-year period from approximately 4.2 to 2.5 Indians per black inhabitant.²¹

To summarize, then, Juan Garrido and a few fugitive slaves may have been the first blacks to enter the tierra caliente, but it was the anonymous free *mulatos* cited in the Pungarabato complaint of 1592 and others like them that foreshadowed later trends. The precipitous decline of the native peasantry, upon which the early colonial economy depended, presented serious obstacles for the development of the region by Spanish colonists, including through African slavery. While few Spaniards were interested in settling the region until the late colonial period, descendants of enslaved Africans were. During the seventeenth and early eighteenth centuries many of these individuals and their children were assimilated into the struggling Indian communities that had welcomed them. The expansion of commercial enterprises in the years that followed initially increased the options available to blacks and spurred further migration to the mid-Balsas Valley. Ultimately, however, agrarian stresses emerged as expanding private estates competed with rebounding Indian villages for scarce arable land. Deteriorating conditions in other areas of the viceroyalty also drove migrants to a region that could no longer accommodate them. As a consequence, the tierra caliente became a tinder box of racial animosity by the late colonial period. Blacks sought ways to negotiate the rapidly colliding Hispanic and indigenous worlds, but they found few options before them and achieved fewer successes than their predecessors.

Free-Black Strategies of Survival

The first generations of black migrants to the tierra caliente had encountered a sparsely populated terrain occupied by a scattering of modest Indian pueblos and a few outlying livestock estates. Given the extent of Spanish disinterest in the region, the surviving Indian villages confronted few significant threats to their land until the eighteenth century. This meant that to ensure access to land many black migrants had to establish harmonious relations with area villagers. As long as land pressures between Indians and Spaniards was minimal, and declining native communities sought to assimilate outsiders, blacks were able to establish themselves in this poor and marginal corner of the colony.

Surviving records from the late seventeenth and early eighteenth century reveal some of the ways blacks were incorporated into village society.

Even if not immediately accepted as full members of the community, newcomers were allowed to settle and work on pueblo land. Indians commonly allowed non-Indians onto communal lands dedicated to the community's patron saints and other holy intercessors. To cite just one example, ten residents lived on lands dedicated to the religious hospital of the pueblo of Coyuca in 1683. Of these ten individuals, eight were *mulato*, one was a free *negro*, and one a *mestizo*.[22] In return, blacks entered an indigenous moral economy, offering various alms to the image or statue of the saint kept in the village's church whose land they occupied.[23] Later, as they and their children came to be accepted more as native villagers, blacks sought other ways to contribute to community welfare, pride and cohesion. Again, religious organizations were important means to this end. In 1730, for instance, Miguel Moxica, who described himself as a "native" (*natural*) and the "elder of the founders" of the pueblo of Pungarabato, initiated a petition with the bishopric court of Michoacán for official approval of the village's brotherhood of Santa Bárbara. In response, the sympathetic parish priest noted that Moxica was actually a free *mulato* rather than an Indian, a point the village's officials did not feel the need to mention, let alone denounce.[24]

Black residents in Indian villages also demonstrated their loyalty by supplying testimony in legal matters, a tradition that endured through the end of the colonial period. It is not surprising that Indians would look to blacks to fulfill this role given that Spanish officials held the testimony of non-Indians in greater esteem than that of indigenous witnesses. The dearth of local Spaniards and the enduring and intimate relationships between blacks and Indians made this a logical choice. To cite just one example, when the pueblo of Axochitlan moved to gain official title to their ancestral lands in 1709, their claims were supported by the testimony of two free *mulatos* and a *morisco*.[25] Two of these men had lived in the area for thirty and fifty years respectively and one was married to an indigenous woman.[26] Clearly, these were individuals well acquainted with the pueblo and with their neighbors.

Circumstances became bleaker for the region's black population during the last decades of the colonial era. To reiterate, migration accelerated in the eighteenth century as living conditions and employment opportunities deteriorated elsewhere in the colony. Indians also experienced their own demographic growth in the tierra caliente, which placed new pressures on village resources and social bonds. Assimilating outsiders into pueblo life no longer made sense at a time when a growing segment of the native-born lacked sufficient land. Making matters worse, villages faced new threats from the expanding commercial estates that dotted the countryside. Because pueblos had been able to retain much of their ancestral lands despite horrific population decline a century earlier, many ranchers were—like black migrants—essentially village dependents, reliant upon the favor of Indian officials to secure the arable land and pasture they coveted.[27]

Spaniards and blacks faced this situation on unequal footing. Ranchers forged alliances with complicit state magistrates to protect their access to village land despite often insistent Indian resistance. Their power and influence also meant that they hardly needed to act the part of good neighbor if such gestures went against their dispositions or interests. When the Spaniard Joseph Agustín Salgado was apprehended for theft in the village of Tetela, for instance, it made little difference that he enjoyed a reputation for indolence and vice while his Indian accuser was a respected village official and industrious rancher in his own right. Salgado's family connections led to his release and to the imprisonment of his accuser on trumped up charges.[28] Such behavior was unimaginable for poorer blacks lacking the elites' political connections. Moreover, as the most vulnerable group of outsiders, blacks risked expulsion, intimidation, and physical violence even when they endeavored to meet Indian expectations of good neighbors and fellow sons of the pueblo.

Whether living among Indian villagers or on the outskirts of pueblo territory, blacks frequently found themselves in harm's way at a time of mounting agrarian stress. This was particularly the case in the many boundary disputes that plagued the region in the late colonial era. Confrontation and violence were common as besieged pueblos battled one another and private estates for control over disputed land. Typically, combatants drove their cattle onto the disputed plots, destroyed their enemies' corrals, fields, and living structures, which they replaced with their own and guarded against any retaliatory measures. Ironically, these Indian conflicts often involved marginal lands traditionally worked and settled by black dependents. Their presence in the outbreaks lent the confrontations a decidedly racial undertone as villagers sought to expel non-Indian outsiders from land they claimed as their own.

The situation faced at the mid-century mark by black residents of the pueblo of San Miguel Totolapan exemplifies this dilemma. For a number of years the village had faced threats to its land tenure from several different quarters, including the pueblo of Poliutla and squatters from a nearby mining camp. Tensions reached a head in 1755 when a border skirmish erupted between peasants from Poliutla and a sole black defender of Totolapan's land claims. Pascual de Santiago was a sixty-year-old *negro libre* (free black) who had lived in the region since his youth. He had worked as a ranch hand for a Spanish hacendado before becoming the custodian of the cattle ranch of one of Totolapan's many village confraternities. While the Indian peasants of Poliutla were fighting another pueblo for control of the land, it was Pascual de Santiago who faced their wrath on behalf of the absent villagers. Abused and fleeced of ten pesos, he watched the villagers torch his home and topple the corral holding the brotherhood's cattle.[29]

As was the case with many land disputes in the region, Totolapan's grievance against the raid was aided by their non-native neighbors. The village presented the testimony of six witnesses, all of casta descent (two mestizos, three *mulatos*, and one negro) and half of whom lived in Totolapan and undoubtedly depended on the goodwill of the village for their livelihood.[30] Despite the rough treatment that Santiago had suffered and the testimony that two other non-Indian residents of the village provided on its behalf, Totolapan's legal representatives still elected to depict the conflict to colonial officials as one pitting "Indians" against "non-Indian" intruders. Thus, while the pueblo faced the threat of a number of squatters at the time of the attack, only those described as *"lobos* or *mulatos"* were singled out as particularly prejudicial to the village due to their wicked disposition.[31] Certainly, Totolapan's legal strategy echoes a familiar discourse that Indians hoped would resonate with the prejudices of Spanish colonial officials, but it could not have been well received by Pascual de Santiago and others like him who had courageously defended the village's land claims at risk of their own personal injury and loss of possessions.

Beholden to the Indian elite for access to village land, other blacks faced dilemmas similar to Pascual de Santiago during a period of heightened village stress. On the one hand, they were to honor the obligations expected of all pueblo "sons" in return for access to collective resources and assistance. In times of conflict this might mean defending the community with their fists, sharing gossip of its enemies with pueblo officials, or offering money and testimony in support of ongoing litigation. Yet, this extension of de facto kinship proved illusory as the sentiment spread that the penetration of racial outsiders and interlopers were to blame for declining conditions and impoverishment. Blacks residing in Indian villages thus faced hostility despite their goodwill, or even because of it.

Such a predicament was faced by *mulatos* who lived in the vicinity of the pueblo of Axochitlan during the intense factional fighting that plagued the town from the 1760s to the 1790s. Again, as with the example of the conflict between Poliutla and Totolapan, on the surface the struggle concerned only Indians. Two principal factions competed over the annual elections that would determine the pueblo's officers and the management of municipal property. Each side sought allies with rival factions in the nearby village of San Cristóbal as well as among notable Spaniards, including Axochitlan's priest and a string of resident *tenientes de justicia* (deputy district magistrates). The Spaniards participated in—even provoked— these disputes so as to gain for themselves access to the town's wealth and land. The resident black population, in contrast, had little to gain and much to lose if they were found supporting the losing faction. Unfortunately, maintaining neutrality proved difficult in a community where bonds of solidarity had been torn asunder by decades of bitter competition.

A couple of examples will illustrate this dilemma. During this extended struggle, in 1781, one of the town's cliques (known as the Vásquez party) approached the *mulato* Lucas Palacios and asked that he contribute forty pesos to support a suit against their enemies. Palacios hesitated initially and pointed out to the villagers that he intended to use his meager savings to roof his house. At the Indians' insistence, he agreed to turn over thirty pesos in return for promised work on the roof, perhaps understanding his participation as one of the many unstated obligations he met to remain in good standing with the pueblo. Palacios turned over most of the cash, but the villagers never reciprocated by fixing his roof. Vásquez leaders also insisted that the *mulato* Miguel Palacios raise funds among the residents of a nearby *ranchería*. He consented to the request, although his nephew Vicente convinced him not to turn over the money, fearful of the consequences for meddling in the village's ongoing dispute.[32]

Such anxieties were not unfounded. Ten years later, on June 30, 1791, an angry crowd representing one of the factions gathered at the home of the town's teniente de justicia, seized the official and dragged him to his adversary, the parish priest. While this was a carefully calculated move executed by the faction's leadership, the disturbance opened a window of opportunity for a more spontaneous demonstration of popular anger and resentment. Upon seizing the teniente, other villagers took advantage of the chaos by hurling rocks at those neighbors they identified as interfering *mulatos*.³³ As had been the case in Totolapan, blacks residing in Axochitlan found it difficult to demonstrate their fealty to their adopted villages. By the end of the colonial period, complex problems were frequently reduced to simpler and more tangible causes related to racial differences and antipathy.

As what had once been a haven from Spanish oppression and slavery vanished, some blacks looked to divorce themselves from pueblo life and establish a third space between Indian society and the ranches and mines of the Hispanic elite. Collective organization offered one possibility. A few attempted to create their own farming settlements along the margins of the territorial claims of Indian villages and Spanish private estates. These could be rather impromptu efforts. Economic downturns in the area's modest mining camps, for example, had always led migrant Indian, *mulato*, and mestizo workers to turn their attention to subsistence farming as a way to support their families.³⁴ Ranch workers also formed their own settlements either on estate property or near their borders. In at least one instance, such a place evolved into its own mini-pueblo of sorts. The multigenerational migrant hamlet of Cacalotepeque originated as a camp of mostly *mulato* migrant ranch hands in the second decade of the eighteenth century, coalescing over many decades into a semiautonomous farming community under the nominal auspices of the village of Tetela del Río.³⁵

Black migrants faced daunting obstacles to these sorts of strategies, however. Most importantly, an informal community lacked official title to its land, and thus its members could suffer eviction by nearby villages or private estates. By the late eighteenth century, when interethnic relations within local villages really began to sour, little land remained available to found new black settlements. Indeed, even a relatively established community like Cacalotepeque could not withstand the growing hostility and pressures. The hamlet succumbed in January 1783 to an attack mounted by several hundred villagers from the nearby pueblo of Apaxtla. Its residents offered a brave defense against overwhelming odds, but to little avail. Government apathy and Indian hostility spelled doom for the community after nearly seventy years of existence.

For most, the only realistic alternative to pueblo life was to seek employment on one of the many ranches or mining camps dotting the landscape. In doing so, however, blacks escaped one hostile environment for another. The personal lives of these mostly illiterate and mobile laborers is difficult to reconstruct, but the life of one rather unusual cowhand suggests the difficulties free blacks faced in the tierra caliente and at least one man's effort to navigate his way in an increasingly polarized society. Of ambiguous racial descent, Pascual Salazar (alias Saucedo) was born on a ranch near the pueblo of Huetamo in 1712 and spent most of his youth under the custodianship of a modest Hispanic ranching family from the district of Zirándaro.[36] As an adult, Salazar relied on his own wits and physical prowess to make his way in a world divided between Indian villagers and Spanish ranchers. His was a difficult and despised existence. A local priest described him as "a poor wretch who has not supported himself by any other means than that of his personal labor, hiring himself out to serve as a farm hand [*gañan*] on the rancherías of this district, [spending] some days on one [estate], and some on others."[37]

Salazar saw in magic a way to carve out his own niche in a society that would rather ignore or marginalize him. Drawing from local indigenous knowledge, he claimed the power to heal and to curse, gaining in the process the respect and fear of an extended network of Spanish, black, and Indian clientele and occasional victims. The role of healer thus enabled Salazar to bridge on occasion both the indigenous and Hispanic worlds.[38] Talismans symbolizing a pact with the Devil also provided him with the equestrian skills that were so critical for his everyday survival. In this respect, Salazar followed a long tradition of social outcasts. In his famous 1629 treatise on Indian idolatry in the modern-day states of Guerrero and Morelos, Hernando Ruiz de Alarcón noted practices similar to Salazar's that many *mulato*, mestizo, and Indian cowhands had developed.[39] The marginal economic and social positions of these dependent ranch workers "constituted what was in many ways a world apart in New Spain," helping to create a subculture of magic and power that drew upon the participation and beliefs of all the colony's ethnic groups.[40]

Unfortunately for him, Salazar's career as a folk healer and sorcerer came to an end in 1765 when a member of his adopted family, Nicolás Saucedo, denounced him to the authorities. Saucedo claimed that Salazar caused him to become sick with rashes all over his body and made his testicles "monstrously inflamed" covered with welts that emitted a foul-smelling discharge. He believed this was all in retaliation for a request that Salazar return a firearm Saucedo had lent him.[41] Despite concerns that Saucedo and others had physically coerced a confession out of him, Salazar eventually repented his crimes and participated in an inquisitorial auto-da-fé in Mexico City in March 1768. Salazar faced a ten-year exile from his home, but died five months later, his health destroyed by the extended imprisonment and the two hundred lashes he had received as part of his punishment.

In his own way, Pascual Salazar had committed an act of hubris similar to José Rosales's slapping the face of the Spanish waxmaker, Carranza, in nearby Tlalchiapa in 1801. In a moment of frustration, he had refused a request from a social superior, albeit a relative, and drove home that point, from Saucedo's point of view, by attacking the core of his affronter's masculinity, his testicles. In both cases local Spaniards and state and church officials intervened and reinforced powerful reminders of expectations of racial boundaries and decorum. For his own part, Salazar denied making a pact with the Devil, but he did admit to posing as a sorcerer and a healer, alluding to his marginal and despised position as a justification for his ruse. He had done so to gain a few material benefits (a handful of coins, bread, bananas, metates, etc.) from villagers and ranchers alike and, perhaps more importantly, recognition as a man of ability.[42] While any trifle or boon may have ameliorated his economic situation, Salazar was motivated by more than material concerns. He was clearly a man of poor public esteem seeking recognition through the use of magic and integration into local society, even if only as the relatively marginal figure of healer.[43] In his final defense, shaped by his court-appointed attorney, Salazar reiterated that his threats to cause harm and his use of magic for good and evil were all feigned efforts to gain money and other gifts, to "earn some respect," and "to intimidate people with the aim that they not cause me any harm."[44]

Conclusion

On July 24, 1819, the parish priest of Cutzamala, Juan José Simón de Haro, wrote to the Holy Office of the Inquisition to criticize the moral decay he witnessed throughout the "hot lands of the South."[45] In particular, he targeted a number of lewd dances—the "Sapo," "Gallinero," and "Abuelo," among others—all of which he considered worse than the better-known "jarabe gatuno." These dances were most likely shaped by African musical influences, but Haro was careful not to condemn any particular group. Indeed, while he alluded to its prominence along the Pacific coast, an area populated largely by *mulato* sharecroppers by the nineteenth century, he also noted the popularity of these licentious dances with all of sorts of people in his own parish. Haro's letter suggests the degree to which a common popular culture had developed in the tierra caliente by the late colonial period, if not earlier.[46] While at some level the region's inhabitants may have been united by the liberating rhythms of dance, by 1819 the tierra caliente was also rent asunder by nearly a decade of insurrection and decades more of racial animosity.

One historian of African slavery in colonial Mexico has noted that although no legal impediments stood in the way of blacks gaining their freedom, no "welcome home party" awaited them either. Colin Palmer criticizes not only the failure of colonial society "to create a secure place for the freedmen," but also the fact that the black population "faced a body of restrictive legislation which limited their upward mobility, doomed them to an inferior status, and permitted them only a limited participation in the Spanish-dominated society on that society's own terms."[47] Building off these insights, this chapter has highlighted the tenuous position that the free-black population faced vis-à-vis both Spaniards and Indians in the tierra caliente. Blacks had played a pivotal role in the maintenance and transformation of area villages, particularly following the darkest years of the indigenous demographic collapse. Yet, later generations faced little opportunity and many risks by the late eighteenth century. This was true for both recent newcomers seeking relief from difficult times elsewhere as well as long-time residents who had endeavored to establish harmonious and mutually beneficial relations with Indian villagers.

Many blacks continued to rely on traditional strategies of survival as a way to secure their subsistence needs, but they often experienced disappointing reversals. A few brave souls responded to growing hostility by asserting their rightful place in a society they and their predecessors had helped create. But such instances were all too quickly used by Indians and Spaniards to confirm their suspicions that blacks were people not to be trusted or embraced. Enjoying neither the privileges of the ranching elite, nor the minimal legal protections the colonial government offered its indigenous vassals, free blacks faced ostracism and condemnation from both quarters.

Haro's reactionary letter offers us one final cautionary lesson. More than just a critique of a vulgar form of popular culture, his diatribe links the perceived relapse of public morality to the treachery of the rebels and the support they receive in a territory, the coast and sierra of Guerrero, well known for its black population. These deep-rooted prejudices concerning black aggression and hostility continue to inform contemporary sentiments. Such is the case for the reputation of the modern-day state of Guerrero, its reputed violence and antipathy toward outsiders long associated with the relative "blackness" of its inhabitants.[48]

⁂ NOTES ⁂

1. Because of the similarity in spelling, in this volume the Spanish word *mulato* will be italicized throughout to distinguish it from the English mulatto.

2. Archivo General de la Nación (AGN), Criminal, vol. 195, exp. 13, fols. 465, 467v, 461v. On the role of honor in plebeian conflict, see several of the essays in Lyman L. Johnson and Sonya Lipsett-Rivera, eds., *The Faces of Honor: Sex, Shame and Violence in Colonial Latin America* (Albuquerque: University of New Mexico Press, 1998).

3. For the sake of clarity and conciseness I have elected to use the English term black as a general descriptor for the Africans and descendants of Africans who lived in colonial Mexico or New Spain. While it has its advantages, the term does tend to mask the remarkable cultural and racial heterogeneity that characterized this population. Thus, I have also elected to retain the colonial racial labels that were used to describe specific historical actors, like José Rosales, discussed in this chapter.

4. Literature on the African Diaspora in Mexico is too extensive to list here. Recent studies in English focusing on the interaction between blacks and Hispanic society and colonial institutions include Herman L. Bennett, *Africans in Colonial Mexico: Absolutism, Christianity, and Afro-Creole Consciousness, 1570–1640* (Bloomington: Indiana University Press, 2003); Ben Vinson III, *Bearing Arms for His Majesty: The Free-Colored Militia in Colonial Mexico* (Stanford: Stanford University Press, 2001); Nicole von Germeten, *Black Blood Brothers: Confraternities and Social Mobility for Afro-Mexicans* (Gainesville: University Press of Florida, 2006). For a recent discussion of historiographical trends, see Ben Vinson III, "La historia del estudio de los *negros* en México," in Ben Vinson III and Bobby Vaughn, *Afroméxico: El pulso de la población negra en México: Una historia recordada, olvidada y vuelta a recordar*, trans. by Clara García Ayluardo (Mexico City: Centro de Investigación y Docencia Económicas and Fondo de Cultura Económica, 2004), 19–73.

5. Works discussing this relationship include Aguirre Beltrán, *Cuijla: Esobozo etnográfico de un pueblo negro* (Mexico City: Fondo de Cultura Ecónomica, 1985 [1958]); Patrick J. Carroll, *Blacks in Colonial Veracruz: Race, Ethnicity, and Regional Development* (Austin: University of Texas Press, 1991); Bernardo García Martínez, "*Pueblos de Indios, Pueblos de Castas:* New Settlements and Traditional Corporate Organization in Eighteenth-Century New Spain," in *The Indian Community of Colonial Mexico: Fifteen Essays on Land Tenure, Corporate Organizations, Ideology and Village Politics*, ed. Arij Ouweneel and Simon Miller, 103–16 (Amsterdam: CEDLA, 1990); Edgar F. Love, "Legal Restrictions on Afro-Indian Relations in Colonial Mexico," *The Journal of Negro History* 4, no. 2 (1970): 131–39; Matthew Restall, ed., *Beyond Black and Red: African-Native Relations in Colonial Latin America* (Albuquerque: University of New Mexico Press, 2005); Brígida Von Mentz, *Pueblos de indios, mulatos y mestizos, 1770–1870: Los campesinos y las transformaciones protoindustriales en el poniente de Morelos* (Mexico City: Centro de Investigaciones y Estudios Superiores en Antropología Social, 1988).

6. Andrew B. Fisher, "Marketing Community: State Reform of Indian Village Property and Expenditure in Colonial Mexico, 1775–1810," in *Commodifying Everything: Relationships of the Market*, ed. Susan Strasser, 215–34 (New York: Routledge, 2003).

7. J. Benedict Warren, *The Conquest of Michoacán: The Spanish Domination of the Tarascan Kingdom in Western Mexico, 1521–1530* (Norman: University of Oklahoma Press, 1985), 75; René Acuña, ed., "Relación de Sirandaro y Guayameo," in *Relaciones Geográficas del siglo xvi: Michoacán*, vol. 9 (Mexico City: Universidad Nacional Autónoma de México, 1987), 262. Garrido and other black conquistadors are covered in Peter Gerhard, "A Black Conquistador in Mexico," *Hispanic American Historical Review* 58, no. 3 (1978): 451–59; and Matthew Restall, "Black Conquistadors: Armed Africans in Early Spanish America," *The Americas* 57, no. 2 (2000): 171–205.

8. J. Benedict Warren, *Conquest of Michoacán*, 184, 194–95; Agustín Millares Carlo and J. Ignacio Mantecón, eds., *Índice y extractos de los protocolos del Archivo de Notarías de México, D.F.*, 2 vols. (Mexico City: El Colegio de México, 1945–46), I:312, II:108.

9. René Acuña, ed., "Relación de Ajuchitlan," in *Relaciones geográficas del siglo xvi: Michoacán*, 29.

10. Elinore M. Barrett, *La cuenca de Tepalcatepec: Su colonización y tenencia de la tierra*, trans. Roberto Gómez Ciriza (Mexico City: Secretaría de Educación Pública, 1975); Gerardo Sánchez Díaz, *La Costa de Michoacán. Economía y Sociedad en el Siglo XVI* (Morelia: Universidad Michoacana de San Nicolás de

Hidalgo, Instituto de Investigaciones Históricas, Morevallado Editores, 2001); Rolf Widmer, *Conquista y despertar de las costas de la Mar del Sur (1521–1684)* (Mexico City: Consejo Nacional para la Cultura y las Artes, 1990).

11. Agustín Millares Carlo and J. Ignacio Mantecón, eds., *Índice y extractos*, I:262, 318.

12. Carlos Paredes Martínez, ed., *"Y por mí visto . . .": Mandamientos, ordenanzas, licencias y otras disposiciones virreinales del siglo XVI* (Mexico City and Morelia: CIESAS and Universidad Michoacana de San Nicolás de Hidalgo, 1994), 191.

13. AGN, Indios, vol. 6 (primera parte), exp. 382, fol. 102v; Magnus Mörner, *La corona española y los foraneos en los pueblos de indios de América* (Stockholm: Almquist & Wiksell, 1970), 202–3.

14. Regarding this phenomenon in the viceroyalty as a whole, see Patrick J. Carroll, "Black-Native Relations and the Historical Record in Colonial Mexico," in *Beyond Black and Red*, ed. Matthew Restall, 245–67. For an insightful assessment of this form of indigenous protest, see Felipe Castro Gutiérrez, "Indeseables e indispensables: Los vecinos españoles, mestizos y *mulatos* en los pueblos de indios de Michoacán," *Estudios de Historia Novohispana* 25 (2001): 59–80.

15. The data is culled from parish counts for the bishopric of Michoacán, which included most of the region's settlements; see Alberto Carrillo Cázares, ed., *Partidos y padrones del obispo de Michoacán, 1680–1685* (Morelia: Gobierno del Estado de Michoacán, El Colegio de Michoacán, 1996), 285, 348–49, 353, 358–59, 365; Carrillo Cázares, ed., *Michoacán en el otoño del siglo xvii* (Mexico: El Colegio de Michoacán, Gobierno del Estado de Michoacán, 1993), 108–9.

16. AGN, General de parte, vol. 21, exp. 219, fol. 257.

17. Cited in Claude Morin, *Michoacán en la Nueva España del siglo XVIII: Crecimiento y desigualdad en una economía colonial* (Mexico City: Fondo de Cultura Económica, 1979), 37–38; Danièle Dehouve, *Entre el caimán y el jaguar: Los pueblos de indios de Guerrero* (Mexico: Centro de Investigaciones Superiores de Antropología Social, 1994), 99–100, 112; Edgar Pavía Guzmán, "Era de los Borbón," in *Historia General de Guerrero: El dominio español* (Mexico: INAH, Gobierno del Estado de Guerrero, JGH Editores, 1998), 261.

18. Jonathan D. Amith, *The Möbius Strip: A Spatial History of Colonial Society in Guerrero, Mexico* (Stanford: Stanford University Press, 2005), passim; Claude Morin, *Michoacán en la Nueva España*, 66–70, 151; John Tutino, *From Insurrection to Revolution in Mexico: Social Bases of Agrarian Violence, 1750–1940* (Princeton: Princeton University Press, 1986), 185–86.

19. Edgar Pavía Guzmán, "Era de los Borbón," 258. As in the past, only a handful of elite families residing in the tierra caliente were wealthy enough to afford a few black slaves, and evidence for their presence is rare. For example, see AGN, Tierras, vol. 636, exp. 6; Genealogical Society of Utah (GSU), roll no. 793289 (microfilmed archival material from the Archivo de la Casa de Morelos [Morelia, Michoacán]).

20. Peter Gerhard, *A Guide to the Historical Geography of New Spain*, rev. ed. (Norman: University of Oklahoma Press, 1993), 136, 292.

21. Andrew Bryan Fisher, "Worlds in Flux, Identities in Motion: A History of the Tierra Caliente of Guerrero, Mexico, 1521–1821," Ph.D. diss., University of California, San Diego, 2002, 265.

22. GSU, roll no. 757227.

23. For example, AGN, Tierras, vol. 237, exp. 3. fol. 7-v.

24. Archivo de la Casa de Morelos, Cofradías, Erecciones, Siglo XVIII, caja 1256, exp. 6. Patrick Carroll discusses the idea of "black naturales" in his chapter in this volume.

25. In colonial New Spain morisco designated an individual of mixed Spanish and African ancestry, who exhibited more qualities of the former than did a *mulato*.

26. AGN, Tierras, vol. 248 (primera parte), exp. 1, fols. 5–6v.

27. For the situation with ranchers, see Peter F. Guardino, *Peasants, Politics, and the Formation of Mexico's Nation-State: Guerrero, 1800–1857* (Stanford: Stanford University Press, 1996), 28, 30.

28. AGN, Acordada, vol. 16, exp. 16.

29. AGN, Tierras, vol. 3694, exp. 2, fols. 7-v, 27v, 30v–31.

30. Ibid., fols. 29v–34.

31. Ibid., fol. 28.

32. AGN, Tierras, vol. 1866, exp. 7, fols. 7–8v.

33. AGN, Criminal, vol. 321, exp. 1, fols. 21, 29, 73v.

34. José Antonio de Villaseñor y Sánchez, *Theatro Americano, descripción general de los reynos, y provincias de la Nueva España, y sus jurisdicciones* (Mexico City: Editora Nacional, 1952 [1746]), I:226.

35. AGN, Criminal, vol. 167, exp. 1. I have explored the origins and historical development of Cacalotepeque elsewhere; Andrew Bryan Fisher, "Worlds In Flux," 188 355, Andrew B. Fisher, "Creating and Contesting Community: Indians and Afromestizos in the Late-Colonial Tierra Caliente of Guerrero,

Mexico," *Journal of Colonialism and Colonial History* 7, no. 1 (2006), available at http://muse.jhu.edu/journals/journal_of_colonialism_and_colonial_history.

36. Regarding his ancestry, Salazar described himself as either a *coyote* or mestizo, while others considered him either mestizo or even español, the latter category due no doubt to his connection to a "Spanish" family (AGN, Inquisición, vol. 1055, exp. 1, fols. 30, 33v, 39v, 54–63, 86v, 88v). On the issue of contesting mestizo versus *mulato* identities, particularly in colonial courts, see Aaron P. Althouse, "Contested Mestizos, Alleged Mulattos: Racial Identity and Caste Hierarchy in Eighteenth Century Pátzcuaro, Mexico," *The Americas* 62, no. 2 (2005): 151–75. After over a century of intermixture, even local elite identified as Spanish by descent were not necessarily free of indigenous and African ancestry.

37. AGN, Inquisición, vol. 1055, exp. 1, fol. 79.

38. On the intermediary role blacks and other castas played in colonial witchcraft, see Laura A. Lewis, *Hall of Mirrors: Power, Witchcraft, and Caste in Colonial Mexico* (Durham: Duke University Press, 2003).

39. Hernando Ruiz de Alarcón, *Treatise on the Heathen Superstitions that Today Live among the Indians Native to this New Spain, 1629*, trans. J. Richard Andrews and Ross Hassig (Norman: University of Oklahoma Press, 1984), 67–68.

40. Fernando Cervantes, *The Devil in the New World: The Impact of Diabolism in New Spain* (New Haven: Yale University Press, 1994), 90–91.

41. AGN, Inquisición, vol. 1055, exp. 1, fols. 13v–16.

42. Ibid., fol. 59v.

43. In this respect, his case seems to echo the conclusions reached by Solange Alberro concerning the desire held by many blacks in colonial Mexico for social integration and recognition of status. See Solange Alberro, *Inquisición y sociedad en México, 1571–1700* (Mexico City: Fondo de Cultura Económica, 1988), 475.

44. AGN, Inquisición, vol. 1055, exp. 1, fol. 112v.

45. Ibid., vol. 1466, fols. 89–90v.

46. For a discussion of elite and ecclesiastical reactions to popular dances in the late colonial period, see Juan Pedro Viqueira Albán, *¿Relajados o reprimidos? Diversiones públicas y vida social en la ciudad de México durante el Siglo de las Luces* (Mexico City: Fondo de Cultura Económica, 1987), 160–69; see also John Charles Chasteen, *National Rhythms, African Roots: The Deep History of Latin American Popular Dance* (Albuquerque: University of New Mexico Press, 2004).

47. Colin A. Palmer, *Slaves of the White God: Blacks in Mexico 1570–1650* (Cambridge: Cambridge University Press, 1976), 179.

48. The late colonial association of "bellicosity and blackness" in Guerrero is noted in Jonathan D. Amith, *The Möbius Strip*, 63. For modern views of Guerrero and its inhabitants—which often take a more specific regional focus—see Gonzalo Aguirre Beltrán, *Cuijla*, 60; Judith A. Boruchoff, "Creating Community Across Borders: Reconfiguring the Spaces of Community, State and Culture in Guerrero, Mexico and Chicago," Ph.D. diss., University of Chicago, 1999), 91–2; Norberto Valdez, *Ethnicity, Class and the Indigenous Struggle for Land in Guerrero, Mexico* (New York: Garland Publishing, 1998), vii–viii. Similar associations of "blackness" and violence are often linked to the "hot lands" of Morelos and Oaxaca, as well; Steve J. Stern, *The Secret History of Gender: Women, Men, and Power in Late Colonial Mexico* (Chapel Hill: University of North Carolina Press, 1995), 289–90.

Black Aliens and Black Natives in New Spain's Indigenous Communities

PAT CARROLL

✣ ON THE NIGHT OF FEBRUARY 28, 1752, EIGHT TO TWELVE ARMED men broke into the home of Antonio Romero and his wife Theresa Xtotl, two natives living in San Pedro de Cholula. They robbed the couple of two hundred pesos, a considerable amount of money, as well as other items valued at over eleven pesos. The thieves meant business. They intimidated Theresa and Antonio Romero into surrendering what wealth they had by beating her severely. The town surgeon testified that he treated Theresa for open wounds to her nose, upper lip, and forearm. Pedro Pérez, identified as a "mestizo" (person of mixed Nahua-white appearance), was the only one convicted of the crime. He testified that his accomplices included transients of various racial backgrounds—indigenous Cholulans and persons of mixed black-Indian and black-white appearance.[1] Colonial criminal and land dispute records abound with all manner of conflictive encounters between native Mexicans and black and racially hybrid individuals, or castas as they were then called, especially Afro-Mexican hybrids. As Andrew Fisher posits, such conflicts may have actually increased toward the end of the colonial period due to eighteenth-century population growth and the attendant pressures on available indigenous communal land and water resources. These pressures, along with a more active late colonial Bourbon judicial system in New Spain, gave native villagers the incentive and the means to expel Afro-Mexican intruders from their midst. Examining the records from the colonial Pacific coastal lowlands of Mexico, Fisher argues that these pressures led to increasingly more conflictive relations between Afro-Mexicans and native Mexicans as the eighteenth century progressed.[2]

Based on often-recorded incidents like the assault and robbery of Antonio Romero and his wife Theresa Xtotl, most scholars agree with Fisher's analysis and describe black-indigenous colonial relations in New Spain as generally hostile in nature. Yet, this conclusion rests on anecdotal evidence much as the assault described above. It overlooks more subtle and mundane documentary evidence that suggests the contrary, that black-Indian relations, especially within native villages, were commonly peaceful and consensual.

Over the course of the colonial period, blacks and their casta (racially mixed) progeny probably settled in nearly all of the indigenous villages in central Mexico.[3] Marginalized and often enslaved, they faced disempowerment at the hands of white masters and authorities in Spanish zones of power; slavery, racism, and legally institutionalized discrimination restricted black opportunity. Native communities provided a potential escape from such limiting conditions and the possibility for increased socioeconomic status. They also offered the likelihood of female companionship, an important consideration during the first century of contact when male African slaves outnumbered females by a ratio of as much as three to one.[4] Runaway slaves either spirited indigenous women away to their palenques (hideouts), or sought refuge in the villages of their Indian wives' families.[5]

African slave culture may have predisposed blacks to seek residence in indigenous communities. In most West African societies, fictive family formation occurred regularly. Slaves became members of their master's lineage group, and family organization was, in the words of John Thornton, "highly variable," following matrilineal as often as patrilineal lines.[6] Such ties were "a formal part of African concepts of kinship relations" according to Igor Kopytoff.[7] Homeland connections between bondage and non-blood kinship ties, coupled with Africans' identification with slavery in the New World and their acceptance of matrilineal lineage patterns may very well have predisposed slaves and free blacks alike to form kinship bonds with Indians who accepted them into their indigenous communities.

The Explicit Historical Record

Despite probably frequent peaceful black incursions into native towns for all the reasons listed above, Hispanic record keepers often failed to report these incidents. Perhaps this omission resulted from poor record keeping.[8] William Taylor recognizes biases in Spanish ecclesiastical records. He has pointed out that, with respect to religious practices in native *pueblos*, "most of the documentation was generated by [Spanish] policing institutions, which were preoccupied with order and orthodoxy, and . . . skewed toward the unusual."[9] The same can be said of records about the lives of blacks and black castas (racially mixed persons of black descent) living within native villages during the colonial period. Spaniards paid far more attention to atypical conflictive encounters between such individuals and indigenous peoples than the more common peaceful ones. The key word in Taylor's quote is "unusual." Spanish authorities reacted more readily to subordinate peoples' unusual/illegal behavior than they did to their normal/legal actions. Thus, Hispanic record keepers were far more likely to record accounts of blacks that acted out of place in native villages than information about blacks that fit into indigenous communities. This suggests an important distinction between those blacks and black castas that took up residence in native villages. One subgroup displayed African or Hispanic cultural characteristics that were alien and out of place in native residential zones. Spaniards referred to these individuals as *bozales* (ethnically African) and *ladinos* (ethnically Spanish). The other black subgroup usually established village kin and cultural ties by marrying into a local indigenous family and by adopting the local indigenous lifestyle. Spaniards labeled a black or casta that lived among and behaved like Nahuas, Totonacs, Mexica, or other indigenous peoples a "natural," a label they normally reserved to designate someone as native to a place. Spanish officials with little or no personal contact with native villages very probably failed to distinguish between indigenous village dwellers and ethnically indigenous black and black *casta naturales* living within indigenous communities.

Villagers proved far more discriminating toward these newcomers than did distant Spaniards. Culture or ethnicity, not race (phenotype), was the principal determinant of identity within native social zones. African and ladino blacks or castas stood out because they failed to assimilate culturally. They retained their alien cultures, making them, to borrow Taylor's word, "unusual." Indigenous residents frequently petitioned white authorities to have these black and casta outsiders removed from their communities. Spanish records of such confrontations with ethnically non-native blacks have contributed to our perception of generally hostile black-indigenous relations in Mexico. Black naturales, on the other hand, blended into indigenous families and communities. Natives seldom brought these individuals to the attention of Spanish authorities, so there is little trace of them in the colonial documentation.[10]

The Implicit Historical Record

Acknowledgment of black and casta naturales within native cultural spaces yields a far more balanced historical perception of black-indigenous relations in Mexico, a core colonial setting in the Americas. Census tally sheets for colonial provinces or districts with large numbers of native settlements provide us with hints of that presence by implying their under reporting.

Population tallies for Jalapa and Jatlazingo compiled by don Juan de Villalva and dated December 15, 1777, divided residents for the two districts into columns by geographic location and race. He then subdivided these two broad designators by gender and age (adult vs. children). Racial categorization had remained relatively consistent over time. The late colonial racial categories Villalva used were the same ones early seventeenth-century clerics had employed in Jalapa: Spaniards, mestizos, *mulatos*, negros, pardos, and indios. Villalva did apply one additional label, "*lobos*," persons who appeared of primarily black and secondarily indigenous phenotype.[11] His designation by site does, however, reveal a certain type of inconsistency within Spanish record keeping. Colonial chroniclers often listed rural villages as totally Indian.

Villalva recorded only "indios" residing in eleven of the thirty-five pueblos outside the district capital of Jalapa in 1777.[12] Such areas, in the words of Gonzalo Aguirre Beltrán, were "regions of refuge" for natives and other non-Hispanics.[13] These villages encompassed Jalapa's indigenous world, a social zone infrequently visited by white public officials and itinerant clergy. It seems highly unlikely that after three centuries at risk for black penetration that this did not happen.

The 1777 census of communicants for the *cabecera* (head town) of San Thiago de Totutla and its environs provides an even more likely example of Spaniards' failure to enumerate black "naturales" in indigenous village counts. Totutla fell within the district of Córdoba, Veracruz.[14] The compiler, a Spanish cleric named Gaspar Antonio Rivera (interestingly with no honorific "*Don*" prefix before his name), enumerated 1,776 individuals in the document. This total broke down into the following cohorts. Spaniards made up twenty-one of the sum, all residing either in urban *barrios* (neighborhoods), or in the countryside on small farms (*ranchos*). Eight adult whites comprised four married couples. They all had a "don" or a "doña" prefix before their names. The children of these unions made up most of the remaining thirteen Spanish residents. Natives comprised the majority of the population, 1,167 individuals, with their highest concentration in the cabecera itself. A minority of the native residents inhabited various other sites such as outlying urban barrios, small farms, and the subject pueblo of Comapa. Forty-three natives served as resident laborers, *gañanes*, on Hispanic-owned livestock ranches located on the district's Acasonica meadowlands. Rivera neither racially nor ethnically identified the remaining eighty-eight persons listed in the census. He merely noted their place of residence and their names.[15] Who were they? How did they identify themselves? How did their Spanish and indigenous neighbors identify them?

The census title offers no direct answers to these questions. It merely purports to list all the communicants in the Totutla parish without mention of racial or ethnic characteristics for the last cohort of eighty-eight individuals. I suspect, for the following reasons, that many in this group were black castas. The district of Córdoba remained one of the last bastions of black slavery in Mexico during the final quarter of the eighteenth century. Its relatively high black and relatively low number of indigenous inhabitants enhances the likelihood that many in this racially unclassified group of eighty-eight persons were either free blacks or free-black castas. Castas represented the fastest growing segment of the colonial population from the early seventeenth century onwards in the districts of Jalapa and Córdoba, as well as in Mexico as a whole.[16] In central Veracruz no group contributed proportionately more to the increasing racially mixed population than did blacks. From 1645 to 1793, they crossed racial lines in choosing marriage partners at twice the rates of whites and indigenous residents.[17] In Spanish-controlled urban centers blacks chose Indian marriage partners as often as they chose white mates. In the countryside where indigenous peoples numerically dominated they must have united with them at a much higher frequency. What else could explain so rapid an increase in the casta population? Córdoba's slave population by 1777 was overwhelmingly racially mixed because of the district's early eighteenth-century retreat from participation in the Atlantic slave trade. This fact, plus the high rate of black/indigenous miscegenation, increases the likelihood that these racially unidentified individuals in the census were black castas.[18]

A late colonial land dispute provides an even more likely example of Spaniards' failure to note blacks' presence in indigenous settlements. In 1773, don Juan de Izazaga, the white owner of three haciendas within the jurisdiction of Zacatula, in present-day Guerrero, brought suit before royal officials against villagers of the native pueblos of San Pedro Churumuco and San Agustín Coahuayutla.[19] He complained that these indigenous communities had encroached on his lands and that he was unable to force them to leave. The accused squatters planted and harvested newly established *milpas* (cultivated plots), and they repeatedly drove Izazaga's cattle off the pasture lands the natives "illegally" occupied. Villagers responded with a countersuit. They argued that they had merely reclaimed their pueblos' lands that Izazaga had earlier usurped.

Litigation dragged on for over twenty years.[20] Documents submitted by both sides always referred to the two villages as "Indian" towns.[21] Izazaga, however, charged that numerous black castas lived like natives in both communities. These black "naturales," by Izazaga's account, had accompanied their indigenous neighbors onto his lands. The hacendado argued that because of heavy "*mulato*" infiltration into the two settlements they were no longer "*pueblos de indios*." In his mind their diverse racial makeups forfeited both villages' rights to communal lands legally reserved for native towns.[22]

The record does not say whether royal judges hearing the case agreed with Izazaga's reasoning. They did, however, hand down a mixed judgment. The court awarded some of the contested land to the two villages and some to Izazaga.[23] This ruling may very well have indicated some basis for Izazaga's claim that the villages no longer met the legal Spanish racial criteria for designation as "*Repúblicas de Indios*" because of the numerous black casta naturales residing within them. If that was indeed the justification for the court's decision then this raises two questions related to our historical assumptions about black-indigenous relations in colonial Mexico. We have already touched on the first of these queries: Why did Spanish census and ecclesiastical records fail to mention the black residents of villages like San Pedro Churumuco and San Agustín Coahuayutla? The probable answer is that living like natives in these indigenous pueblos, the blacks failed to attract the notice of white record keepers. This, however, raises a second question: Why did the natives of these two villages tolerate black outsiders living among them when they had the legal means to expel them?

Indian vs. Spanish Construction of "Otherness"

Woodrow Borah, who authored one of the most extensive studies to date of native Mexican participation in the Spanish judicial system, recorded numerous examples of indigenous legal actions to thwart black and other non-native penetration into their villages.[24] Understandably, those aliens who moved into spaces occupied by natives and failed to socially interact successfully with indigenous neighbors or, worse, began to exploit or assault them, often appeared in Spanish legal records. Colonial documents describe incident after incident of antagonistic encounters between natives and blacks and black castas.[25]

In 1579, residents of the Nahua town of Zumpango, a subject village of Guautitla, in today's state of Mexico,[26] petitioned the provincial capital's alcalde mayor (district magistrate) to remove a group of Hispanic (ladino) blacks and castas who had commandeered native houses and repeatedly stolen chickens and other food items from the villagers.[27] Later in the same year, the alcalde mayor of Pánuco, in northern Veracruz,[28] received a complaint from the Totonac Pueblo of Huejutla that *mulato* and mestizo ladino muleteers who passed through the area routinely forced their way into native homes demanding lodging and food without compensation.[29] The following year natives from the fishing village of San Pablo, in present-day southern Veracruz, sought legal redress against ladino castas who had taken up residence on the edge of their village and from there repeatedly paddled out to indigenous fishermen as they returned with the day's catch to rob them of their fish.[30] In another case, Nahuas from several villages adjacent to the provincial capital of Tehuacan petitioned the alcalde mayor to take action against ladino blacks and castas who had invaded their towns and engaged in theft and violent crimes against the native villagers.[31]

In extreme cases, Spanish, black, and casta invasions of indigenous communities even led to rebellions. In 1745 one such incident broke out in the pueblo of Santa María de la Ascunción de Theloloapán, jurisdiction of Ygualpa (Guerrero[32]). Captain don Joseph Rodríguez Vásquez, district magistrate and commander of the region's militia, put down the uprising. He charged the indigenous governor and members of the town council with revolt and then jailed them. The accused tried to justify their actions at the ensuing trial by claiming that during the years leading up to the revolt local officials, including Rodríguez, had both encouraged and legally sanctioned ladino blacks' and castas' seizure of the village's lands and their taking up residence in Theloloapán. The defendants charged that these actions represented deliberate strategies on the part of whites and Hispanicized (ladino) blacks to undermine the racial integrity of Theloloapán in order to gain legal access to its communal lands. Violence, the natives claimed, represented their last and only resort.[33]

Examples of hostile black ladino incursions into native settlements may have been common, but they may also slant the overall picture of black and casta behavior within indigenous living spaces.[34] The following incident, although ultimately resulting in conflict between an eighteenth-century black casta and his Nahua neighbors, suggests that was not always the case. In 1759, officials from the town of Tepecoacuilco, near Taxco, petitioned the Viceroy, the Marquis de Amarillas, to remove a troublesome *mulato* by the name of Miguel de Chabarria from their village. The natives admitted that Chabarria had resided among them for some time. He had evidently adopted the indigenous lifestyle and blended into the community. Several years later he hired on with a mule team that plied trade among Hispanic settlements throughout the region. At that point his demeanor changed. He no longer fit into the social life of the village. He acted like a ladino and became estranged from his neighbors. Eventually he even began to engage in criminal activities including assault, extortion, and destruction of property.

Earlier in the same year (1759) Spanish officials levied a tributary census for Tepecoacuilco. This count enumerated no non-natives residing within the town, despite the presence of Chabarria and, in all probability, other black *naturales* like him.[35] Their absence from the census is loaded with social implications. The fact that neither Spaniards nor Nahuas recorded Chabarria as a *mulato* in the official tributary count suggests that at that time he was well integrated into village life. Living and behaving like a native had earned him acceptance. His acquired ethnicity apparently overrode his inherited phenotype in the minds of the indigenous villagers. As long as Chabarria's behavior remained within the bounds of Nahua culture, natives had no objection to his living among them. When he began acting like a ladino outsider they lodged criminal complaints and petitioned to have him removed from the village.

Evidence presented to a Mexico City ecclesiastical judge in 1789, concerning the degree of kinship between a couple seeking permission to marry, demonstrates multigenerational black integration into native families and communities. Victoriano de la Cruz and María Josefa, the prospective groom and bride, as well as the witnesses they brought with them from their Nahua hometown, identified the two as "naturales." The fact that neither had a Hispanic surname further reinforces their native identifications. Bachallier José de Guzmán, the university-educated clerical magistrate that heard their case, however, noted in the record that the bride "*al parecer* (appeared to be) mulata."[36] This statement implies a significant difference in how Hispanics and indigenous peoples defined individuals. The bride, groom, and witnesses were all part of the same native community, Tenango del Valle, south of Toluca.[37] They were neighbors and friends. In their minds, María Josefa's lifestyle, not her race, determined her identity. She lived among them and behaved much as they did. The couple, their families, and the rest of the villagers considered both of them Nahuas because they acted like Nahuas, and they were members of Nahua village families. Victoriano and María Josefa even belonged to the same extended kin group. That was the very reason they stood before de Guzmán. One of her grandmothers was one of his grandfather's sisters, making the bride and groom second cousins. Their native world accepted them as Nahuas. But once they stepped outside that space and into the Hispanicized zone of Mexico City, markers other than culture defined their identities. In the viceregal capital, their appearance, not their ethnicity, determined who they were, and nothing they or their Nahua neighbors said could change that. Within a Hispanic social environment Victoriano was a Nahua because his phenotype matched that of a Nahua in the ecclesiastical judge's eye. María Josefa, on the other hand, looked like a mulata, so the white cleric designated her so. To the white Hispanic priest, her racial identity trumped her Nahua cultural identity.

On rare occasions Spaniards did record blacks who peacefully resided in indigenous towns. This happened within the district of Izúcar, Puebla, despite the fact that native villagers had apparently accepted a number of blacks and black-casta naturales into their communities. In 1754, Hispanic clerics enumerated four families *"de color quebrado"* (a burnt skin color, probably pardo) that lived alongside 209 Nahua families in the pueblo of Santiago Theopantla.[38] This represented a clear racial construction of identity. Pardos were even more heavily concentrated in the indigenous village of Izúcar de Tepexoxomac. There black castas accounted for 104, and natives 174, of the settlement's total families.[39] The pueblos of San Martín Contiguo, San Matheo, Ahuatlán, San Francisco, Santo Thomas de Aquino Tlapanalan, San Juan Evangelista Calmecatitlán, San Augustin Tepecho, San Bartholome Quetzpalar, San Phelipe Quauhpecho, and Tlilapan, too, had pardo families residing within them.[40] These Izúcar patterns of racial distribution invite the same social conclusions we drew above for Victoriano and María Josefa's native town of Tenango del Valle. Black castas had peacefully integrated into indigenous villages and families throughout Mexico by the end of the colonial period. Their native neighbors and family members readily accepted them as long as they met the two principal criteria for identification as natives. They had to adopt indigenous culture, and they had to become members of extended native families. If they behaved like natives, if they married natives, natives defined them as natives. In contrast, living like a native did not make one a native within the Hispanic social sector. To Hispanics, physical appearance, principally skin color, weighed most heavily in determining identity.

Black Naturales and the Specter of United Subordinate Peoples

White officials had good reason to oppose close black/native relations like those that developed when blacks integrated native villages and became naturales. As Colin Palmer speculated, black and casta incursions into indigenous communities created the potential for alliances between persons of color that threatened whites' control over all aspects of New Spain's sociopolitical life.[41] The fact that this threat did periodically materialize over the course of the colonial period justified these anxieties. As early as 1537, plans were uncovered for rebellion involving black and Azteca conspirators in and around Mexico City. The rebels intended to surprise and kill all Spaniards in the city and then seize control of the entire Valley of Mexico. Just a few hours prior to its outbreak, white authorities learned of the plot and quickly arrested the ring leaders. Each conspirator received a quick trial and exemplary justice; Spaniards hung them all.[42]

In 1579, Spanish authorities in Guadalajara complained of attacks by bands of cimarrones (renegade black slaves) and natives.[43] Six years later, runaway black bondsmen joined indigenous insurgents in Zacatecas and Coahuila.[44] In 1627 Thomas Gage, the English priest and traveler to Mexico, noted a widespread insurgent alliance between escaped black slaves and indigenous peoples in Guatemala. These rebels concerned Mexico's viceregal authorities.[45] Nearly a century later (1756) in Actopan, within present-day Hidalgo, a revolt broke out over a special labor draft to help drain the nearby mines of Pachuca. More than two thousand natives and other persons of color joined the uprising. Ensuing violence caused widespread property loss and eight Spaniards died in the fighting. After a royal investigation, Spanish officials charged a black casta with leading the tumult.[46] Later in 1768, blacks and Totonacs of the Papantla region in Veracruz rose up against the local Spanish district magistrate over fishing rights and tribute levies.[47]

Despite Spanish fears and opposition, blacks and natives continued to peacefully interact with each other and to unite in hostility against whites throughout the colonial period. In 1582, don Pablo Suarez, district magistrate for Zacatula (Guerrero[48]) identified the root cause of the problem. He warned Mexico City authorities that numerous runaway black slaves had married native women and taken up residence in their wives' villages throughout the region. From these native refuges the blacks and some of their indigenous neighbors and kinsmen preyed on white travelers and white agricultural estates. The allied black and indigenous marauders committed assaults, thefts, extortion, and destruction of property. Suarez cautioned that these deprivations threatened not only the local economy, but Spaniards' political control over the area as well.[49]

This type of danger to the colonial political economy emerged even more clearly in events that occurred within the Valley of Mexico's district of Coatepeque. Nahuas from the pueblo of Chimalhuacán rose up in 1702. According to Manuel de Castro y Romero, district magistrate for Coatepeque, the insurgents first marched on the neighboring rival indigenous village of Suchiaque, sacking and pillaging it. From there they took to the road leading to Texcoco, attacking and robbing travelers all along the way. Spanish forces led by don Francisco Andrés de Vargas, lieutenant general of the district militia, converged on Chimalhuacán within days of the uprising. He tried to arrest the pueblo's native governor, Pedro Melchor, for the latter's efforts to hide some of the rebels in his home. At that point, the governor rallied his supporters by ringing the village chapel's bell. Residents rushed to his aid forcing the Spanish forces to retreat under a hail of stones and insults. During his escape de Vargas noticed individuals who he suspected were the cause of the tumult. He counted several pardo naturales among the throng that attacked him. They resided within the village and, according to de Vargas, illegally produced and peddled large quantities of the native intoxicant *pulque*. De Vargas concluded that a combination of blacks and alcohol had transformed this peaceful indigenous village into a hotbed of unrest.[50]

Placing Our Findings in Context

Spaniards' under recording of black naturales in native communities deserves historical attention for it reveals a level of social interaction between these two groups that researchers seldom take into consideration. Perhaps even more importantly, such omissions in the historical record obscure an even more fundamental social development in colonial Mexico, the existence of parallel and somewhat overlapping social orders instead of a single imperially imposed Spanish social environment. The evidence presented above suggests that the much-studied "sistema de castas," which operated within white Hispanic zones of influence, did not stand alone. Within this schema for social stratification, race or physical appearance became the principal designator of identity and social rank. However, an alternative yet little-examined indigenous social system held sway within predominately native living spaces. And how did this developmental dichotomy come about? How did natives manage to maintain control over village social conditions in the aftermath of Spanish conquest and colonial control? The answer to this question lies in events that took place during the early formative years of the colonial period.

At the mid-point of the sixteenth century, royal and ecclesiastical authorities tried to create an apartheid physical setting separating natives from whites and blacks. They did this in response to a demographic crisis. Woodrow Borah and Sherburne Cook estimate that between 1519 and about 1610, central Mexico's indigenous population fell from an estimated 25 million to around one million individuals. They and most other present-day scholars attribute this loss of life to the introduction of Old

World diseases to which Native Americans had no previous exposure and, therefore, little natural resistance.[51] At the time colonial Europeans thought otherwise. They blamed high native death rates on mistreatment at the hands of white settlers and their black slaves.[52] In order to protect natives the crown attempted to limit their contact with the newcomers. Royal officials adopted this dramatic new settlement strategy because they viewed indigenous peoples as valuable human resources. Politically, natives enhanced royal power by swelling the ranks of vassals to the Spanish crown. Economically, they provided the backbone of the labor force for emerging colonial economies in core settlement areas such as New Spain. And socially, natives represented potential converts to Catholicism, an apparent divinely sent offset for the loss of faithful in Europe to the Protestant Reformation.[53] In order to protect these new vassals, laborers, and converts, the crown legally institutionalized two living zones in Mexico—a *República de Españoles* and a *República de Indios*.[54] From 1549 onwards non-Indians, with the exception of appointed crown officials and church clerics, were prohibited by law from residing in indigenous communities.[55] This physical division created the potential for natives' and non-natives' semi-independent social development. I use the prefix "semi" because these "New Laws" did not eliminate all contact between natives and others. They simply reduced the level of interaction between these groups. Consequently, both resulting social orders, Hispanic and indigenous, would have influence over each other as the colonial period progressed, creating a degree of developmental overlap between the two. James Lockhart takes this into account when he cautions against drawing too strong a sociocultural dichotomy between natives and Hispanics. He adds that common features between both social environments did grow over time. Nevertheless, Lockhart acknowledges that despite these expanding commonalities, by the end of the colonial period and beyond indigenous peoples of central Mexico "remained highly conscious of their micro-ethnic distinctions" between both other native and non-native societies. As a result, partial isolation of Indians in their rural communities and urban barrios did create competing and sometimes conflicting criteria for individual and group constructions of identity between both republics.[56]

Initially, the two alternative Hispanic and indigenous social systems created an especially strong identity dilemma for African slaves and their descendants. White masters tried to forcibly deconstruct blacks' ethnically based African identities in order to racially marginalize them within the emerging sistema de castas. In this social setting most blacks had difficulty in identifying themselves on an individual and a community basis along the same kin and ethnic lines they and their forbears had used in their homelands. The new sistema de castas encouraged them to make such connections on the basis of their physical appearance, especially their skin color. Blacks soon learned that this new order competed with an existing native social system that emphasized ethnicity in the process of social stratification, just as most West African societies did. Blacks just as quickly realized that pluralistic social development provided them with a potential advantage. It gave them agency to negotiate privilege in one or the other social setting. Blacks might even attempt to construct their own colonial social identity by playing European-imposed and existing indigenous social systems off against one another.[57] They could join one or the other, or they could help forge a casta-inspired middle social environment between Spanish and native social realities.[58] An awareness of the distinctions in the nomenclature used to classify individuals within the Spanish and indigenous social orders represents a necessary first step toward discerning how blacks brokered advantage in this increasingly complex and organic Mexican social climate.

As Immanuel Wallerstein observes, western culture has used constructs such as race, ethnicity, and nation for centuries to distinguish between different subpopulations. To quote him, race "is supposed to be a genetic category, which has a physical form." A "nation," on the other hand, represents a sociopolitical category. Ethnicity, in turn, more or less equates to the concept of culture.[59] Race acted as the principal identifier of persons and groups in New Spain's sistema de castas. Therein, physical appearance, or phenotype, determined race. Extended familial membership and ethnicity provided the main determinants of identity within Mexico's Indian republics.[60] This marker, ethnicity, rested on acquired lifestyle characteristics such as language, beliefs, and customs, in a word—culture.

We know most about New Spain's sistema de castas. Spaniards created it and kept most of the records related to it. The system designated Spaniards as *"blancos,"* or whites, derived from physical appearance, most notably Iberians' white skin color.[61] Operationally, within colonial central Veracruz (the Jalapa, Córdoba, Orizaba districts) the sistema de castas normally utilized just six racial phenotypes in their record keeping. In addition to blanco, the term "negro" identified a black or very dark brown–skinned person. "*Mulato*" designated an individual who appeared to represent white/black miscegenation. "Pardo" denoted a skin tone that commonly derived from black/Indian unions.[62] Mestizo identified someone who looked like the product of a white/Indian union. "Indio" represented the sixth racial term in common usage. It, too, derived from skin color. Early sixteenth-century descriptions of Mexican natives often included the phrase "*de color aindiado*," bronze or coffee colored.[63] By the second quarter of the seventeenth century the prefix "de color" largely disappeared from parish and notarial records. The association of race with skin color had become so accepted that using the prefix de color seemed superfluous. From about 1630 onwards Spanish documents used color terms alone—blanco, mestizo, *mulato*, negro, and pardo—to designate a person's race.[64] The principal guardian of the Spanish social order, the Ibero-Catholic church, actually organized their ecclesiastical records around the concept of race. Marriage, death, baptismal, confirmation, and lay brotherhood (cofradia) registries were all cataloged by race. Royal census and private notarial records also included these labels. Clearly race, primarily determined by skin color, served as the foundation for social differentiation within Spanish-dominated social zones.

As suggested by the contrasting experience of black naturales (natives) and black ladinos (aliens) within native pueblos, an indigenous social order existed side by side with the Spanish sistema de castas from the late sixteenth century onwards in colonial Mexico. Spaniards tacitly acknowledged and partially accommodated this alternative native social reality in Jalapa by utilizing a number of cultural categories as secondary considerations to race in both constructing identity and ascribing social rank. The phrase "*gente de razón*" (rational beings) was applied to persons adhering to European-based cultures. Spaniards designated non-European-based cultural groups, such as Africans and indigenous Mexicans, "*gente sin razón*," or irrational beings.[65] These cultural terms appeared in all types of Spanish records throughout the colonial period. They generally corresponded to the previously mentioned two republics Spaniards created in the mid-sixteenth century to divide and protect the diminishing native population from whites and blacks. African slaves fell into the Republic of Spaniards even though they did not initially adhere to Spanish culture. Iberian record keepers also referred to indigenous Mexicans as naturales, as opposed to labels like "*macehualtin*" or "*timacehualtin*," which the natives themselves used. Within a generation or two even natives began using the Spanish ethnic term naturales in distinguishing themselves from non-natives. The Hispanic racial designation "indio" did not commonly appear in Nahuatl documents until at least the eighteenth century.[66] We should note, however, that Hispanic record keepers seldom bothered to distinguish between specific indigenous ethnic groups, relying instead on the catch-all racial term—indio, and the general cultural term—natural. Spaniards nearly always identified unacculturated Africans as bozales, and Hispanicized ones as ladinos. Whites also considered indigenous residents of native republics, as well as African bozales, to be "gente sin razón." These ethnically rooted descriptors operating within the racially based sistema de castas, along with natives' eventual acceptance of the Spanish term natural, represented examples of overlap between the Hispanic and indigenous social worlds.

The language used in Spanish ecclesiastical registries to describe indigenous couples provides yet another indicator of intersection between the two social systems. Despite strong Iberian pressure for natives to sanction their conjugal unions through ceremonies conducted by the Catholic Church, most indigenous peoples failed to do so. Priests and ecclesiastical scribes seldom recorded indigenous couples as *"casados"* (married). In baptismal and death registers they listed females as male partners' *"mujeres"* (women) instead of as their *"casadas"* (wives). This indicated that the couples had not married within the Catholic Church. Some of the explanation for natives' failure to embrace the sacrament of marriage may have resulted from the church fees charged for such ceremonies. Just as likely, noncompliance with colonial civil and ecclesiastical law simply reflected the peaceful operation of indigenous cultural patterns in native pueblos. Native men and women united as they had before Spanish and African arrival, through kin and ethnically based indigenous ceremonies and customs. Hispanic record keepers' descriptive language for non-church-sanctioned indigenous unions reveals yet another example of overlap between Spanish and native social systems.

Natives' decisions to accept one dimension of Hispanic naming patterns and to reject another, represents one more example of interconnectedness between the two social environments. Although indigenous peoples did accept Christian first names at baptism they seldom appropriated Hispanic surnames. Church records listed only Christian first names for most Indians in central Veracruz. In San Pedro de Cholula parish registries, natives more commonly appeared with appropriated Christian first names and their own native surnames. James Lockhart documented this pattern of natives' nonadoption of Spanish surnames throughout central Mexico. He found that, generally, only those holding village leadership positions and those natives on the cultural margins of both worlds account for the few deviations from this pattern.[67] Individuals who did take Hispanic surnames, such as native governors or *caciques* (headmen) and migrants from home villages to Spanish towns or agricultural estates had to interact in both social environments. This placed them at higher risk to appropriate sociocultural traits from both orders. Combined, these native male-female union and naming patterns support the notion that separate but somewhat overlapping Hispanic and indigenous social systems coexisted in colonial Mexico.[68]

Conclusions

Our examination of black ladino (alien) and natural (native) experiences in indigenous communities as well as our deconstruction of the language used in Spanish records yields four general conclusions. We can first conclude that blacks did frequently infiltrate indigenous communities. Second, we found that blacks underwent two types of general experiences while living in native towns. One group, ladinos, entered and lived as intruders, again, as aliens. They commonly developed antagonistic relationships with indigenous villagers because those neighbors saw them as "others," not on the basis of their Hispanic marker of identity, their race, but because of the principal native identifying criterion, their ladino ethnicity. Black naturales had a quite different experience. They usually enjoyed amicable relations with inhabitants of indigenous pueblos. Indians accepted them because these blacks had assimilated native culture and married into indigenous families. Our third overall conclusion holds that black ladinos' and naturales' contrasting experiences in native communities reveal the existence of an indigenous social system coexisting alongside, and distinct from, the better-documented Spanish sistema de castas social order. Limited Spanish contact with, and presence in, native villages and barrios, as well as somewhat overlapping customs, beliefs, and value systems, masked the operation of the indigenous social order. Often, the black ladino presence in native social zones invited antagonistic culture clash. Native responses varied from petitioning Spanish authorities to remove these cultural "others," to conflict between the alien black intruders and the natives within the village, to outright indigenous rebellion against all Spanish authority (the Chimalhuacán, Theoloapan, and Papantla revolts of 1702, 1745, and 1768 respectively). Finally, our last and most tentative conclusion is that this type of sociocultural conflict may help to explain some of the general social unrest that Mexico suffered during the period leading up to independence and continuing, off and on, through the first quarter of the twentieth century.

We glimpse these four broad conclusions through the narrow window of black naturales' and black ladinos' experiences in colonial Mexican indigenous communities. These conclusions remain tentative because they rest on largely anecdotal and circumstantial evidence. Despite this shortcoming they deserve further testing because of their potential interpretive power in explaining black/Indian relations in particular and overall Mexican social development in general.

✢ NOTES ✢

1. Theresa counted twelve intruders; two witnesses placed the number at eight. Puebla (Archivo del Poder Judicial, Fondo Real de Cholula, Instituto Cultural Poblano, caja 1751–1753, fols. 1–12v.

2. Andrew B. Fisher, "The Free-Black Experience in Guerrero's Tierra Caliente," in this volume.

3. Gonzalo Aguirre Beltrán, *Población negra de México* (México, D.F.: Fondo de Cultura Económica, 1972), 237–38; Colin Palmer, *Slaves of the White God* (Cambridge: Harvard University Press, 1976), 47; Patrick Carroll, *Blacks in Colonial Veracruz: Race, Ethnicity, and Regional Development* (Austin: University of Texas Press, 1991), tab. A.6, 166.

4. Palmer, *Slaves of the White God*, 47, 56; Patrick Carroll and Adriana Naveda Chávz-Hita, "Familia esclava y resistencia en Veracruz colonial," *Anuario* IX (diciembre, 1994): cuadro 2, 20.

5. Patrick Carroll, "Mandinga: The Evolution of a Runaway Mexican Slave Community, 1735–1827," in *Comparative Studies in Society and History* 19, no. 4 (October, 1977): 489–90, 501–3.

6. John Thornton, *Africa and Africans in the Making of the Atlantic World* (New York: Cambridge University Press, 1992), 206–7.

7. Igor Kopytoff and Suzanne Meirs, "African Slavery as an Institution of Marginality," in *Slavery in Africa*, ed. Igor Kopytoff and Suzanne Meirs, 10 (Madison: University of Wisconsin Press, 1977).
8. Patrick J. Carroll, "Black-Native Relations and the Historical Record in Colonial Mexico," in *Beyond Black and Red*, ed. Matthew Restall, 245–67 (Albuquerque: University of New Mexico Press, 2005).
9. William B. Taylor, *Magistrates of the Sacred: Priests and Parishioners in Eighteenth Century Mexico* (Stanford: Stanford University Press, 1996), 47.
10. As in other historical settings a certain amount of inconsistency in record keeping existed within colonial Mexican documents across time and space in the application of identifying labels for individuals and racially and ethnically distinct subpopulations. Yet, at least in the area I studied most, central Veracruz, these inconsistencies appeared the exception rather than the rule. To dismiss the social significance of racial, ethnic, and national markers because of some inconsistencies in their application understates the significance of race and ethnicity within New Spain's evolving society. Immanuel Wallerstein underscores this point. While acknowledging variance in the use of racial and ethnic identifiers, he argues that they nevertheless retain social importance. Describing the broader post-1665 Atlantic basin social environment, Wallerstein observes that, "People shoot each other every day over the question of labels." See Immanuel Wallerstein, "The Construction of Peoplehood: Racism, Nationalism, Ethnicity," in *The Essentials of Wallerstein* (New York: New Press, 2000), 293.

    In order to resolve labeling inconsistencies, some scholars have invented new nomenclatures that the historical actors themselves never knew or used. Gonzalo Aguirre Beltrán introduced terms for racial hybrids. He scrapped *mulato* and *pardo*, replacing them with Afromestizo. He substituted Euro-Mestizo for historical terms denoting white-Indian racial mixture, labels such as mestizo and *castizo* (both describing persons who appeared to be of varying degrees of white-Indian miscegenation). Aguirre Beltrán continued to use the Spanish colonial label for native peoples, "indio," even though the natives themselves did not normally identify themselves with this term.

    Some scholars object to racial indicators altogether because of their inherent imprecision in any temporal and spatial context. This position posits that social concepts like race and ethnicity were and are too limited and had/have less influence on peoples' daily lives than more inclusive designators such as economic class or, even more broadly, terms like "peoples." The problem with this logic is the same as that for Aguirre Beltrán's invented terminology. All of these more "precise" and applicable constructs of "otherness" represent an ahistorical imposition on historical realities. Modern terms were not used by the historical actors themselves. They therefore represent present scholars' perceptions of what colonial Spaniards, indigenous peoples, and blacks thought about otherness, as well as how they applied those thoughts in everyday interaction with one another. Instead of adding to our understanding such hindsight logic may actually distort our comprehension of past social realities. From my perspective a less dangerous route to discovering the colonial Mexican social environment involves the deconstruction of language Spaniards, blacks, natives, and castas used to designate otherness. Individually and collectively these labels provide insight into the multidimensional nature and dynamics of New Spain's organic colonial social setting.

Having said all this, I must acknowledge my own shortcoming in this respect. I criticize others for imposing modern markers of identity on colonial Mexican social contexts, and then proceed to do nearly the same thing. Colonial record keepers almost never attached the word "natural" to their descriptions of blacks or black castas. I do. My only justification for this license is that Spaniards seemed to use the terms indio and natural interchangeably. Yet, natural most commonly appeared to represent more a place of origin than a racial or ethnic designation. On the other hand, natural may have taken on a different meaning, a designation of ethnicity, when juxtaposed in the documents with the term ladino. The label "ladino" identified a non-European (a black African or an indigenous person) who had adopted Hispanic culture. I have tried to appropriate only the colonial ethnic connotations of natural when attaching it to blacks and black castas living within indigenous communities. Thus, in this essay I have appropriated natural to differentiate between black ladinos, or Hispanicised blacks, and black naturales, culturally indigenous blacks, living within native-dominated social spaces.

11. Archivo General de la Nación (AGN), Historia, vol. 522, fol. 239; Notaria Eclesiástica de la Parroquia del Sagrada Corazón (NEPSC), Registros de Bautizos, Entierros, y Matrimonios, passim.

12. These eleven native rural *pueblos* included: San Juan Miahuitlán, San José Miahuitlán, San Pedro Ciconquiato, Santa María Yequatla, San Andres Tlalnequayoacan, Santa María Magdalena, San José Paxtepeue, San Miguel Aguazuelas, San Marcos, San Bartolomé Xalatzingo, and San Pedro Hatatila.

13. Gonzalo Aguirre Beltrán, *Regiones de refugio: el desarrollo de la comunidad y el proceso dominical en mestizamérica* (México: Instituto Nacional Indigenista, 1987), passim.

14. Peter Gerhard, *A Guide to the Historical Geography of New Spain* (Cambridge, UK: Cambridge University Press, 1972), 83.

15. Archivo de las Indias (AGI), México, vol. 2580, fols. 1–19. I wish to thank Susan Deans-Smith for graciously providing me with a photocopy copy of this census document.
16. Carroll, *Blacks in Colonial Veracruz*, table A.10, 168.
17. Ibid., tables A.15 and A.20, 174 and 180–81 respectively.
18. Adriana Chávez-Hita, "Esclavitud negra en la jurisdicción de Córdoba en el siglo XVIII," tésis de Maestro en Historia, Universidad Veracruzana, Jalapa, 1977, 10, 12, 68–69, 74–77, 97.
19. Gerhard, *Guide to the Historical Geography of New Spain*, 393.
20. AGN, Tierras, vol. 1043, exp. 1, passim.
21. Ibid., vol. 1044, fols. 209–10v.
22. Ibid., vol. 1044, exp. 3, fol. 25.
23. Ibid., vol. 1044, last exp. (unnumbered), fols. 1–5.
24. Woodrow Borah, *El juzgado general de indios en la Nueva España, traducido por Juan Utrilla* (México: Fondo de Cultura Económica, 1985), 109, 181–83.
25. Matthew Restall provides a good overview of changing black-Maya relations over a 250-year period in the Yucatán region. He argues that Mayans initially adopted a somewhat neutral attitude toward black intruders in their villages, but by the end of the colonial period Mayas' neutrality had switched to suspicion and distrust. Matthew Restall, "Otredad y ambigüedad: las percepciones que los españoles y los mayas tenían de los africanos en el Yucatán colonial," *Signos históricos* II, no. 4 (2000): 30–31.
26. Gerhard, *Guide to the Historical Geography of New Spain*, 127.
27. AGN, General de Parte, vol. 2, exp. 259, fol. 52v.
28. Gerhard, *Guide to the Historical Geography of New Spain*, 211.
29. AGN, General de Parte, vol. 2, exp. 382, fol. 79v.
30. Ibid., exp. 938, fol. 201.
31. Ibid., exp. 305, fol. 201.
32. Gerhard, *Guide to the Historical Geography of New Spain*, 148.
33. AGN, Criminal, vol. 5, exp. 7–9, fols. 216–318.
34. Christopher Lutz and Matthew Restall make this same point in an essay on black-Maya relations in the Yucatán and Guatemala. See their "Wolves and Sheep: Black-Maya Relations in Colonial Guatemala and Yucatan," in *Beyond Black and Red*, ed. Matthew Restall, 186, 188, 195, 197–204, 212–13 (Albuquerque: University of New Mexico Press, 2005).
35. AGN, Bienes Nacionales, vol. 497, exp. 3, fols. 1–8.

36. Ibid., vol. 93, exp. 170, fols. 1–2.
37. Gerhard, *Guide to the Historical Geography of New Spain*, 270–71.
38. AGN, Inquisición, vol. 937, fol. 296v.
39. Ibid., fol. 295v.
40. Ibid., fols. 295–97v.
41. Colin Palmer, *Slaves of the White God: Blacks in Mexico, 1570–1650* (Cambridge: Harvard University Press, 1976), 60.
42. Ibid., 133–34.
43. Philip Powell, *Soldiers, Indians, and Silver* (Berkeley: University of California Press, 1952), 172.
44. Silvio Zavala, *Estudios Indianos* (México: Colegio de México, 1948), 192–93; David Davidson, "Negro Slave Control and Resistance in Colonial Mexico, 1519–1650," *Hispanic American Historical Review* XLVI (August, 1966): 243, 247; Jack Forbes, *Africans and Native Americans: The Language of Race and the Evolution of Red-Black Peoples* (Urbana: University of Illinois Press, 1993), 186.
45. Thomas Gage, *Travels in the New World*, edited by J. Eric Thompson (Norman: University of Oklahoma Press, 1958), 22, 96.
46. William B. Taylor, *Drinking, Homicide, and Rebellion in Colonial Mexican Villages* (Stanford: Stanford University Press, 1979), 124–25.
47. AGI, México, legajos 1934–35. These two volumes combined contain 1,614 pages of materials on this threatening late colonial revolt involving an alliance between the majorities of this district's native, black, and casta populations. What made this uprising even more threatening was the fact that most of the black and casta insurgents were armed militiamen married to native women. See also: Ben Vinson III, *Bearing Arms for His Majesty: The Free Colored Militia in Colonial Mexico* (Stanford: Stanford University Press, 2001), 32–33.
48. Gerhard, *Guide to the Historical Geography of New Spain*, 394–95.
49. AGN, Indios, vol. 2, fols. 154v–155.
50. Ibid., Criminal, vol. 1, exp. 25 (*sic* 27–28), fols. 484–95.
51. Sherburne F. Cook and Woodrow Borah, *Essays in Population History*, 3 vols. (Berkeley: University of California Press, 1963), III:10, 100–101; Alfred Crosby, *Columbian Exchange* (Westport, CT.: Greenwood Publishing, 1972), 37–39.
52. Cheryl Martin, *Rural Society in Colonial Morelos* (Albuquerque: University of New Mexico Press, 1985), 24.
53. Carroll, *Blacks in Colonial Veracruz*, 7–8, 43.

54. James Lockhart, "Views of Corporate Self and History in Some Valley of Mexico Towns: Late Seventeenth and Eighteenth Centuries," in *The Inca and Aztec States, 1400–1800*, ed. George Collier et al., 391–93 (New York: Academic Press, 1982).

55. Collier et al., *The Inca and Aztec States*, 43, 85.

56. James Lockhart, *The Nahuas After the Conquest: A Social and Cultural History of the Indians of Central Mexico, Sixteenth Through Eighteenth Centuries* (Stanford: Stanford University Press, 1993), 443–44; and Lockhart, "Views of Corporate Self and History in Some Valley of Mexico Towns," 392–93; Martin, *Rural Society in Colonial Morelos*, 122.

57. Both Ben Vinson III and Herman Bennett illustrate black agency in their recent works, but they demonstrate it within the white sistema de castas. Vinson argues that through solidarity based on membership in the free-colored militia, blacks negotiated socioeconomic opportunity for themselves. Bennett contends that blacks played white interest groups' (slave masters, clerics, and royal officials) claims of authority off against each other to obtain privilege for themselves. My argument for black agency goes beyond the white-controlled social order, and extends black negotiation to arenas within the Indian world, as well as between the Indian and white social spaces. See Vinson, *Bearing Arms for His Majesty*, especially chap. 6, and 215–19; Herman L. Bennett, *Africans in Colonial Mexico: Absolutism, Christianity, and Afro-Creole Consciousness, 1570–1640* (Bloomington: University of Indiana Press, 2003), passim.

58. For a broader discussion of the emergence of the casta social order, see Patrick J. Carroll, "Los mexicanos negros: El mestizaje y los fundamentos olvidados de la 'raza cósmica,' una perspectiva regional," *Historia Mexicana* 44, no. 3 (1995), 403–38.

59. Immanuel Wallerstein, "The Construction of Peoplehood: Racism, Nationalism, Ethnicity," in *The Essentials of Wallerstein* (New York: New Press, 2000), 293–94, 300.

60. Lockhart, *The Nahuas After the Conquest*, 99, 102–3, 106, 108, 110–12.

61. Aguirre Beltrán, *Población negra de México*, 163.

62. Note that the use of the term "pardo" varied greatly in Mexico according to region and time period. As will be seen in the following chapters, the term is also used in a variety of ways in this book. For instance, the word pardo could also serve as a substitute for the word mulatto. Census takers and some bureaucrats in the eighteenth century used the term in this fashion. Similarly, pardos could also be interpreted as individuals who had a slightly higher social status (and even educational levels) than mulattos. But as signaled in this chapter, in its most classic expression, the term pardo referred to the

mixed-race offspring of indigenous and black individuals. Keep in mind that colonial residents probably had some understanding of all the various nuances of the term.

63. Aguirre Beltrán, *Población negra de México*, 166.
64. NEPSC, caja 1, libro 1, 1607 (*sic*, 1605)–1646; Forbes, *Africans and Native Americans*, 66–67.
65. Archivo Parroquial de Jalapa (APJ), passim; Nettie Lee Benson Latin American Collection of the University of Texas at Austin, W. B. Stevens Collection, "División del curato de Jalapa," exp. 960, fols. 247, 264.
66. Lockhart, *Nahuas After the Conquest*, 115–16.
67. NEPSC, passim; Archivo Parroquial de San Pedro Cholula, passim; Lockhart, *Nahuas After Conquest*, 119–23.
68. In the province and later district of Jalapa, for example, the percentage of endogamous marriages remained very high from 1645–1715. It vacillated between 97 percent and 98 percent in the area's indigenous-dominated (population-wise) rural zone. In this zone endogamous godparent- and marriage-witness selection patterns remained high as well—95 to 97 percent—throughout the period. See Carroll, *Blacks in Colonial Veracruz*, tabs. 14–15, 173–74. James Lockhart documented these patterns in much of the rest of central Mexico (Lockhart, *Nahuas After the Conquest*, 118–24).

From Dawn 'til Dusk

Black Labor in Late Colonial Mexico

BEN VINSON III

❧

❦ ON APRIL 18, 1793, MEXICAN MILITARY INSPECTOR DON BENITO Pérez drafted a lengthy letter to the viceroy detailing the state of affairs among the free-colored communities and militiamen that he had spent several months reviewing. Contained within the pages of his report were opinions that were probably consistent with the views of many elites of the time. In his estimation, the colony's interior was crowded with unemployed blacks who congregated on the outskirts of major urban areas such as Mexico City. He wrote that the best way of dealing with this potentially troublesome lot was to be zealous in charging tribute, which would have the effect of pushing blacks to the coasts as they sought to evade the heavy burden of unwanted taxation.[1] On the one hand Pérez's comments revealed an interesting understanding of the black predicament: the quite sizeable free black population found itself struggling to survive financially in freedom. Any efforts to circumscribe their freedom even more (in this case, through exacting straining financial demands) produced visceral reactions. Black populations would move in order to defend their liberty. But while Pérez's letter offered some astute understandings of colonial black life, they were also a bit misguided. He ignored some of the complex realities of black life with which even he must have been quite familiar. The colonial archives are filled with evidence of gainful black labor and enterprise. Indeed, urban blacks in particular were probably found employed more often than not.

However, as evidenced in Pérez's dispatch, it was easy for free coloreds to be misunderstood by their society. Even when they worked a trade, sometimes for the government itself, innocent and industrious activity could be egregiously mistaken for criminality and deviancy. In October of 1785, Leberina Azevedo, the wife of Vicente Medina, wrote an impassioned letter to the viceroy begging that her husband, a free-colored militiaman, not be incarcerated and shipped to Puerto Rico for being found on the streets of Mexico City carrying sharp scissors. He was not a vagabond toting an illegal weapon she pleaded, but a hired employee of the Royal tobacco factory where he had responsibilities in the cigar-making industry. He had been found simply carrying a tool of his trade.[2]

Similarly, at 8:00 p.m. on the night of July 20, 1789, Lucio Antonio Rodríguez (another black soldier) was apprehended on the streets of Mexico City for carrying a knife. According to his testimony, he had recently gotten off work from the Royal custom's house where he held a job as an artisan. Like Medina, his knife was his occupational tool, and he had been using it that evening to cut wineskins and boots at the house of don Juan Marañon. Rather than being caught committing a crime, he had been apprehended while innocently going about his daily business. After several rounds of testimony lasting for over a year, proof of his impeccable character and service record were provided and all charges were cleared. However, until then, he had to endure the humiliation of being dragged through the courts.[3] In a world where stereotypes and laws inhibiting the black population lingered, distortions regarding black laborers and black employment persisted.

From the standpoint of scholars, labor has been one of the great topics of study regarding black life in the colonial Americas. In many ways, research on slavery has captivated and monopolized historical scholarship, yielding tremendously important results that have greatly improved our understanding of the colonial and modern worlds. We now know more about how slavery contributed to the development of capitalism, global economies, world systems, Western notions of modernity, and colonial/metropolitan relationships. We have sharper understandings of how slavery contributed to the structuring of social hierarchies and racial systems, as well as how it impacted independence movements and the mundane operation of everyday politics.[4] But while slavery certainly occupied a foundational and prominent role in the colonial black experience, it is important to remember that it was only a part of black life. Particularly in the Latin American context, free coloreds such as Vicente Medina and Lucio Antonio Rodríguez, comprised a substantial workforce that also strongly influenced broader social, political, and economic processes.[5] Their activities in places such as Brazil, Venezuela, and Cuba are well known but, in other colonial contexts, such as Mexico, Bolivia, and Guatemala, their worlds are less understood. At least for Mexico, this is not necessarily due to scholarly neglect. Over the past several decades, a number of important studies have been produced that have either featured free coloreds, or have included them in broader analyses of regional and local economies.[6] However, few attempts at achieving a general synthesis of free-colored labor have been achieved.

This chapter is an initial attempt at expanding our knowledge of free-black Mexican labor, especially for the late eighteenth century. There may have been few moments in Mexican history that present better circumstances for evaluating free-colored labor. The 1790s marked the eve of independence and the close of the colonial era. If, as some have argued, the eighteenth century was a period of general prosperity in Mexico, where greater social mobility for blacks was possible due to a weakening caste system, a stronger class system, and greater racial hybridity, then these years offer one of the richest opportunities to take the pulse of Afro-Mexican socioeconomic progress. Second, the production of an extraordinary colony-wide census, commissioned by viceroy Revillagigedo between 1790 and 1793, provides an unparalleled opportunity to examine free-colored occupational habits. Since the census was raised to identify potential recruits for military duty, detailed information on women (including their professions) was largely excluded, as was data on the native population. Nonetheless, combined with other sources, such as parish registers and tribute data, the late colonial period is one for which we may be able to know the Afro-Mexican population intimately.

It is important to stress that for Afro-Mexicans, the eighteenth century was in many ways a *mulato* and pardo century and that, at some level, blackness and the black experience should be evaluated on these terms. As a colony, Mexico experienced tremendous demographic growth, nearly doubling in size from four to seven million inhabitants between the 1650s and the late 1700s. The Afro-Mexican population grew, too, more than tripling from roughly 116,000 in the 1640s to almost 370,000 by the 1790s.[7] But with the decline of the slave trade after the 1640s, much of the expansion of the Afro-Mexican population came not through substantial increases in the shipment of new slaves, or by large measures of endogamous natural growth among free blacks (negros), but rather through the miscegenation of existing slaves and free blacks with mestizos, whites, natives and other groups.[8] By the 1790s, the Revillagigedo census only identified a scant five hundred morenos, or "pure blacks," throughout New Spain, along with another 6,100 black "Africans."[9]

Apart from being a mulatto century, one might also argue that the 1700s were an era of Afro-Mexican success. Using the lens of "success" to discuss the black experience offers an important alternative to some traditional models of studying black life. Particularly in Latin American contexts, life after slavery is often processed within the framework of assimilation and mestizaje. Interpreting life after slavery through the "success" lens opens new opportunities for engaging blacks on different terms, notably ones that compel us to measure free-colored populations in light of their respective societies and that demand us to reckon with blacks as a group struggling for their own internal cultural, political, and social cohesion.

Two potential barometers for measuring black success rest in comparing the economic livelihood of blacks in the 1700s against benchmarks from the previous two centuries, as well as against the conditions of black life in the greater Atlantic world. In simplest form, an argument can be made that because so many of Mexico's blacks were free in the eighteenth century, their liberty should be celebrated over the more pervasive slavery that governed a great deal of New Spain's black life from the 1500s into the 1600s, and that shackled so much of the black population in slave regimes throughout the French and British Caribbean in the 1700s. Some might also be persuaded to argue that the very prevalence of black freedom in New Spain during the eighteenth century partially compensated for the many misfortunes that some blacks encountered when they took marginal and menial positions.

Of course, this vision of eighteenth-century black success in New Spain comes with some caveats. While most Afro-Mexicans were indeed free during the 1700s, the truth is that slavery persisted as an institution until 1829.

In the years preceding emancipation, anywhere from three thousand to ten thousand slaves worked in a range of professions including mining, textiles, and sugar cultivation. Some of the regions where slaves continued working included the cane fields of Córdoba, the developing frontier areas of northern Mexico (Sonora, Durango, and Sinaloa), the textile center of Querétaro, as well as select coastal regions including Tamiahua and Acapulco. As strict trade controls and monopolies were removed from ports throughout Mexico in the eighteenth century, a small, renewed slave trade appeared in tropical regions like Tabasco. Essentially, what these factors mean is that any discussion of eighteenth-century Afro-Mexican success must be situated in a context in which slavery continued to exist, even if only on a small scale. In some of the locations where slavery remained visible, the cultural impact of the system may have borne implications upon free-colored social relationships, as well as their prospects for advancement in society.

The meaning of free-colored economic progress must also be situated in a society characterized by great inequality. In broad measure, the eighteenth century was generally one of economic growth for Mexico on the whole. The colony ranked first among the world's silver producers and mining triggered the development of a variety of industries, including agricultural, ceramic, and textile production. Yet at the same time, the story of Mexican economic progress was greatly disjointed. Equal opportunities were not available for all, and while more millionaires were created in New Spain than anywhere else in the Spanish empire, the Mexican working masses saw a 25 percent drop in real earnings during the last half of the eighteenth century, thanks in part to inflation, crop failures, and epidemics. While some free coloreds were absorbed into the middle class, others who occupied the lowest strata of the economy were exposed to extreme income volatility, squalid poverty, and exploitation by a supremely powerful elite class. Was this a fate better than slavery? Indeed, was this success? Arguably yes, arguably no. However, such observations only seem to beg the question: to what degree should black success be measured against the benchmark of slavery or against the material opportunities and livelihoods of others who were free?[10]

The following sections, essentially a series of economic narratives, do not pretend to fully answer the questions raised here, but they help provide a context for resolving them. By providing a broad understanding of the general contours of free-colored economic life, and highlighting the roles that blacks played in specific local and regional economies, we can arrive at a better grasp of how free coloreds lived, articulated, and defined their freedom, as well as how they translated it into opportunities that intersected with the most powerful forces of the colonial economy.

Colonial Snapshots: A Portrait of New Spain's Free-Colored Labor Scene

Throughout the second half of the eighteenth century and up until the outbreak of the wars for independence, Afro-Mexicans comprised roughly 10 percent of New Spain's population.[11] Table 5.1 provides occupational information on 11,730 free coloreds (mainly males) who came from twenty different provinces, districts, and urban centers throughout the viceroyalty (see Maps 5.1 and 5.2). Combined, these regions housed approximately 64,000 free coloreds, or roughly 17 percent of the nearly 370,000 Afro-Mexicans who lived in Mexico during the 1790s.[12]

In a predominantly agricultural society, it should not surprise us that agriculture was the largest arena of work for free coloreds.[13] Entire provinces, such as Igualapa, Guazacoalcos (Acayucan), and Tampico housed scores of *labradores* (farmers) and *baqueros* (cowboys), almost to the near exclusion of other professions. Indeed, the labrador may have been the most common black male occupation in colonial Mexico. Using census records alone, it is hard to distinguish among the labradores and baqueros who owned their own plots or flocks, and those who were sharecroppers, hacienda laborers, and ranch hands.[14] Of those who worked as employees on the larger estates, differences in salary existed between seasonal workers and year-round hacienda residents. While seasonal workers could generally benefit from high wages paid during harvest seasons, they did not always have access to adequate housing and their employment was irregular throughout the year. Meanwhile, laborers who lived permanently on an estate might have enjoyed better lodging facilities and more continual employment, yet at the same time they could incur greater debts there, where they also typically bought their goods and wares. All of the earnings of agriculturalists and ranchers were further subjected to market forces. Fluctuations in product value and levels of occupational experience also affected wage differentials.[15]

Some of the free-colored agricultural workforce was mobile. As evidenced in regions such as the Pacific coast as early as the sixteenth century, black populations both enslaved and free, moved from estate to estate, or

TABLE 5.1. Free-Colored Labor in Late Colonial Mexico, 1780–1794

Economic Sector	Number of Workers	Percentage of Workforce (%)
Transport and services	1,113	9.5
Construction	133	1.1
Metal, wood, pottery	261	2.2
Textiles, dress, shoes, leatherworking	982	8.4
Arts and entertainment	15	.1
Food and drink	119	1.0
Commerce	86	.7
Administrative, professional, church, military	17	.1
Agricultural, fishing, and pastoral	6,160	52.5
Tobacco	170	1.4
Mining and refining	1,961	16.7
Mill workers[a]	101	.9
Other industry[b]	306	2.0
Other	230	2.6
Unknown	76	.7
Total	**11,730**	**99.9**

Source: AGN, Padrones, vols. 11, 12, 13, 16, 17, 18, 21, 35, and 37; AGN, I.G., vol. 53-A; I.G., vol. 416-A, Acayucan, 1795, Biblioteca Nacional de Antropologia y Historia (BNAH) Archivo Judicial de Puebla, rollos 43–44, Tributos Expediente formado en virtud de las diligencias hechas por los alcaldes ordinarios al gobernador intendente Don Manuel de Flon, Puebla, 1795; Archivo Historico de la Ciudad de México (AHCM), Ciudad de México, vol. 1; Juan Andrade Torres, *El comercio de esclavos en la provincia de Tabasco (Siglos XVI–XIX)* (Villahermosa, Mexico: Universidad Juarez Autonoma de Tabasco, 1994), 60–61; Jorge Amós Martínez Ayala, *Epa! Epa! Toro Prieto, Toro Prieto* (Morelia: Instituto Michoacano de Cultura, 2001), 67–69; Bruce Castleman, "Social Climbers in a Colonial Mexican City: Individual Mobility within the Sistema de Castas in Orizaba, 1777-1791," *Colonial Latin American Review (CLAR)* 10, no. 2 (2001): 242–44; David A. Brading, "Grupos étnicos: Clases y estructura ocupacional en Guanajuato (1792)," in *Historia y población en México (Siglos XVI–XIX)*, ed. Thomas Calvo, 256 (Mexico City: El Colegio

from village to village in search of better livelihoods.[16] In some instances, black residential and occupational mobility even helped anchor the development of certain townships, such as the village of Tonameca located in the Pacific province of Guamelula (see Map 5.1).[17] By the second half of the eighteenth century, this town had come to possess the highest population density of blacks in the district. Although market forces did produce important moments of opportunity that helped push and attract black agriculturalists to various parts of the colony, not everyone heeded the logic of the market. In the second half of the eighteenth century, as cotton and sugar production reinvigorated the Pacific basin's economy, causing some free coloreds to move onto or near estates in areas such as Zacatula (see Map 5.1), others opted not to leave their homes or change their long established lifeways. In the province of Igualapa, also in the Pacific basin, as some blacks moved to take advantage of special economic opportunities, others solidified their roots in the orbit of the great estates, forming a number of black settlements in the Costa Chica whose cultural legacies remain felt even today.[18]

New Spain's black agricultural and pastoral workers included a number of individuals categorized as *sirvientes* (servants) and *operarios* (workers) who labored on estates, small farms, and ranches. It was generally understood that many "servants" in rural areas did not always perform domestic labor, but also worked in the agricultural and ranching professions as assistants, peons, and farmhands. Their servant status probably signaled a lower position within the labor hierarchy. A few rural servants

---

de México, 1994); Wu, "The Population of the City of Queretaro in 1791," *Journal of Latin American Studies* 16, no. 2 (1984): 293; Guillermina del Valle Pavón, "Transformaciones de la población afromestiza de Orizaba según los padrones de 1777 y 1791," in *Pardos, mulatos y libertos, Sexto encuentro de Afromexianistas*, 88–93 (Xalapa: Universidad Veracruzana, 2001); and Juan Carlos Reyes G., "Negros y afromestizos en Colima, siglos XVI–XIX," in *Presencia africana en México*, ed. Luz María Montiel Martínez, 301 (Mexico City: Consejo Nacional para la Cultura y Artes, 1993).

Note: The study includes seven cities (Guanajuato, Valladolid, Querétaro, Orizaba, Mexico City, Puebla, and Oaxaca), and thirteen provinces/districts (Acayucan, Tabasco, Guamelula, Tixtla, Acapulco, Tlapa, Chilapa, Motines, Tampico, Colima, Igualapa, San Juan del Rio, and Irapuato).

[a] These workers were all in the mining industry.
[b] Includes thirty-eight workers in the sugar industry, some of whom were agriculturalists.

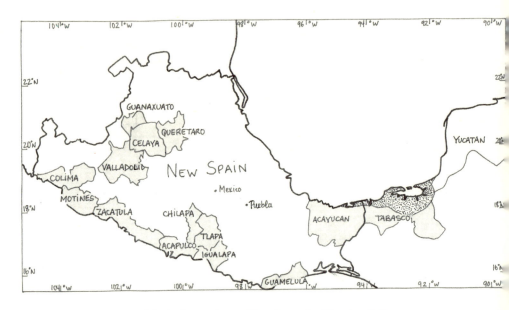

MAP 5.1. Mexico's provinces. Map drawn by Séverine Rebourcet.

MAP 5.2. Mexico's cities. Map drawn by Séverine Rebourcet.

were more specifically categorized as *sirvientes de trapiches*, meaning that they worked on sugar cane mills. Operarios, meanwhile, typically referred to unskilled industrial workers and manufacturers, particularly in urban settings. But in the rural world of New Spain, many operarios worked on plantations, haciendas, and cotton estates—sometimes as machinists, but not necessarily. This intriguing group of all-purpose black laborers probably resembled the indiscriminate category of rural *"trabajadores"* (workers) found in regions like Tabasco.[19]

After the agricultural and pastoral professions, the second largest employment arena for the free coloreds surveyed in this sample was mining (see Table 5.1).[20] It is almost certain that as future research allows us to acquire more data on New Spain's free-colored labor force, mining's role will diminish within the hierarchy of eighteenth-century Afro-Mexican professions. As with the labradores and baqueros, the particularities of the census make it hard to distinguish among miners. The category included refiners, pick and blast men (who extracted ore from its deposit), whim-minders (who hoisted ore from shafts), smelters, amalgamators, foremen, and peons alike. Needless to say, the skill level and pay scale of these workers varied tremendously. Virtually all of the mining jobs in the data sample were located in Guanajuato, the premier silver center of the late colonial empire. In the 1790s, Guanajuato had a large black labor force, much of which was born in the city or its surrounding province, and that had ancestral roots stemming back into the sixteenth and seventeenth centuries.[21] Despite the presence of black miners in other areas of the colony, such as Taxco and Sultepec, it is unlikely that any mining center in the eighteenth century came close to matching Guanajuato's black workforce. Consequently, the total number of blacks in the Mexican mining industry must have assuredly been overtaken by other sectors of free-colored employment.

Among these were the transport and service industries, which included porters, water carriers, muleteers, domestics, cooks, servants, laundresses, and coachmen (see Table 5.1). If complete employment information was available for women, we would also find more wet nurses, nannies, housekeepers, and attendants.[22] One surprise is that muleteers (*arrieros*), who have long been perceived as a niche profession for blacks, were relatively few among employed free-colored males in the transport industry. Their strongest representation came in the colony's western highland regions (Tixtla, Tlapa, and Chilapa) and in Guanajuato, which possessed over 250 black arrieros. Elsewhere, and especially in the major regional market cities of Puebla, Oaxaca, Valladolid, and Orizaba, muleteers were almost absent. What this suggests is that except for a few instances, many free-colored muleteers tended to live in smaller towns along major thoroughfares that tied together the colony's primary markets.[23] Another trend, more noticeable in the Pacific highlands than elsewhere, was evidence for the employment of free coloreds as muleteers' assistants (*sirvientes de arrieros*). These workers were mainly responsible for helping pack and feed the animals, while also assisting with driving mule trains from various mountainous passageways down to the colony's coastal and heartland zones.

Artisans in the textile, dress, leatherworking, and shoemaking industries competed fiercely with the service and transport sector for third place within the free-colored occupational hierarchy (see Table 5.1). These professions included tailors, seamstresses, cobblers, textile mill workers, hatters, cloth cutters, needle makers, spinners, tanners, weavers, and ribbon makers, among others. Some of these trades, such as cloth cutters, involved minimal expertise and were mainly considered to be manufacturing professions. Others demanded superior craftsmanship and even guild membership. During the colonial period, and especially during the eighteenth century, free coloreds were known to have access to the upper ranks of several guilds and many emerged as examined masters in their trades. However, in the census documents examined here, not a single free-colored master artisan was found among the 11,000-plus laborers.[24]

When combined with workers in the metal, woodworking, and pottery sector, as well as candlemakers, wax producers, and cigar makers, the total population of free-colored artisans actually outnumbered those employed in the service and transport industries. Of course, the lack of information on women complicates matters.[25] Like their male counterparts, free-colored women were also employed as artisans, with perhaps their heaviest representation coming in the textile industry. There were probably significant numbers of black female confectioners and tobacco factory workers as well. All of this begs the question: what was the likely impact of females on the overall free-colored workforce? It is hard to say with certainty, but it is highly probable that the number of female artisans never overtook the number of female service workers.[26] Consequently, women most likely affected the free-colored labor force by substantially increasing the representation of service and textile workers in the labor hierarchy. Moreover, it is likely that female representation increased the variety of trades to be found in the services, while raising the number of workers in both the food industry and petty commerce—women worked as waitresses, tortilla makers, street peddlers (selling stockings and combs), fruit vendors, and druggists, among other positions.[27] With female help, the service industry probably surfaced as the second most important free-colored occupational arena (over mining), followed by the textile-related craft trades.

A Tale of Four Cities: Free-Colored Big City Labor

No single colony in the Spanish empire had two urban centers that rivaled the size of Mexico City and Puebla in the late eighteenth century and, quite possibly, few could boast the economic diversity and complexity of Mexico's four largest metropolises, including Guanajuato and Querétaro (see Map 5.2). All dominated the political and economic landscapes of their regions by buying goods and supplying manufactured wares, furnishing credit for business ventures, as well as administering the greater affairs of governance, justice, and military order. Collectively, these centers also offered opportunities that were simply unavailable in smaller towns and the rural countryside. Whereas one might be hard pressed to find a silversmith, painter, or teacher in less populated zones, in New Spain's first-order cities, such professions were more commonplace. Similarly, whereas only a handful of occupational options existed in smaller towns, in places like Mexico City there were well over six hundred different professions available between 1790 and 1842.[28] Of course, the industrial and service functions of most cities meant that artisans and unskilled laborers comprised the lifeblood of urban economies. In a typical Latin American metropolis anywhere between 20 and 40 percent of the population worked as artisans, while another 30 to 40 percent were unskilled laborers.[29] As might be expected, the status of these professions varied widely, and arguments can be made that the social position of many artisans did not match their actual worth in the economy.[30]

By and large, free coloreds found themselves navigating the colonial urban world of honor, position, and status by maximizing and exploiting whatever opportunities (big and small) their professions allowed. As a general rule, free blacks found some of their best access to jobs in the focal industries of the larger metropolises, in part because of the cities' overwhelming need to furnish workers in these trades. These professions, in turn, linked free coloreds professionally to large swathes of the urban populace, creating opportunities for important shared identities that were occupationally based and that could enable other forms of success. Like other urbanites, free coloreds also found an impressive range of job opportunities within the service and artisan sectors, but unique pressures shaped the degree to which they were able to enter certain professions. Studying the leading free-colored occupations among Mexico's "big four" urban centers uncovers some of the mixed patterns of opportunity and restraint that structured these key sites of the Spanish colonial world.

Mexico City

With a population of between 100,000 and 200,000, Mexico City in the 1790s was by far the largest colonial capital under Iberian control and definitely one of the great world metropolises.[31] Employing a workforce of over 38,000 people, the amount of available adult human capital alone was larger than most cities and, with steady flows of immigrants, Mexico City was a place whose productive capacity continued to rise. The city was also an important center of black life. At least seven thousand mulattos resided in the capital, and combined with other blacks of varying hues, the free and enslaved black population probably approached ten thousand, making it one of the single greatest concentrations of blacks in New Spain.[32] In studying the phenomenon of urban black labor, it makes sense to start here.

Although records have survived of approximately fifty thousand of the city's residents in 1790, just three quadrants (*cuarteles*) will be analyzed (see Map 5.3).[33] Cuartel 1, located downtown, was situated within the principal site of commerce, government, and religious activity, being home to some of the wealthiest and most powerful magnates of the colony. It was also among the most homogenous and whitest parts of the city.[34] Given that the town center was the oldest section of the capital, it tended to conservatively replicate many staid and traditional social hierarchies. This was despite heavier immigrant settlement here than elsewhere in town.[35] Most newcomers were rapidly channeled into domestic service, which worked to solidify the vertical hierarchical relationships that had operated in this part of the capital since early colonial times.

Moving toward the western periphery (cuartel 23), Mexico City became decidedly more working class. Despite housing the Alameda, a splendid

MAP 5.3. Mexico City and *cuarteles* 1, 20, and 23.
Map drawn by Séverine Rebourcet.

park that was an attraction for the elite, most residents lived modestly. They flocked into cramped quarters within large apartment complexes, they resided in larger artisan workshops and suites, or, toward the outer extremities (especially in the northwest), they dwelled in single household shacks (*jacales*) and multifamily *corrales* that had adjoining farming plots.[36] Wage and day laborers abounded, some working in the numerous convents and churches, others for a variety of workshops and local businesses, and still others in the nearby tobacco factory, the largest of its kind in Mexico.[37]

Finally, near the southern periphery (cuartel 20) the city's character shifted again. Many of the areas surrounding Mexico City were thickly populated with natives, especially regions that had been designated as Indian "barrios" shortly after the conquest. Here, natives had access to their own governing officials and administrative structures, much like in the indigenous townships that dotted the colony's landscape. By the end of the colonial period the more rigid boundaries had weakened, but native influences remained strong. The southeastern edge of the city enveloped some of the old Indian barrio of San Juan and, in cuartel 20, life was largely agricultural, with farms, jacales, and corrales being prominent residential structures.

When compared to the city as a whole, the black population in these three sections of town was small, numbering just around five hundred individuals. Nevertheless, their role in the urban labor scene is illuminating. Previous work on Mexico City has shown that by the middle of the eighteenth century, the urban workforce apparently adhered to a certain racial logic whereby different casta groups reflected, mimicked, and resembled the employment patterns of their parent populations. In other words, natives, who had traditionally fulfilled roles as the colony's primary lowskilled laborers, continued to occupy these posts in the eighteenth century. In a similar vein, mestizos, who had partial native ancestry, could be found filling positions as laborers to higher degrees than others, although their partial white ancestry also opened opportunities in the artisan sector. Meanwhile, the legacy of slavery affected blacks and mulattos as freedmen. Because slavery had been heavily associated with domestic labor in urban Mexico, it may have been more than a coincidence that overwhelming numbers of free negros were found working as servants in the 1753 census.[38] On the other hand, mixed-race mulattos, like the racially mixed mestizos, had large numbers of artisans at midcentury. Still, over half of mulatto males worked as servants or as members of the service sector.

Gender drew the boundaries between race and labor more starkly. Black and mulatto women, for instance, who joined the workforce in far greater proportions than did their white and mestiza counterparts, dominated the realm of domestic service. In fact, in 1753, 45 percent of the city's servants were *mulatas*. Few free-colored women found employment as seamstresses, spinners, or in other artisan trades. In interpreting the racial logic of Mexico City's labor scene, it is important to stress that bloodlines alone did not simply "create" or "restrict" employment opportunities. Rather, it was the networks that the different races had access to and, quite possibly, the different socialization processes of these groups that, along with skin color, influenced the functioning of race in the urban employment arena.

Several of the basic labor market features found in 1753 continued to apply in 1790 (see Table 5.2). The artisan trades and domestic service continued to offer important employment options for mulattos. However, just 13 percent of the total mulatto population in the three cuarteles worked as artisans. Mulatto men enjoyed an advantage in accessing these professions, as roughly one-quarter were craftsmen, but these numbers paled in comparison to midcentury, when approximately half of the mulatto men surveyed were artisans. The substantially lower figure probably did not reflect broader, city-wide patterns in the 1790s, since it is unlikely that within a forty-year time span, the artisan professions would have closed so tightly to mulattos. In fact, there are indications otherwise. Among all races, roughly twenty thousand people were employed as artisans in the 1790s, corresponding to approximately half of the capital's workforce.[39] Moreover, as the artisan class grew in late eighteenth-century Mexico, guild membership dwindled. Being released from the corporate protections and protocols of guild membership meant that more artisans worked independently out of their homes or in the city's emerging factories. Correspondingly, access to the artisan trades should have been easier, opening up greater opportunities for the black population.

It is hard to determine from the available information how wide these doors opened, but some patterns are clear. First, as in the mid-eighteenth century, access to artisan positions fluctuated for free coloreds according to skin color. In our three parts of town, negros were virtually excluded from the artisan ranks in 1790, with only one shoemaker among them. Even among mulattos, color mattered. Light-skinned mulattos, known as moriscos, enjoyed greater access to artisan posts than their brethren. A full 60 percent of moriscos (most of whom were men) were artisans (see Table 5.2).[40]

Second, one's location in Mexico City partly determined access to the artisan trades. Certain professions were also clustered in specific neighborhoods. While well over half of free-colored artisans were located in the

TABLE 5.2. Free-Colored Workforce in Three *Cuarteles* of Mexico City, 1790

Race	Service Sector	Artisans	Commerce and Government	Other	Total
Mulatos	208 (82%)	33 (13%)	7 (3.0%)	4 (2.0%)	252 (100%)
Moriscos	5 (28%)	11 (61%)	1 (5.5%)	1 (5.5%)	18 (100%)
Negros	10 (91%)	1 (9%)	0 (0.0%)	0 (0.0%)	11 (100%)
Total	223 (79%)	45 (16%)	8 (3.0%)	5 (2.0%)	281 (100%)

Source: The information from this table is drawn from a database compiled by Herbert S. Klein and Sonia Pérez Toledo that analyzes the following census records: AHCM, Ciudad de México, vol. 1, exp. 2; vol. 4, exp. 6; and vol. 4, exp. 9. These records were initially found by Manuel Miño Grijalva who coordinated the database entry and analysis effort.

city center, in actuality seemingly better chances for entering the artisan ranks could be found away from downtown. In the two peripheral cuarteles, although free coloreds were few in number, many were artisans. Over one-third of the employed mulattos and all working moriscos were artisans in cuartel 23. In the predominantly Indian environment of cuartel 20, every employed free colored was an artisan, except for a mulatto government official, a morisco bread merchant, and a lone, anomalous, morisco servant. Conversely, for free-colored women, opportunities for working in artisan crafts remained small. In fact, only one, a seamstress, emerged in the sample.[41] It is telling that she was a light-skinned morisca who resided in the central part of the city, where employment rates for free-colored women ran highest and where the range of professions was greatest.[42]

By and large, domestic service predominated among free-colored laborers in the center of town, where opportunities for working in elite households abounded. In 1790, the four largest professions for mulatto men and women included cooks, coachmen, young male attendants (*mozos*) and female house cleaners (*recamereras*). Combined, they accounted for well over half of the adult working population in the city center. Other domestic professions were also well represented. Between kitchen helpers, wet nurses, nannies, assistants (including female attendants called *damas de compañia*), caretakers of the elderly, washerwomen, convent servants, male lackeys, porters and pages, roughly another quarter of the workforce was accounted for. The remaining mulatto workers in the downtown area were artisans, laborers, and petty merchants, including a street vendor and the owner of a small-time game of chance.

In Mexico City, household economies, and even the composition of families, mattered a great deal toward securing economic prosperity. Although relatively few free-colored women listed a profession in the outer regions of the city, it is highly unlikely that they did not work. Instead of laboring outside of the household, many worked at home for their families in tasks that included sewing, farming, and cooking. Some may have sold extra or leftover food to supplement their household's income. Children, too, were important in a household's economy, and although many did not formally declare a profession until age eighteen, it was customary to help around the house and even take small jobs requiring little skill.[43] Indicators further reveal that toward the end of the eighteenth century, family arrangements became more complex in Mexico City as households expanded to incorporate friends, relatives, and strangers. Appended household members (*agregados*) formed part of an urban strategy to pool and maximize resources for economic survival.[44] Free coloreds certainly participated in this practice, albeit to varying degrees. In the three cuarteles, well over half (64 percent) of all households where free coloreds lived either included agregados or featured free coloreds as agregados themselves. Negros were more commonly encountered as agregados than any other group, while moriscos stood at the other end of the spectrum.[45]

Puebla

New Spain's second largest city was Puebla, lying just eighty miles east of the capital. With a population of over fifty thousand in the late eighteenth century, Puebla ranked third or fourth in size among all Latin American urban centers.[46] But the city's development had an uneven history, especially during the 1700s. From a peak of over 65,000 in the late seventeenth century, the eighteenth century witnessed considerable population decline that was both demographic and economic in nature. Prior to the 1650s, Puebla had been one of the principal suppliers of woolen goods in the Spanish kingdom, as well as a major grain and flour producer. Agricultural production was supplemented by products produced in the region's tanneries, particularly ham, soap, and lard. Trade also thrived and merchants took advantage of their relative proximity to the port of Veracruz. Puebla was so successful that rumors even circulated of relocating the viceregal capital there. But the eighteenth century brought dramatic change. Stiff competition in agriculture and industry saw other areas of Mexico supplant Puebla's dominion over the marketplace. Wheat and grain production moved into the Bajío and Guadalajara, and a surging Querétaro became a prime competitor in the textile industry. Eventually, residents began leaving Puebla for better opportunities elsewhere, generating a disturbing pattern of out-migration. Much like Boston during a comparable period, eighteenth-century Puebla became subject to spurts of growth and longer periods of decline.[47] Agricultural expansion did help the economy recover between 1760 and 1780, but modest gains were tempered by epidemics and agricultural crises that hit hard between 1759 and 1773.[48]

Because of the rhythms of these economic cycles, Puebla found itself in a slightly different position than Mexico City in the 1790s. As the colony's capital was experiencing the early stages of economic crisis that would magnify in the nineteenth century, Puebla was actually enjoying a growth spurt, albeit a short one.[49] European wars and their New World theaters interrupted the normal pace of international market flows, enabling the city to export flour and foodstuffs to places like Havana at advantageous prices. Textile manufacturing also enjoyed prosperity, as cotton was woven on an unprecedented number of looms. But the cycle of war and peace upon which Puebla's economy rested during the late eighteenth century was an acutely volatile one that would ultimately inhibit commercial modernization efforts and sustained economic growth.[50] Yet at the same time, these forces brought nearly a decade of prosperity in the 1790s that helped condition the workforce, giving the city's black working population a specific occupational profile.

Puebla's free-colored population was smaller than Mexico City's. Its urban core and surrounding district housed just 2,930 negros and mulattos in 1777 (4.1 percent of the total population), a number that was probably not greatly surpassed in the 1790s.[51] Regardless, this group had become rather influential, producing important merchant and artisan families, as well as a host of high-ranking military officers.[52] By the late eighteenth century, the free-colored population had seemingly acquired distinct niches in the marketplace.[53]

The city's 1794 tributary census summarily described Puebla's free-colored male workers as pardos[54] who could primarily be subdivided into three main groups: (1) a poorly paid and semiskilled majority, (2) a more highly skilled middle stratum of artisans, and (3) a sizeable but variegated third group that included a wide range of social classes (see Table 5.3).[55] The first and largest group of laborers, accounting for nearly half (44 percent) of the male free-colored workforce, incorporated just three professions—*tejedores* (weavers), tobacco factory workers, and *cocheros* (coachmen). Meanwhile, just six professions comprised the second group, which in turn accounted for roughly a quarter of the free-colored workforce. These included hat makers, bakers, blacksmiths, cobblers, and tailors. The final group was much harder to define. Consisting of almost one-third of the overall labor pool, these men included merchants, musicians, businessmen, and artisans, as well as a smattering of peons, laborers, construction workers, agriculturalists, muleteers, and so on. Many of the free coloreds working in the food industry, including confectioners and cooks, were located here, as well as nearly all woodworkers, especially carpenters and coach makers.[56]

Despite the variety of professions, this was not a very prosperous group. There was only one high-status merchant among them and two petty businessmen with small shops and street stands. A pardo coach maker did operate in the city. Within the artisan trades, coach makers commanded attention and respect, given that considerable expenditures were needed to buy the supplies and facilities to start a business. Coaches also tended to be bought by a well-to-do clientele, and prices climbed into the hundreds of pesos.[57] However, it is unclear whether Puebla's pardo coach-maker actually owned his business. This definitely would have impacted his wealth. Prosperity may have more reliably touched the city's black tanners (*tocineros*), an occupation that regularly drew sufficient earnings to qualify for solid middle class standing in Puebla during the eighteenth and early nineteenth centuries.[58] Highly regulated through trade guilds, tocineros possessed a strong identity and political power that translated into key seats on the city council. Moreover, as a measure of their wealth, each tocinero was required by law to demonstrate the use of at least thirty pig carcasses per week. This steady and high volume of carnage was needed to display their financial solvency to the government, particularly their ability to provide certain municipal services, such as furnishing horses to the militias.[59]

TABLE 5.3. Free-Colored Workforce in Puebla, 1794

Occupation	Number of Workers	Percentage of Workforce
Tejedores (weavers)	91	19
Cigarreros (tobacco factory workers)	66	14
Cocheros (coachmen)	52	11
Sombrereros (hatters)	33	7
Herreros (blacksmiths)	26	5
Zapateros (cobblers)	25	5
Panaderos (breadmakers)	21	4
Sastres (tailors)	16	3
Albañiles (masons)	15	3
Others	139	29
Total	484	100

Source: BNAH, Archivo Judicial de Puebla, rollos 43–44, Tributos, Expediente formado en virtud de las diligencias hechas por los alcaldes ordinarios al gobernador intendente Don Manuel de Flon, Puebla, 1795.

While opportunities for wealth existed throughout the occupational spectrum, it is difficult to know which individual artisans were able to translate their craft trades into profitable business enterprises. By and large, it seems, the city's free-colored workforce stood with Indians near the bottom of Puebla's social order.[60] This observation needs some explanation. In many respects, the city's male free-colored workers appeared to resemble other non-Indians. For starters, as with castizos,[61] mestizos, and whites, the proportion of artisans among free coloreds towered over the percentage of artisans in the native workforce and probably well outpaced the share of black artisans employed in Mexico City's workforce during the 1790s. In fact, in 1794, over 80 percent of Puebla's pardo males were craftsmen, being largely employed in the clothing and textile industry.[62]

But a closer inspection of Puebla's pardo population yields other important details. Within the textile and clothing industry, free coloreds were more likely to find jobs as tejedores (weavers) than any other occupation. Over half of all male, free-colored textile workers in the 1794 census were weavers, which corresponded to 19 percent of the total male free-colored workforce. No other occupation enjoyed such prominence. While access to the trade definitely contributed to the large number of free-colored artisans, on the other hand, a weaver's earnings were among the lowest in the city. Although weavers had long enjoyed a strong and proud tradition in Puebla with a historically powerful guild, by the late eighteenth century the average tejedor was earning around two *reales* a day, approximately the pay of an agricultural peon and barely enough for subsistence.[63] Unfortunately, these wages would dip further during the early 1800s. Broadcloth weavers apparently earned more. Their greater skill commanded higher prices, but there were only two free-colored *tejedores de ancho* in the city during the early 1790s.

The second most common employment for Puebla's pardos may have been more lucrative. Along with Mexico City, Puebla was one of a few locations in the colony with tobacco factories.[64] These factories employed about one thousand workers, almost equally balanced between men and women. Puebla's pardos comprised around 13 percent of the overall male workforce in the industry, a figure that well exceeded their representation in the general population. Most were bachelors, meaning that, by and large, their earnings did not support wives and children, although some may have given financial assistance to their relatives, illegitimate children, and girlfriends. There was a wide variety of specialization among tobacco workers, including a limited number of relatively well-paid "masters of the table" and foremen who could earn in excess of one peso per day. Yet there were also large numbers of low-skilled workers, such as rollers, who earned as little as one peso per month.[65]

The third largest profession for Puebla's free coloreds was cocheros, who regularly served as chauffeurs for the wealthy. At least 11 percent of Puebla's pardo males were coachmen in the early 1790s, who in turn comprised over half of all free-colored men working in the service and transport sector. As with weavers, compensation for this line of work was meager, with the average coachman struggling to earn a paltry two reales per day.

Turning to the middle tier of Puebla's workforce, *panaderos* (breadmakers) probably lived some of the most challenging lives. Historically, their profession enjoyed a notorious reputation, with employees being chained and locked in bakeries, sweating profusely under the heat of sweltering ovens. But by the second half of the eighteenth century working conditions had improved substantially. Prisoners were not to be impressed into bakeries, hours were standardized, wages were to be paid daily (with no unfair deductions), workers were allowed to live offsite, and earnings could reach up to two reales per oven load of bread. Under these circumstances, no less than half of Puebla's free-colored panaderos were married and lived with their families in the community. However, opportunities in the profession were limited. No free-colored overseers were recorded as managing the city's bakeries, and it is unlikely that any were entrepreneurs, owning their own *panaderías*.[66]

Other members of the middle tier of Puebla's free-colored male workforce enjoyed greater material well-being. Once they landed steady employment, they worked long hours in stores and shops typically owned by others, or in small operations they owned themselves. The most prosperous could afford to hire managers and assistants, who, working alongside them, added to profit margins and enabled commercial expansion. Success was never assured. Of the middle strata, hat makers, who were the most numerous, probably also possessed the greatest range in earning potential. Depending upon their skill, clientele, the quantity of production, and the quality of their materials, hat makers could earn anywhere between one and four reales per day, with master hatters faring even better. A steady daily income of four reales was not quite middle-class income, but it definitely distanced someone from the urban underclass. The most accomplished hat makers in the city could easily break through the middle-class ranks and into the elite. In the 1820s, some elite master hatters earned in excess of twenty-five reales per day, which exceeded the earnings of many merchants.[67]

The city's free-colored hatters were in small but good company in the 1790s. Blacksmithing, shoemaking, and tailoring provided staple employment opportunities for the city's free-colored population, as elsewhere in urban New Spain. Within the textile industry, tailors probably fared better than the more numerous weavers and may have enjoyed more prestige. Being one of the occupations furthest removed from the actual process of cloth production, and with its employees having direct contact with the consumer market, tailors enjoyed a certain cachet, although from the elite perspective they remained the subject of ridicule.[68] Overall, the number of pardo tailors in Puebla was small, especially when compared to places like Mexico City where, in the 1750s and possibly into the 1780s, tailoring may have been the most accessible artisan trade. Tailors, like cobblers, had fairly low overhead costs in starting their businesses. This made both professions attractive to a wide range of individuals. However, between the two occupations, cobblers enjoyed a lower status. Status differences were reflected in earnings. By the 1820s, a typical tailor in Puebla might earn between one and eight reales per day, whereas cobblers more consistently earned wages hovering at the one real mark.

Guanajuato and Querétaro

North of Mexico City, in a low-lying plain called the Bajío, rested one of the most fertile and productive regions in the colony. Staple crops, including maize, wheat, beans, chilies, and fruit, grew abundantly here and silver mining prospered, specifically in Guanajuato, which by the early 1800s was generating more than five million pesos annually.[69] Unsurprisingly, the Bajío would become home to some of the largest population densities in Mexico. By 1803, the province of Guanajuato alone boasted half a million inhabitants.[70] In its vicinity were other important centers, including Celaya, León, and Querétaro. Of these, Querétaro had gained a well-earned reputation as a textile center in the eighteenth century. Easy access to the markets of the north, which both supplied wool to the city's factories and served as consumers of woolen products, greatly facilitated the city's prominence. Combined with a tobacco factory and a leatherworking industry, Querétaro had much to offer prospective settlers.[71] Despite hard years (smallpox epidemics erupted nearly every eighteen years after 1750), agricultural failures, and testy politics (Guanajuato's residents vociferously protested unfair monopolies, policies, and taxes), the Bajío region grew.[72] Querétaro and Guanajuato, in fact, became the third and fourth largest cities in Mexico, with populations of approximately thirty thousand in the 1790s. In their hinterlands were secondary townships that anchored growth.[73]

Overall, the late colonial Bajío was an atypical region of Mexico. Natives did not comprise a majority of the population, and most individuals (including natives) lived in racially mixed townships, cities, or rural estates. In this sense, the Bajío represented a prototype of what Mexico would eventually become—a landscape where mestizos thrived as the predominant racial type. But in the 1790s, the region had not quite achieved this state and free coloreds were part of the reason. Of the 400,000 persons counted in Guanajuato's 1792 provincial census, over 72,000 (18 percent) were mulattos. In the city proper, mulattos numbered as many as seven thousand individuals, or 22 percent of the urban population.[74] Querétaro offered a slightly different scenario. The province's free colored population in 1791 was remarkably low, numbering just over three thousand persons, or barely 4 percent of the regional population. Over half was located in the city of Querétaro itself.[75] Free coloreds had historically been more numerous; just eighteen years earlier the 1778 census had recorded as many as seven thousand living in the city alone. The disappearance of the black population may have been a harbinger of future events to come throughout Mexico. Although smallpox wreaked havoc between the censuses of 1778 and 1790, the rapid and almost wholesale decline of Querétaro's free-colored population probably had little to do with disease. Instead, black losses were most likely attributable to their being rapidly absorbed by other racial groups—at least in the official record. In other words, changes in the racial criteria used by government census takers may have been the real reason why, almost overnight, individuals who were once deemed mulattos were now reclassified as mestizos.[76]

Given the centrality of mining and textiles to the economies of Guanajuato and Querétaro, it is unsurprising that both would appear as major areas of free-colored employment. What is surprising, however, is the degree to which blacks occupied them. In Guanajuato, between 1791 and 1792, no fewer than 4,659 individuals were employed in this sector, comprising approximately 49 percent of the male, non-Indian workforce.[77] Remarkably, mulattos, with over 1,800 workers, represented a full 40 percent of the mining industry, and six out of every ten working mulatto males were miners. The related charcoal makers and refining industries also employed large numbers of blacks (30 percent). No other racial group had larger numbers in the mining sector.

Similarly, in Querétaro, free coloreds formed nearly 20 percent of the non-Indian, male textile workforce. As in Guanajuato's mining sector, these figures significantly exceeded their representation in the city's population, with nearly four out of every ten black males working in textiles. In the larger factories, free coloreds worked in almost every aspect of the industry, although mainly as weavers, workers, and spinners. A few labored in the finishing processes, that is, generating coarse cotton cloth and making fine shawls. However, there were no black administrators and dyers, although admittedly there were just a small number of these positions available in the city. A handful of Querétaro's mulatto textile workers operated cottage industries of their own. There were seven recorded *trapicheros*, who, in all likelihood, ran small family-style operations consisting of one or two looms.[78]

While the Querétaro census offers only a glimpse of an industry that may have employed well over three thousand men and women during the late colonial period, it is nevertheless a compelling view. Combined with the data from Guanajuato, we clearly see that two of the most important industrial fields in each city generously employed free people of color. This suggests that as the Mexican economy expanded in these areas, material opportunities arose for blacks. While their occupations may not have been the most coveted or lucrative positions, they were opportunities nonetheless, and ones that placed free coloreds directly in the mainstream workforce.

When Guanajuato's and Querétaro's free-colored occupations are ranked according to the number of blacks they employed, a slightly different picture emerges. In Querétaro, the four positions in which free coloreds were occupied the most were split between the artisan and service industries, with weavers and cobblers outpacing coachmen and servants. In Guanajuato, the top six positions were divided between the mining, farming, transport, and service industries (see Tables 5.4 and 5.5). These differences most likely reflect the unique economic orientation of a mining center, as opposed to an industrial/manufacturing center. Querétaro resembled Puebla in many ways and, to some extent, Mexico City. The major difference was that in Querétaro there may have been greater occupational diversity among the top half of black laborers. In other words, the four most commonly cited free-colored professions only represented 28 percent of the male workforce in Querétaro, whereas in Mexico City and Puebla, roughly half of all male laborers fell into the top four trades.[79]

Guanajuato stood at the other end of the spectrum. Its top six positions employed over three-quarters of the male workforce. Such extreme lack of differentiation among free-colored workers may have been the way of life in the largest mining towns, where the preponderance of mining jobs was complemented with significant employment in the agricultural and transportation sectors. In Guanajuato, however, as in many of the urban areas examined in this chapter, blacks could not escape the pull of the service economy. But in Guanajuato, service positions did not fall as heavily on free-colored males as in the major manufacturing cities. In fact, Spaniards actually composed the largest number of servants, with mulattos emerging as one of the least likely groups to be employed in this task.

TABLE 5.4. Free-Colored Workforce in Guanajuato, 1792

Occupation	Number of Workers	Percentage of Workforce
Mineros (miners)	1,881	60
Sirvientes (servants)	143	4
Labradores (farmers)	139	4
Arrieros (muleteers)	108	3
Molineros (millworkers)	101	3
Rescatadores (petty refiners)	79	2
Zapateros (cobblers)	73	2
Tratantes (dealers)	39	
Carboneros (charcoal-makers)	38	
Sastres (tailors)	35	
Albañiles (masons)	32	
Panaderos (breadmakers)	32	
Herreros (blacksmiths)	24	
Tocineros (tanners)	13	
Carpinteros (carpenters)	11	
Total[a]	3,132	78

Source: Brading, "Grupos étnicos," 256.
[a] Represents the total of only the seven most numerous professions.

TABLE 5.5. Free-Colored Workforce in Querétaro, 1790

Occupation	Number of Workers	Percentage of Workforce
Tejedores (weavers)	79	14
Zapateros (cobblers)	33	6
Cigarreros (tobacco factory workers)	29	5
Cocheros (coachmen)	28	5
Criados (manservants)	23	4
Others	375	66
Total	567	100

Source: Wu, "The Population of the City of Queretaro in 1791," 293.

Conclusion

In no uncertain terms, by the end of the eighteenth century, Afro-Mexicans were deeply embedded within the major occupational arenas available to most colonists. In the hinterlands and countryside, free coloreds participated in the cotton boom of the Pacific. They worked on estates and smaller farms that generated key foodstuffs in the Mexican heartland; they toiled in cane fields; and they labored tirelessly as fishermen, ranchers, and shepherds. The evidence reveals that blacks contributed to the larger export economies of their regions while also supplying local markets; free coloreds even joined the legions of subsistence farmers throughout New Spain. Of course, niche industries emerged, and some were partly determined by racial status. Interestingly, this pattern was found to some degree in the colony's two great urban centers, as service labor soared within the downtown quarters of Mexico City and low-paying weavers disproportionately occupied large numbers of Puebla's free coloreds. While historians have often cited cities as being the vanguard of class transformation and change, as well as sites where a plebian (rather than a racial) consciousness came into being, at the same time we have seen here how cities could preserve elements of caste hierarchy. Ironically, this was expressed precisely *within* class mobility. In other words, as class mobility happened, and as it touched those members of colonial society who belonged to subordinate castes, the social hierarchies of race and caste were not necessarily ruptured (although in some instances they could be). Instead, these social hierarchies could be reworked and restructured to accommodate the occupational mobility of groups such as free coloreds. Therefore, as broader economic opportunities opened in certain urban areas, caste hierarchy could correspondingly shift to accommodate the changes to a city's economic structure. As a result, seeming advancements in job status could actually represent stasis in social standing. Mexico City and Puebla, two of the colony's oldest cities with some of the longest-serving elites, were natural places where one might find such trends. On the other hand, some of the great bastions of the new economy—Guanajuato and Querétaro—offered other possibilities. In both centers, mining and textiles generated seemingly wholesale opportunities for all. But even here, black advancement to many of the best positions tended to be restricted, thereby presenting a limited window of economic opportunity for the free-colored population. When stopping back and looking at the overall portrait of black labor in the colony, without a doubt we can say that free coloreds were very much a part of the economic life of New Spain, and quite possibly in ways that both mirrored and rivaled the participation of mestizos and other caste groups. But it is still unclear whether, as blacks lived their freedom, they were as fully vested in all the opportunities that the colonial economy had to offer and, more importantly, what such a shortcoming may have meant on an individual and collective basis for free-colored life.

✣ NOTES ✣

1. Archivo General de la Nacíon (AGN), Tributos, vol. 34, exp. 7, don Benito Pérez to Revillagigedo, April 18, 1793, fols. 163–73.
2. AGN, Indiferentes de Guerra (I.G.), vol. 307-B, Leberina Azebedo para que no se remita a presidio a su marido, Vicente Medina, soldado del batallona de pardos de México.
3. AGN, I.G., vol. 307-B, exp. 5, Causa formada por el tribunal de la Acordada contra Lucio Antonio Rodríguez, soldado del batallón de pardos de México por portador de arma corta.
4. Some classic works include: Eric Williams, *Capitalism and Slavery* (Chapel Hill: University of North Carolina Press, 1944); Walter Rodney, *How Europe Underdeveloped Africa* (Dar-Es-Salaam: Bogle-L'Ouverture Publications, London and Tanzanian Publishing House, 1973); Frank Tannenbaum, *Slave and Citizen: The Negro in the Americas* (New York: Vintage Books, 1946); Paul Gilroy, *The Black Atlantic: Modernity and Double Consciousness* (Cambridge: Harvard University Press, 1993) especially chap. 2; Gilberto Freyre, *The Masters and the Slaves: A Study in the Development of Brazilian Civilization*, trans. Samuel Putnam (New York: Alfred A. Knopf, 1946); and Carl N. Degler, *Neither Black Nor White* (New York: Macmillan, 1971). See also: David Eltis, *The Rise of African Slavery in the Americas* (New York: Cambridge University Press, 1999); Aline Helg, *Our Rightful Share: The Afro-Cuban Struggle for Equality, 1886–1912* (Chapel Hill: University of North Carolina Press, 1995); Laurent Dubois, *A Colony of Citizens: Revolution and Slave Emancipation in the French Caribbean, 1787–1804* (Chapel Hill: University of North Carolina Press, 2006); Aline Helg, *Liberty and Equality in Colombia, 1770–1835* (Chapel Hill: University of North Carolina Press, 2003).
5. Throughout this chapter the term "free colored" is used to refer to a variety of black populations, including racially mixed pardos (black/native mixture), mulattos (black/white mixture), and moriscos (light skinned mulattos).

Morenos and negros were synonymous terms referring to blacks who were not racially mixed.

6. Some examples can be found in the following edited collections: Luz María Martínez Montiel and Juan Carlos Reyes G., eds., *Memoria del III Encuentro Nacional de Afromexicanistas* (Colima, Mexico: Gobierno del Estado de Colima y Consejo Nacional para la Cultura y las Artes, 1993); Adriana Naveda Chávez-Hita, ed., *Pardos, mulatos y libertos, Sexto encuentro de afromexicanistas* (Xalapa, Mexico: Universidad Veracruzana, 2001); and Luz María Martínez Montiel, ed., *Presencia africana en México* (Mexico City: Consejo Nacional para la Cultura y las Artes, 1994).

7. Gonzalo Aguirre Beltrán, *La población negra de México: Estudio etnohistórico*, 3rd ed. (Mexico City: Fondo de Cultura Económica, 1989), 219, 230.

8. For more on the period from the 1640s into the eighteenth century, see: Dennis N. Valdés, "The Decline of Slavery in Mexico," *The Americas* 44, no. 2 (1987): 167–94; Frank Proctor III, "Slavery, Identity, and Culture: An Afro-Mexican Counterpoint, 1640–1763," Ph.D. diss., Emory University, 2003; Herman L. Bennett, *Colonial Blackness, Sin, Sex, and Emergent Private Lives in New Spain, 1622–1778* (Bloomington: University of Indiana Press, 2009). For good material on miscegenation see: Patrick J. Carroll, "Los mexicanos negros, el mestizaje y los fundamentos olvidados de la 'raza cósmica,' una perspective regional," *Historia Mexicana* XLIV, no. 3 (1995): 403–48; and Mónica Leticia Gálvez Jiménez, *Celaya: sus raíces africanas* (Guanajuato, Ediciones la Rana, 1995).

9. The number of five hundred morenos is most likely a low figure since not all of the colony's provinces are accounted for in the archives. The number of "Africans" most likely corresponds to blacks who were not racially mixed, but there is no way to completely confirm this.

10. Some interpretations of Mexican slavery show how the system offered a variety of challenges to the power of masters and perhaps even a few material advantages over Mexico's underclass. For good examples of scholarship on the autonomy that slaves were able to acquire, see: Herman L. Bennett, *Africans in Colonial Mexico: Absolutism, Christianity, and Afro-creole Consciousnsess, 1570–1640* (Bloomington: Indiana University Press, 2003); Javier Villa-Flores, "'To Lose One's Soul': Blasphemy and Slavery in New Spain, 1596–1669," *The Hispanic American Historical Review* (*HAHR*) LXXXII, no. 3 (2002): 435–69; Joan Cameron Bristol, "Negotiating Authority in New Spain: Blacks, Mulattos, and Religious Practice in Seventeenth Century Mexico," Ph.D. diss., University of Pennsylvania, 2001; and Proctor, "Slavery, Identity, and Culture."

11. Aguirre Beltrán, *La población negra*, 223–30. There has been a great deal of guesswork involved with understanding the dimensions of Afro-Mexican demography; however, the figures provided by Aguirre Beltrán still remain fairly reliable.

12. These are estimates. Unfortunately, we may never be able to get a complete portrait of free-colored demography during these years. For all of its strengths, the surviving documents of the Revillagigedo census only allow us to closely examine some of the free-colored population. Note that the sampling technique I have used to obtain occupational information in the west coast provinces results in an undercount of the male population. To obtain information for these areas, I used the military census summary sheets of the Revillagigedo census. These records yield information on the most active segment of the male population, generally men between the ages of eighteen and forty-two who were in good physical condition and were not exempted from duty. Exemptions included men with disabilities or who were "demented" and unable to work. However, men already serving in the militias were also exempted. Only eight provinces were affected by these sampling techniques, resulting in the exclusion of 1,141 individuals from the occupational survey.

13. When all of the various agricultural and pastoral professions are accounted for, Mexico's black population was still less agriculturally centered than in the neighboring United States. Over 74 percent of all Americans were agriculturalists in 1800, and even more blacks (mainly slaves) as opposed to just over half of free Afro-Mexicans. See: Thomas Weiss, "U.S. Labor Force Estimates and Economic Growth," in *American Economic Growth and Standards of Living before the Civil War*, ed/ Robert E. Gallman and John Joseph Wallis, 22 (Chicago: University of Chicago Press, 1992).

14. Those who have wrestled with such questions include Brígida von Mentz, *Pueblos de indios, mulatos y mestizos, 1770–1870. Los campesinos y las transformaciones protoindustriales en el poniente de Morelos* (Mexico City: CIESAS, 1988), 130–37; and Cheryl English Martin, *Rural Society in Colonial Morelos* (Albuquerque: University of New Mexico Press, 1985).

15. Isabel González Sánchez, "Sistemas de trabajo, salarios y situación de los trabajadores agrícoloas, 1750–1810," in *La Clase Obrera en la Historia de México*, ed. Enrique Florescano, Isabel González Sánchez, Jorge González Angulo, Roberto Sandoval Zarauz, Cuauhtémoc Velasco A., and Alejandra Moreno Toscazo, 157 (Mexico City: Siglo XXI, 1980). For full treatment on rural workers' lives and conditions see 125–72. Note also that good distinctions between dependent and independent labor are made in Matthew Restall,

The Black Middle (Stanford: Stanford University Press, 2009). See especially Chapter 4, entitled "Ways of Work."

16. For an interesting interpretation of black labor mobility in the Pacific region see: José Arturo Motta Sánchez, "Derrota a la Mar del Sur; trazas de una senda de afrosucesores libres y cautivos en la segunda mitad del siglo XVIII," in *Diaspora, Nación y Diferencia: Poblaciones de origen Africano en México y Centro America*, CD ROM (Mexico, Universidad de Guanajuato, 2008). For additional analysis of free-colored labor in the Pacific basin, see Ben Vinson III, "West Side Story: Free-Black Labor in the Mexican Pacific during the Late Colonial Period as Seen Through the Revillagigedo Census," *Journal of Colonialism and Colonial History* 10, no. 3 (2009), available at http://muse.jhu.edu/journals/journal_of_colonialism_and_colonial_history.

17. Peter Gerhard, *A Guide to the Historical Geography of New Spain* (Cambridge: Cambridge University Press, 1972), 124–26.

18. Daniéle Dehouve, *Entre el caimán y el jaguar: Los pueblos indios de Guerrero* (Mexico City: Centro de Investigaciones y Estudios Superiores en Antropología Social, 1994), 104–7, 111, and 114; Jesús Hernández Jaimes, "El comercio de algodón en las cordilleras y costas de la mar del sur de Nueva España en la segunda mitad del siglo XVIII," in *Mercaderes, comercio y consulados de Nueva España en el siglo XVIII*, ed. Guillermina del Valle Pavón, 237–44 (Mexico City: Instituto Mora, 2003); Ben Vinson III, "The Racial Profile of a Rural Mexican Province in the 'Costa Chica:' Igualapa in 1791," *The Americas* (*TAM*) 57, no. 2 (2000): 269–82.

19. The specific tasks performed by operarios could be more defined in larger urban areas. In Mexico City, for instance, there were operarios who worked specifically in bakeries and others who toiled in the treasury. But in large cities like Guadalajara and Guanajuato, operarios could equally remain part of an amorphous and anonymous mass of low-wage laborers. For more, consult: Rodney D. Anderson, "Race and Social Stratification: A Comparison of Working-Class Spaniards, Indians and Castas in Guadalajara, Mexico in 1821," *HAHR* 68, no. 2 (1988): 209–43; Cuauhtémoc Velasco Ávila, "Los trabajadores mineros en la Nueva España, 1750–1810," in *La Clase Obrera*, 291–99; and Sonia Pérez Toledo and Herbert S. Klein, *Población y estructura social de la Ciudad de México, 1790–1842* (Mexico City: Universidad Autónoma Metropolitana Unidad Iztapalapa (UAMI), 2004), 295.

20. Slaves continued to have a presence in mining as well, see Brígida von Mentz, "Esclavitud en centros mineros y azucareros novohispanos. Algunas propuestas para el estudio de la multietnicidad en el centro de México," in *Poblaciones y culturas de origen africano en México*, ed. María Elisa Velásquez and

Ethel Correa, 259–67 (Mexico City: Instituto Nacional de Antropología e Historia (INAH), 2005).

21. David A. Brading, "Grupos étnicos; Clases y estructura ocupacional en Guanajuato (1792)," in *Historia y población en México (Siglos XVI–XIX)* (Mexico City: El Colegio de México, 1994), 244; and Colin A. Palmer, *Slaves of the White God: Blacks in Mexico, 1570–1650* (Cambridge: Harvard University Press, 1976). Note that in Guanajuato, as in other Mexican mining regions, many of the sixteenth- and early seventeenth-century black miners were slaves. As slavery subsided, the offspring of the unions between slaves and freedmen generated an appreciable free-colored population. Many of them also became miners, but migratory flows brought new infusions of black workers. Again, the phenomenon was not unique to Guanajuato. In Sultepec, for instance, a local priest recounted that "mining attracted many 'foreigners, the whitest of which look black.'" See Von Mentz, "Esclavitud en centros mineros," 264.

22. Some excellent occupational information for women in Mexico City can be found in María Elisa Velázquez, *Mujeres de origen africano en la capital novohispana, siglos XVII y XVIII* (Mexico City: INAH, Universidad Nacional Autónoma de México (UNAM), 2006), 161–228; and Elisa Velázquez, "Amas de leche, cocineras y vendedoras: Mujeres de origen africano, trabajo y cultura en la ciudad de México durante la época colonial," in *Poblaciónes y culturas africano*, 335–56.

23. Matthew Restall finds this trend in a rural Yucatecan census from 1700 where all three free-colored muleteers lived in the transportation hub of Maxcanú; see Restall, *The Black Middle*, chap. 4.

24. A wonderful survey of Mexico's artisan trades remains: Manuel Carrera Stampa, *Los gremios Mexicanos: La organización gremial en Nueva España, 1521–1861* (Mexico City: EDIAPSA, 1954). For information on blacks in the gold and silversmithing trade see: John E. Kicza, *Colonial Entrepreneurs: Families and Business in Bourbon Mexico City* (Albuquerque: University of New Mexico Press, 1983). For discussion of the career of Juan Correa, a famous free-colored artist and guild overseer, see: Elisa Vargas Lugo, *Juan Correa. Su vida y su obra*, 4 vols. (Mexico City: UNAM, 1985–1994). Norah Andrews has also found a handful of black guild masters in Puebla in 1800. They included furniture makers, cobblers, blacksmiths, hatters, and tailors. See Norah Andrews, "'I Could not Determine the Truth': Ambiguity and Afromexican Royal Tribute," Master's thesis, Johns Hopkins University, 2009, 23.

25. Evaluating the role of women in the colonial period's labor force has posed a particular challenge in places such as the United States, but in Latin

America, more data is available. Although richer, problems persist given the inconsistent and spotty reporting of female occupations. This situation can be found in late colonial Mexico's census records, especially the Revillagigedo census.

26. This is speculative, but also fits with observations found in Mexico City by Silvia Arrom, *The Women of Mexico City, 1790–1857* (Stanford: Stanford University Press, 1985), 158–66; Patricia Seed, "The Social Dimensions of Race: Mexico City 1753," *HAHR* LXII, no. 4 (1982): 569–606; and María Elisa Velázquez, "Juntos y revueltos: Oficios, espacios y comunidades domésticas de origen africano en la capital novohispana según el censo de 1753," in *Pautas de convivencia étnica en la América Latina colonial (Indios, negros, mulatos, pardos y esclavos)*, ed. Juan Manuel de la Serna Herrera, 331–46 (Mexico City: UNAM, 2005). Note, however, that there is only limited utility in making colony-wide generalizations from the Mexico City case.

27. Again, for excellent treatment see Arrom, *Women of Mexico City*, 154–205.

28. Pérez Toledo and Klein, *Población y estructura social*, 285–99.

29. Susan M. Socolow, "Introduction," in *Cities and Society in Colonial Latin America*, ed. Louisa Schell Hoberman and Susan M. Socolow, 15–16 (Albuquerque: University of New Mexico Press, 1986).

30. Lyman Johnson, "Artisans," in *Cities and Society in Colonial Latin America*, 234–36.

31. Note that population figures for Mexico City are a matter of debate for the 1790s. Viceroy Revillagigedo ascertained that the population stood at 112,000. Other contemporaries argued larger numbers and recent research has shown that the city may have possibly held up to 300,000 individuals. See Manuel Miño Grijalva, "La población de la ciudad de México en 1790. Variables económicas y demográficas de una controversia," in *La población de la ciudad de México en 1790: Estructura social, alimentación y vivienda*, ed. Manuel Miño Grijalva and Sonia Pérez Toledo, 21–74 (Mexico City: UAMI, 2004). Sonia Pérez Toledo has weighed into the argument, calculating the number closer to 117,000. See Pérez Toledo and Klein, *Población y estructura social*, 64. Keith Davies's pioneering study calculates the population at 130,000. See Keith Davies, "Tendencias demográficas urbanas durante el siglo XIX en México," in *Historia y población*, 281–82. Whatever the actual number, the city was extremely large by contemporary standards in the Western world.

32. The figures for mulattos are derived from Alexander von Humboldt, *Political Essay on the Kingdom of New Spain*, 2 vols., trans. John Black (New York: I. Riley, 1811), I:192.

33. These quadrants are cuarteles 1, 20, and 23, and had a total population of over thirteen thousand individuals. The database for these cuarteles has been generously provided by Herbert S. Klein. Note that these quarters have also been studied in depth by members of the urban history seminar run by the Colegio de México.

34. For an excellent graphic representation of the ethnic composition of Mexico City at the outset of the nineteenth century see: Lourdes Márquez Morfín, "La desigualdad ante la muerte: Epidemias, población y sociedad en la ciudad de México (1800–1850)," Ph.D. diss., El Colegio de México, 1991, 59.

35. Pérez Toledo and Klein, *Población y estructura social*, 94.

36. A good study of the use of residential and public space in the center and western parts of Mexico City can be found in Diana Birrichaga Gardida, "Distribución del espacio urbano en la ciudad de México en 1790," in *La población de la ciudad de México*, 311–41.

37. In the late colonial period, the tobacco factory was responsible for employing up to 11 percent of Mexico City's population. Many employees were women who were paid competitive wages. Some incomes even rivaled several artisan trades. For more, see Amparo Ros, *La producción cigarrera a finales de la Colonia. La fábrica en México* (Mexico City: INAH, 1984). For more on the industry, see Susan Deans-Smith, *Bureaucrats, Planters, and Workers: The Making of the Tobacco Monopoly in Bourbon Mexico* (Austin: University of Texas Press, 1992).

38. Patricia Seed records that 81.5 percent of free black males were servants. Seed, "Social Dimensions of Race," 582.

39. Concentrated mostly in the textile, food, leatherworking, metal, and barbering industries, many of these staple arenas of the workforce had long been important niches for free coloreds, particularly the professions of *zapateros* (shoemakers) and *sastres* (tailors). See Pérez Toledo, *Los hijos del trabajo. Los artesanos de la ciudad de México, 1780–1853* (Mexico City: El Colegio de México, UAMI, 1996), 78; Miño Grijalva, "Estructura social y ocupación de la población en la ciudad de México, 1790," in *La población en la ciudad de México*, 160; and Felipe Castro Gutiérrez, *La extinción de la artesanía gremial* (Mexico City: UNAM, 1986), 97, 172–80.

40. There were only seventeen employed morisco men in the sample. Of these, ten were artisans and one was a foreman.

41. There was also a *bolero*, a professional shoe polisher. I would categorize her as being employed in the service sector, but Pérez Toledo and Klein's categorization of professions in *Población y estructura social*, 287, listed her as an artisan. If this person was considered by contemporaries to be an artisan, it is telling that this lower status trade (when compared to the seamstress) was

held by a *mulata* (phenotypically darker than the morisca seamstress), and that she also worked in the city center.

42. For an excellent study of the range of professions open to men and women in Mexico City in the late colonial and early national period, see Pérez Toledo and Klein, *Población y estructura social*, 285–99. The definitional description of many professions can be found in Pérez Toledo, *Los hijos del trabajo*, 55–56 and 269–74. Note that nearly half of the forty-four professions listed for mulattos in cuartel 1 incorporated women, whereas in the other two parts of town, just four out of seventeen professions included them. Also, over half of all free-colored females were listed as being employed downtown, whereas almost none were recorded as working in the southern and western peripheries. Of course, this statistic is somewhat misleading since, in actuality, labor was a daily reality for most free-colored women.

43. In the literature on North America, age ten has been identified as a typical age for children entering the workforce in pre-industrial and early industrial societies. A similar case might be made for Latin America. Of course, some exceptions exist. See John E. Murray and Ruth Wallis Herndon, "Markets for Children in Early America: A Political Economy of Pauper Apprenticeship," *Journal of Economic History* 62, no. 2 (June 2002): 356–82.

44. Indeed, the importance of family as an economic survival mechanism may have been more pronounced in Mexico than in Europe. Michael C. Scardaville, "Trabajadores, grupo doméstico y supervivencia durante el periodo colonial tardío en la ciudad de México, o 'la familia pequeña no vive mejor,'" in *La población de la ciudad de México*, 227–79.

45. Eighty percent of households with negros had agregados (or featured negros as agregados) as opposed to less than 50 percent for moriscos. Note that free-colored households with agregados in Mexico City were harder to find outside of the city center, with barely one-third of free-colored households in the urban periphery possessing them. Surprisingly, morisco families were almost twice as likely to have agregados in the city as mulattos. Although more research is needed, suffice it to say that in the outskirts of town, members of the working classes, including free coloreds, probably lived in smaller family units than in the urban core, although one frequently encountered multiple families living together in the same household. Moreover, unlike elite families of the era, with their large number of retainers and domestic staff, free-colored working-class households in the periphery probably did not regularly incorporate individuals who were not their relatives. Consequently, although household living arrangements generally grew more complex over time in Mexico City, among the black working classes, unrelated agregados did not comprise a large part of their expanding households. For a slightly different

interpretation of the circumstances in Mexico City, see Velázquez, "Juntos y revueltos," 331–46. She contradicts notions that many laborers in the central part of town lived with coworkers, and so on.

46. Socolow, "Introduction," 5.

47. Carlos Contreras Cruz, Francisco Téllez Guerrero, Claudia Pardo Hernández, Melitón Mirto Tlalpa, "La población parroquial en la Puebla de los Ángeles hacia 1777. El caso del Sagrario, San Marcos, y San José, análisis preliminar," in *Población y estructura urbana en México, siglos XVIII y XIX* Carmen Blázquez Domínguez, ed. Carlos Contreras Cruz, and Sonia Pérez Toledo, 21–23 (Xalapa, Veracruz: Universidad Veracruzana, 1996); Guy P. C. Thomson, *Puebla de los Angeles: Industry and Society in a Mexican City, 1700–1850* (Boulder: Westview Press, 1989), xx.

48. Miguel Marín Bosch, *Puebla neocolonial, 1777–1831. Casta, ocupación y matrimonio en la segunda ciudad de Nueva España* (Zapopan, Jalisco: El Colegio de Jalisco, 1999), 65.

49. Grijalva, "Estructura social y ocupación," 158–59.

50. Thomson, *Puebla*, 14–26 and 42–46.

51. Ibid., 63. Note that the total district population was 71,366.

52. Ben Vinson III, *Bearing Arms for His Majesty: The Free-Colored Militia in Colonial Mexico* (Stanford: Stanford University Press, 2001), 60–61.

53. The 1790 census is limited in that it provides information on only four parishes, corresponding to roughly a third of the population, all of whom lived in the eastern and western peripheries of the city. Downtown elite households were excluded, meaning that many individuals working in the service sector were probably not accounted for. The 1794 census, which was actually initiated in 1791, is more comprehensive and may cover all free-colored residents in the city. But given that this census was raised to count tributaries and followed a different format than parish or even military censuses, it is not possible to carefully reconstruct where residents lived in the city (Subdirección de Documentación de la Biblioteca Nacional de Historia (BNAH), Archivo Judicial de Puebla, rollos 43–44, Tributos, Expediente formado en virtud de las exigencies hechas por los alcaldes ordinaries al gobernador intendente don Manuel de Flon con el fin de cobrar tributos de negros y mulatos, Puebla, 1795).

54. In this census, the term pardo is considered synonymous with mulatto and referred to racially mixed individuals, but was not specific as to whether the black admixture was with native, white, or other mixtures. It is unlikely that

the entire population was pardo—but for uniformity, this was the designation used. Also note that the 1794 tributary census excluded female professions.

55. Professions qualifying for the first group employed 10 percent or more of the free-colored population. For group 2, professions employing 5 percent or more of the free-colored population were considered.

56. By 1800 the black labor force experienced some minor shifts in focus. Cobblers surpassed weavers as the leading black profession and hatters rose to claim the third most prominent role. Combined, these three professions claimed about 35 percent of the black labor pool. Cigar factory workers virtually disappeared, while coachmen slipped into a tertiary position. This reshuffling of occupational rankings probably reflected change in Puebla's broader economy; but at its core, the main occupational opportunities remained, although their emphases altered slightly. One could argue that in some ways, by 1800, there were slightly better financial opportunities open to free coloreds, given the way in which occupations were realigned and the number of master artisans found in the census record. See Andrews, "I Could not Determine the Truth," 23.

57. Kicza, *Colonial Entrepreneurs*, 218–19.

58. Tanners included both *curtidores* and tocineros—but the tocineros were the higher status of the two. There were ten free-colored curtidores and six tocineros in Puebla in 1794.

59. Thomson, *Puebla*, 85.

60. An interesting examination of this can be found in Marín Bosch, *Puebla neocolonial*, 147–68.

61. A castizo was a light skinned mestizo—technically the mixture of a white and a mestizo.

62. Anywhere between 20 and 30 percent of Puebla's urban workforce was employed in textiles. But more significantly, over 40 percent of non-Indians worked in these trades during the early 1790s, a trend closely mirrored by free coloreds. Natives, by contrast, tended to be more heavily concentrated in the agricultural, food, and construction professions, where blacks were only minimally involved. See Thomson, *Puebla*, 69; and Marín Bosch, *Puebla neocolonial*, 147–50. Marín Bosch's numbers tend to be lower than those of Thomson's, favoring the 20 percent overall figure. His analysis covers more time and includes parish data. Note that the large proportion of artisans found among the pardos was probably similar to the city's mestizo and castizo workforce. It is hard to accurately gauge the number of artisans among these populations using available sources, but it is possible that, as with free coloreds, they may have comprised between 60 and 80 percent of mestizo,

castizo, and even white laborers. The number of artisans is roughly calculated by totaling the number of white, mestizo, and castizo workers in the textile, dress, metal, leather, wood, and "other" industries (data from Thomson, *Puebla*, 69). Because this is incomplete data for the entire city in 1790, there are gaps in our knowledge, but the information still provides us with a loose guide for understanding what may have been the overall employment situation.

63. González Sánchez, "Sistemas de trabajo," 150–72. For more explanation of the cloth manufacturing process see: Manuel Miño Grijalva, *La manufactura colonial. La constitución técnica del obraje* (Mexico City: El Colegio de Mexico, 1993).

64. Other locations included Querétaro, Oaxaca, Guadalajara, and Orizaba.

65. Ros, *La producción cigarrera*, 58.

66. Kicza, *Colonial Entrepreneurs*, 187–96.

67. Salary figures for hatters and coachmen come from 1823 estimates. See Thomson, *Puebla*, 83.

68. AGN, Alcaldes Mayores, vol. 2, exp. 254, Joseph Enereno to Bucareli, December 21, 1771, Puebla.

69. A still relevant, perceptive, and classic study of mining in Guanajuato is David Brading, *Miners and Merchants in Bourbon Mexico, 1763–1810* (Cambridge: Cambridge University Press, 1971).

70. Humbolt, *Political Essay*, II:129.

71. Celia Wu, "The Population of the City of Querétaro in 1791," *Journal of Latin American Studies* 16, no. 2 (1984): 277; and Humbolt, *Political Essay*, I:129–31.

72. Angela T. Thompson, "To Save the Children: Smallpox Inoculation, Vaccination and Public Health in Guanajuato, Mexico, 1797–1840," *TAM* 29, no. 4 (1993): 435.

73. Humboldt, *Political Essay*, II:131; Gerhard, *Historical Geography of New Spain*, 123.

74. Information on the racial dynamics of the Bajío is well covered in Brading, *Miners and Merchants*, 227–30. For Guanajuato census information, see pages 227 and 247–60. Note that there are two differing census figures for Guanajuato. One is based upon a summary sheet and estimates the urban population at over 32,000. Another, based upon a military census that excludes many Indians, places the population at over 21,000. In the second census record, the number of mulattos is lower (3,481). The figure of seven thousand mulattos is based on the summary sheet.

75. Statistics are from Wu, "Querétaro," 278–79. Note that free coloreds may have comprised up to 7 percent of Querétaro's population in 1791. The figure of 7 percent for the free-colored population in Querétaro is my estimate based upon blending figures from summary sheets and the military census. I calculate the 1,755 mulattos in Querétaro, against the 27,000 figure for the city, as opposed to the 14,847 found in the Revillagigedo census, which leaves out many of the natives.

76. These arguments are put forth by Wu, "Querétaro," 279. It is unclear if the enumerators were primarily responsible for the change, or if individuals declared themselves to be of a different casta from one census to another. Another possibility is that the quality of census taking changed over time.

77. Brading, *Miners and Merchants*, 258. Note that Indians were largely excluded from this military census and their numbers cannot be fully determined in the workforce. Female professions were also excluded.

78. Wu, "Querétaro," 294–95.

79. Of course, more work needs to be done to support this conclusion. The greater diversity of Mexico City's economy, for instance, probably yielded greater potential for increasing free-colored occupational options.

Colonial Middle Men?

Mulatto Identity in New Spain's Confraternities

NICOLE VON GERMETEN

❧

☥ IN 1766, MATHIAS NICOLÁS DUARTE EXPRESSED SOME BITTER feelings toward some of the other members of his Catholic brotherhood (confraternity) based in the church of Saint Augustine in Valladolid (a city to the west of Mexico City, now called Morelia). He was tired of the way some of the brothers wasted money on parties and banquets. These men had raised the dues for membership, but wasted the extra funds carousing. Duarte was so upset that he took his complaints to the highest local church authority, the bishop of Michoacán, who was based in Valladolid and had authority over a large region of western New Spain. What is special about this case was the way Duarte described himself, his allies, and the members he disliked:

> The native brothers, having controlled the finances of this confraternity until the present, in total exclusion of *ourselves, the mulatos*, said Indians have taken advantage of these goods and alms for their private utility. For example, before they paid two pesos alms for the confraternity's masses, and today they pay four *reales*, with

the extra twelve reales spent in their amusements and feasts [*sus bureos y festines*], without the slightest augmentation or benefit for the brotherhood. For this reason, and for other inconveniences that come out of this, I beg your grace to disempower said natives of the control of these goods and the wealth of the above mentioned confraternity, commanding that the *brothers of reason* and not said natives take over the accounts and the other aspects of good government.[1] (italics mine)

Duarte defined himself and his fellow mulatto brothers both as people of reason and sensible, sober men who knew how to spend money wisely. They were not, according to Duarte, prone to the feasts and festivities typical of Indians. In this case, men called *mulatos* defined themselves in contrast to Indians—Duarte formulated his self-image in opposition to other races, especially local Indian residents.

While we generally think of colonial race labels as insulting and degrading, many times individuals of African descent took advantage of their assigned race label in order to promote their interests to colonial authorities. Common race labels in colonial Latin America, especially those used to describe Afro-Mexicans, often derived from names of animals, such as coyote, lobo, and *mulato*, although *mulato*, by the end of the colonial period, was the most common label used for individuals of African descent.

The label *mulato* was used in New Spain to refer to a person thought to have both European and African ancestry. This word implies the word mule, the sterile offspring of a donkey and a horse. When referring to criminal activity or other disruptive actions involving a person with some African descent, authorities used the term *mulato* to describe perpetrators, while pardo was a label used with a degree of respect to describe some literate, high-status *mulatos*, especially those born in Spain, although the day-to-day use of labels such as moreno, pardo, negro, and *mulato* varied according to region.[2] While clearly every time these words were used a person might have felt dehumanized, this chapter will show that sometimes Afro-Mexicans seemed to have a sense of pride in the labels given to them by colonial authorities, especially as they contrasted themselves with other groups, as seems to be the case when Mathias Duarte brought his case before the bishop of Michoacán. From reading this case, we might conclude that the mulattos in Valladolid thought of themselves as middle men in colonial society—descended from slaves, they did not have the full status of Spaniards with *limpieza de sangre*, that is, lineage free from non-Christian, non-European ancestors, but they lived within the Hispanic urban world or in rural areas connected to Spanish-run agricultural enterprises. What were some of the other life patterns associated with people labeled as *mulatos*?

Individuals of African descent were more likely to be considered *gente de razón*, or "people with reason" than Indians.³ The officially mandated separation between colonial Indians and people of Spanish descent, based on language differences, segregation laws, legal status, eligibility for military service, Inquisition jurisdiction, and taxation, was much clearer than the division between Spaniards and Africans. Although subject to the tribute tax, Afro-Mexicans were under the jurisdiction of the Inquisition and could serve in the militia. Occupationally, as seen in Ben Vinson's chapter, many *mulatos* were urban craftsmen or tradesmen, such as tailors, shoemakers, builders, and painters. For women, the occupations of domestic servant and market seller were common, although Indian women also typically did these jobs.

Due to these patterns of life, mulattos often lived next door to Spaniards. New Spain's urban residential patterns reveal little segregation between Afro-Mexicans and Spaniards, especially because non-Spaniards lived in Spanish homes as servants. However, many towns included outlying Indian barrios, and Indians also lived semiautonomously in their own villages.⁴ Confraternity conflicts revolved around the mulatto/Indian distinction as those individuals who identified as mulattos chose to de-emphasize their association with what they may have considered less successful colonial subjects. Regardless, as non-Europeans in at least a part of their lineage, Afro-Mexicans and Indians all suffered legalized racism in the colonial era. They were excluded from many professions. Earlier in the colonial period, authorities attempted to keep Africans and Indians separate and to control their mobility and living arrangements. It is clear that, by emphasizing and encouraging subtle distinctions between different subject groups, Spanish authorities prevented a unified rebellion against their rule.

Furthermore, Spanish government and customs in the Americas tended to organize colonial subjects in groups and taking advantage of these group ties was the best way to advance one's personal goals. Descendants of Mexico's indigenous peoples often petitioned the authorities in groups based around their villages. This was less possible for people of African descent, because they lacked this traditional village structure. Without comparable access to villages as corporate structures, Afro-Mexicans took advantage of two colonial institutions: religious confraternities and militias. Although sometimes racially integrated, both confraternities and militias frequently divided their membership along the lines of racial divisions. Ben Vinson writes that militiamen may have had a sense of communal identity with others of their color, not inherently, but in response to the concrete benefits to be derived from institutionally linked racial affiliations. Access to corporate privileges provided the cornerstone toward building their racial consciousness.[5]

Racial labels were used in self-description only when Afro-Mexicans could gain from describing themselves in these terms. Self-deprecation was often a useful technique. As in society in general, more pejorative terms for race were used by authorities when they perceived the militia men in negative, belligerent ways. They used the more polite term pardo, also often used in self-description, when they discussed Afro-Mexicans in a positive light. The authorities also seemed willing to accept Afro-Mexicans' precise self-labeling. Similar to Afro-Mexican confraternity brothers, Vinson found that militiamen sometimes bickered over privilege based on fine racial distinctions. In other cases they united, disregarding if they were labeled pardo, moreno, or *mulato*, when they felt threatened from outside their institution. "Racial differences had to be subsumed ... when the basic privileges and integrity of their institution were in jeopardy."[6] This pattern is also seen in disputes involving confraternities.

Confraternities were one of the most fundamental social and religious organizations in New Spain, because they helped bring the diverse population into the powerful institution of the Catholic Church. In many places, the Catholic Church was far more dominant and prevalent than colonial government. In rural villages, often the only local Spaniard living in the region was a parish priest. Throughout Latin America, Africans and Afro-Latinos founded confraternities under the auspices of religious orders, parish churches, and, less officially, on haciendas.

Although it was embraced by Indians and Africans, the long-established tradition of the confraternity came along with the Spaniards arriving in the New World. Laypeople, priests, and friars all organized confraternities, recognized by the ecclesiastical hierarchy through the approval of an official confraternity constitution. The primary function of a confraternity was to celebrate a saint's day or honor a less tangible religious doctrine, such as the Holy Sacrament or the Rosary or a moment in the Passion of Christ. Confraternity members maintained an image of their advocation, located in a parish or convent church or chapel. The members cleaned, dressed, and decorated their image. Every year on the holiday connected to the advocation, the image could be taken out for a procession or celebrated through masses, sermons, and fiestas. Confraternity leaders, called majordomos, were elected during the yearly fiesta to take charge of accounts and confraternity activities. People joined confraternities by paying a small fee, having their name entered in a confraternity book or receiving a patent that stated the benefits they would receive through membership. Members depended on their confraternity membership to pay for their funeral mass and burial, and they especially trusted other members to pray for their souls.

Although Spanish confraternities were based on local identities and social divisions, the confraternal system had adapted to incorporate non-Spanish populations in the medieval period. Confraternities based on African origins were already known in Spain by the 1400s. Medieval confraternities were also established in towns recently colonized as Spain slowly came back into Christian hands after centuries of Islamic control. When a Creole society began to grow after a generation or two of European settlement in New Spain, confraternities based on place of origin were affected by new divisions of birth or lineage, whether indigenous, Spanish, African, mestizo, or *mulato*. Confraternities in Spain and New Spain were always connected to some kind of social division and in the New World became part of the process and formation of a racially divided society. The fact that confraternities had labels such as *de los mulatos*, morenos, pardos, mestizos, or negros indicates that this institution contributed to racial divisions and to an idea of what each of these race labels meant. Many towns in New Spain had several different racially designated confraternities, and these labels might have attracted a range of members in each locale. Confraternities were part of social divisions and social mobility.

Even before Africans came to the Americas, the term *mulato* was used in Spain and Africans and their descendants founded racially exclusive confraternities in cities in southern Spain such as Seville and Cádiz. From the 1500s, people described as *mulatos* began to create organizations around this racial identity. The first documented confraternities specifically organized around a *mulato* membership date from mid-sixteenth-century Seville, although traditions say they existed long before.

Brotherhoods dedicated to celebrating Christ's passion with penitential processions during Holy Week were especially popular among Afro-Mexicans. In Catholic villages, towns and cities all over Europe and the Americas, many different brotherhoods reenacted the events leading up the crucifixion on the Wednesday, Thursday, and Friday before Easter. Participants in these processions focused on carrying large statues and dioramas of scenes of Christ's passion as well as ritualistically flagellating themselves while walking in public streets, garbed in long robes and hoods to protect their anonymity. In the sixteenth century, Catholics in Rome showed immense enthusiasm for flagellant processions and passion plays—hundreds of people participated and riots broke out in reaction to recreations of Christ's suffering. Roman Catholics (Spain was closely tied to the Pope and had a large presence in Rome at the time) wanted to emphasize their belief in penance in opposition to the new interpretations of Christianity asserted by Protestant reformers.[7]

In the sixteenth and seventeenth centuries, the most devout and celebrated Catholics in the New World, such as Saint Rose of Lima, believed that physical pain represented the most effective way to demonstrate their love for the Christian god.[8] Rose inherited this belief from ancient and medieval saints, who understood that the undergirding of the Christian religion, which began with Christ's crucifixion, was self-sacrifice and pain. Baroque Catholicism is one overarching term for this complex mixture of the physical and the spiritual, with a constant recognition of social hierarchies and an emphasis on the sensual and the lavish as well as excruciating pain and decay. Afro-Mexicans actively forged their own form of Baroque Catholicism, especially in their penitential confraternities. In colonial Spanish America, a culture of inversions thrived: fantastically wealthy miners founded ornate churches decorated in gold and silver and donated large portions of their wealth to the church for masses to pray for the fate of their souls, and slaves and freed slaves might celebrate their position as the lowliest and most humble Christians. While most Afro-Mexicans did not have to feel guilt for being greedy or wealthy, their suffering, as slaves or as penitents freely choosing to flagellate themselves in public processions, represented a kind of expiation and intercession in the name of the sins of their society. Spaniards were enthusiastic about these penitential displays and brotherhoods, as can be documented by their desire to join or donate to black brotherhoods and the way they viewed their piety as "enslavement" to the Virgin Mary or Christ.[9]

In 1568, a group of men who described themselves as *mulatos* petitioned the king for the foundation of a hospital to serve their needs.[10] The petitioners complained that, as *mulatos*, they received neither treatment nor last rites, since the existing hospitals only admitted Spaniards, mestizos, and Indians. The leader of this group, a tailor named Juan Bautista claimed that many of the six thousand *mulatos* living in the capital were poor and in need of charity. In a revealing summary of their heritage, the petitioners described themselves as born in New Spain, the "sons of negros and Indians or *negras* and Spanish men that live in this land in service of Spaniards and practicing all crafts" (hijos de negros y de indias o de españoles y negras que viven en dicha tierra en servicio de españoles y en los officios de todas artes) and also stated they worked "as cow herders." Since Spaniards and Africans only came to Mexico in 1519, these petitioners were part of only the first or, at most, second generation of people of racially mixed heritage born in America. Juan Bautista also mentioned that a *mulato* servant helped organize sixty men to guard the city in the "time of rebellion," although the specific details of this rebellion were not given. Perhaps Juan Bautista was referring to the 1536 slave rebellion documented in the Codex Telleriano-Remensis. Witnesses described these guards as diligent and careful men, and those founding the hospital as educated in the Catholic religion and virtuous. All witnesses testified to Juan Bautista's good character and the need for a hospital, but unfortunately no action was taken in response to this petition. However, this petition shows that very early in Mexican history, individuals of African descent united with European authorities to advance their fundamental needs and rights as part of colonial society. The petitioners used the term *mulato* to describe themselves, but emphasized how it tied them to Spaniards, whom they both served and defended as loyal colonial subjects.

A few decades later, Mexico City's mulatto community again tried to organize and again faced difficulties, despite good intentions. In this case, a group of free and enslaved mulattos strove to take part in a penitential procession, marching in the streets and flagellating themselves.[11] In a complaint to the archbishop, a church official said that on Holy Thursday of 1601, a group of mulattos met in front of a convent church and started to form a penitential procession. They carried a banner representing their group and a green cross. Ringing a small bell and playing a trumpet, the men tried to draw attention to the images of Christ's passion they were carrying. Instead, according to the representative of the church, these marchers caused "whispers" and deserved punishment because they did not have official church approval for their confraternity. Men of African descent flagellating themselves publicly in an organized fashion aroused alarm among the Spanish observers. The best tactic to suppress this movement, despite its pious Catholic intentions, was to resort to complex Spanish rules and regulations and deny the brotherhood an official license.

The early 1600s was a time of fear of rebellion for Spanish colonial authorities, as the numbers of Africans in the population of New Spain were quite high and, clearly, the mulatto population was also increasing rapidly. In this era, the indigenous people of Mexico were still suffering a precipitous decline in numbers, although they always made up the largest percentage of New Spain's residents. Spanish overlords most feared a union between Africans and Indians, which could easily overthrow their empire. But where did those colonial subjects described as *mulatos* fit into this potentially threatening scheme? The above examples indicate that mulattos, who by definition were born in Spain or New Spain, not Africa, and were probably Spanish-speaking Catholics from birth, wanted to play a role within the Spanish system, not against it. Their participation in and leadership of confraternities was one way that mulattos showed this desire to become part of Hispanic society, while maintaining their separate race label.

Despite threatened and real African and slave revolts in seventeenth-century New Spain, mulattos did not lead rebellions in the 1600s. Instead this was an era when Afro-Mexican confraternities flourished throughout New Spain. In 1659, a group of Veracruz men, led by a mulatto militia captain and a lieutenant, met to organize a confraternity dedicated to Our Lady of the Immaculate Conception and the Humility and Patience of Christ. Veracruz, on New Spain's east coast, was an important slave port in the first half of the 1600s and had a large Afro-Mexican population. This population was large and complex enough to form distinct internal divisions, as can be seen in the set of rules laid down by the confraternity founders.

Every confraternity had to write down a constitution for their organization, specifying their membership requirements, dues, financial arrangements, leadership, and activities. The detailed constitution of the Veracruz confraternity demonstrates not only a desire to be led only by mulattos, but also a great preoccupation (almost forty rules worth) with their public conduct.[12] The first rule was quite specific in designating free mulattos as the only acceptable office holders. The writers of the constitution clearly stipulated "only those who are *legitimately* mulattos and not of any other *color*, even if they are brothers and benefactors of our said confraternity, will have a vote in the councils."[13] The majordomo, the highest-ranking leader of the confraternity, also had to be "an exemplary man, modest and of good habits." But, when voting, even people who "were capable and useful to the confraternity" could not vote if they were not—again the rules repeated these terms—"legitimately mulatto." The Veracruz brothers viewed themselves as different in appearance or color from individuals with more (or less) African ancestry.

Most of these concerns were packed into the first rule. The confraternity constitution went on to specify appropriate behavior during their penitential processions. To avoid any conflict with other brotherhoods in the city, the mulatto organization had their "blood procession" between six and seven p.m. on Tuesday of Holy Week. At the head of the procession would be a gilded banner marked with a white cross. At the penultimate position of the procession would be an image of Christ accompanied by friars. Last would come the confraternity's image of the Virgin. While marching in the procession, the members carried large candles and were exhorted to be silent, modest, and composed. Female members could accompany the procession, separated from the men's group, if they maintained a devoted and "decent" demeanor. Any person who spoke out, especially in a "profane" way, during the procession would suffer immediate expulsion both from the line of marchers and the group as a whole forever. In the confraternity's twenty-ninth rule, the members were again ordered to avoid "indecency" in the procession and, instead, to behave and dress in a modest fashion, invoking their humble and patient advocation. Specific rules of dress ordered the wearing of hoods and tunics and never carrying a sword. Even beyond the yearly procession, the rules stated that members should strive toward the humility of their patron Jesus Christ. If they presented a negative public image or became involved in fights, members faced ejection from the confraternity. While financial status was clearly delineated in this constitution and the organization it represented, the members also valued charity for their fellow members.

Similar to the Veracruz confraternity, in the early years of the eighteenth century, another group of mulattos formed a brotherhood whose rules emphasized their commitment to certain behavior patterns. These men met in the hospital of San Juan de Dios and had the advocation of Our Lady of Sorrows.[14] Using a symbolic number referring to the years Jesus lived on earth, according to Christian tradition, thirty-three official founders initiated the confraternity and were obligated to pay nine reales upon entrance and one real every month, along with a four-real payment for their fiesta. If any member failed to fulfill this financial obligation, thereafter "they had no right to ask anything of the confraternity." The founders of the confraternity dedicated to Dolores emphasized in their constitution that they were quiet men and promised to expel any members who did not approach their confraternity duties in a caring and peaceful way. The constitution explicitly mentioned a desire for order, good organization, and a decent and clean presentation of the confraternity's image of the Virgin of the Sorrows. The founders and their wives were promised lavish funerals worth twenty-five pesos. Besides caring for their own needs, the founders promised to care for and pray for the poor in the hospital of San Juan de Dios.

Outside Mexico City, racial divisions were at least as influential on small-town society, if not even more divisive. For example, the small Bajío town of Salvatierra had five confraternities defined by their non-Spanish membership. These included the mulatto-led Remedios confraternity established shortly after the town's official founding in 1643; the confraternity of Tránsito founded by free blacks around 1650 in the hospital of San Juan de Dios; the mestizo confraternity of the Humility and Patience of Christ founded in 1663; the confraternity of Saint Nicolás Tolentino, founded around 1672 by mulattos; and the confraternity of Saint Peter founded by mulattos and mestizos in 1677.[15] These foundations leave a record of a strong racially defined local panorama, clustered in an era (from about 1643 to 1677).

In 1673, the confraternity of Saint Nicolás Tolentino in Salvatierra experienced conflict over an election dispute based on racial divisions. The case shows that, by this time, mulattos in Salvatierra had already achieved some degree of status and sought the same for their confraternities.[16] In 1673, two members of the confraternity protested the election of Pedro Ruano as majordomo. The petitioners complained that although Ruano had been elected by twenty-four votes, nine of these were by members who had recently joined, including one Spaniard whose vote officially did not count, they argued, this being a mulatto confraternity. Ruano was "in debt and an upstart" (adeudado y advenedizo). Another candidate, who had lost the popular vote, was a more suitable majordomo because he had helped found and maintain the confraternity as majordomo for many years. The petitioners simply wanted to protect the confraternity's possessions and guarantee that it had a legitimate leader, so they asked for a new election. This dispute, despite its racial dimension, was not exclusively a debate over race, but rather a conflict involving race as well as the public reputation of Salvatierra's mulatto residents and how it reflected on their confraternity.

Throughout the territory of New Spain, several other groups of mulattos organized to create confraternities specifically defined by this racial identity and membership. These brotherhoods were most often founded in the 1600s. However, not every constitution document was as clear as the constitution of the Veracruz confraternity in specifically forbidding non-mulatto leadership, especially because it was common for some confraternities to be very open and welcoming to the general population. For example, in 1686, a group of men in Querétaro, just to the north of Mexico City, met in the Santa Clara Convent to organize a confraternity in honor of the Virgin. The leaders wrote that "in the name of virtue and charity, all the *mulato* residents of this city are in agreement" about making a set of rules for their group.[17] Although the race label of the founders was given, the constitution emphasized the duties of taking care of the statue of the Virgin and attending mass, but did not stress an exclusive membership.

This is also the case for a flagellating, penitential confraternity founded in 1635 in the northern mining town of Zacatecas in the name of Saint John.[18] This group of men, all described as free and enslaved *mulatos* and also claiming to represent all other local mulattos who were absent from the meeting, organized to found a brotherhood dedicated to making a "blood procession to make penance for our sins, to serve God and commemorate his passion and death." They specifically chose a time for their procession, only Tuesday of Holy Week, when "no other confraternity, either of Spaniards, Indians or Blacks" made a procession, so as not to cause conflicts. Similar to the Veracruz confraternity, the Saint John brothers had strict rules regarding behavior and appearance during their procession. They ruled that no one could march in the procession without wearing the proper clothes or they would face ejection. Throughout the 1600s and 1700s, all documents related to this organization refer to the members as *mulatos*.

Some confraternities had a more general Afro-Mexican membership and constitutions indicated that both blacks and mulattos made up the founding members and were welcome to join and hold leadership positions. On the other hand, often the change of leadership from one specifically designated as negro to the specific designation of *mulato* indicated a change over time. As decades went by in the 1600s, fewer slaves came to New Spain from Africa and the Afro-Mexican population was more frequently given the label of *mulato*. Confraternity documents, where members often expressed a strong desire to be differentiated from African and enslaved ancestors, show that the individuals who received this label were well aware of this historical process and change over time.

Far to the south of Mexico City, a group of men described as negros founded a confraternity dedicated to Our Lady of the Snow, a famous image of the Virgin originally located in a church in Rome.[19] This confraternity had been founded in 1595, but its first documents date back only to 1660. By that time, the members had race labels of both negro and *mulato*. In 1682, the *mulato* members made a petition to the bishop to improve and reorganize their confraternity. They stated that the confraternity was "erected and founded in its earliest days by petitions made by blacks from Guinea [*morenos de Guinea*] that lived in this city, but have since then disappeared." They continued, stating that currently the confraternity "remains in the hands of brown people of the mulatto nation [*pardos de nación mulato*]." (The term nación was often used in the colonial era to refer to what we now might call an ethnic group.) These new leaders wanted more officially documented privileges and indulgences from the church because their original documents had disintegrated due to lack of care by the original founders. When the bishop of Oaxaca responded to their petition, he also repeated the distinction between the current "free brown mulattos" (*mulatos libres pardos*) members and the original founders, the latter described as "*negros bozales esclavos*" or black slaves recently arrived from Africa.

Everyone involved in this case was well aware of the difference between the race labels of negro and *mulato* and the different statuses of being free or enslaved. However, emphasizing the humblest possible social status in an appeal to the authorities' pity and piety was extremely common in cases involving non-Spanish petitioners. Another section of the petition stressed that these *mulatos* were "miserable poor people, almost all subject to a state of servitude." One of the longest-lasting mulatto organizations in New Spain, the Confraternity of the Rosary in Valladolid, a town that was the seat of the Diocese of Michoacán and is now the city of Morelia, also resorted to this tactic. As did many other confraternities in the Diocese of Michoacán, Rosary officials were not ashamed to emphasize their poverty and humility in an attempt to gain the bishop's consent for alms-gathering outside the city of Valladolid. In a 1679 petition they stated:

> This confraternity always has been sustained by alms, which members beg for outside this jurisdiction, with the permission of the bishops and the most illustrious council. Within the city and the jurisdiction they cannot collect sufficient alms for the ornaments and wax of the most holy Virgin, nor for her masses, nor the anniversaries said for the souls of the *poor slaves our fathers*. We also pay to succor the sick and for the wax at the funerals of the poor that we attend punctually and devotedly.[20] (emphasis added)

This petition not only presented their piety, charitable activities, and poverty, but also sought pity from the bishop for the souls of their "poor slave fathers," although in reality it was free mulattos, blacks, and mestizos, along with a few slaves, that were the early leaders of the confraternity. While charitable concerns drew in the bishop's interest, an emphasis on humble slaves reminded him of the connection between low social status and charitable piety. On the other hand, the late-seventeenth-century Rosary members emphasized the fact that their *fathers*, not themselves, were slaves.

Many small-town confraternity members of African descent worked as agricultural laborers or craftsmen and distinguished themselves in their confraternity rules from other urban Spaniards, Indians, mestizos, and even among others with African heritage, by their specific race label, not their occupation or economic class. Moderately prosperous *mulatos* living in small towns did not form organizations with other non-elite colonial subjects, but instead fought for confraternity segregation. However, the continued self-perpetuation of race labels among colonial subjects may have simply disguised a growing awareness of class distinctions expressed in the more familiar vocabulary of racial distinctions. Small town *mulato* confraternity rules were explicit about forbidding non-*mulatos* from taking control of confraternity offices: in smaller settlements in the late seventeenth and early eighteenth century, local racial hierarchies were still in formation. Therefore, access to power and wealth, including confraternity power, was often negotiated through confraternity rules and conflicts brought to ecclesiastical courts.

In a 1712 ecclesiastical court case, mulatto residents of Pinzándaro, in the sugar-growing region of Michoacán, argued that their numeric domination of the local population meant they should control the local confraternity.[21] The residents of Pinzándaro brought a case to the bishop over the election of a Spaniard as majordomo of the confraternity of the Solitude. The mulatto majordomos strongly defended their position, opening their arguments with assertions that the confraternity was canonically approved and "the said confraternity of Our Lady of Solitude, is controlled by *mulatos* because they founded it and paid its expense with care and zeal, without the intervention of any Spaniard in its foundation, offices or burdens, as stated in the original election records."[22] Pinzándaro's Spanish faction, supported by a hacendado, claimed that "as is publicly known and notorious in this entire jurisdiction . . . negro slaves of the great hacienda" were the actual founders, not "free *mulatos* nor Spaniards." The Pinzándaro brothers took up their role in this paternalistic scheme and described themselves as "pobres desamparados" (poor abandoned ones). Although most of the testimonies favoring a slave foundation for Solitude came from dismissive Spaniards, one witness was an eighty-year-old slave. Born in 1632, he certainly lived through the entire era of this confraternity's existence.

The 1712 Pinzándaro case provides insights into the financial arrangements and membership patterns of a rural confraternity. Unlike most urban, non-Indian confraternities, livestock provided income for the Solitude in Pinzándaro. Testimonies stated that "after many free *mulatos* and slaves of several haciendas and areas (including some Spaniards) joined, the confraternity was in the hands of the *mulatos* that had joined and it lost its principal two or three times." Witnesses reported that the *mulatos*, especially those that brought up the case, simply lacked the funds and financial stability to maintain the costs of a confraternity. In response, the *mulato* brothers testified that they had to sell some cattle to buy ornaments and clothes for the Virgin, justifiable expenses for a confraternity. They claimed the sale of cattle had nothing to do with "poverty or their 'broken' color" (color quebrado). Those advocates of *mulato* control in Solitude argued that the hacienda slaves were the ones who lost control of the confraternity while the free *mulatos* actually brought the confraternity stability and, most importantly, orchestrated the bishop's approval of the confraternity (probably in the 1680 *visita* of Aguiar y Seixas). The testimony of the above-mentioned elderly slave stated that *mulatos* were active in their collection of alms to finance the slave confraternity. Other than the apparent acceptance of Solitude as a *mulato* institution, further results of this case are not given in available documents, but *mulato* numeric dominance continued to grow in Pinzándaro.

The 1776 list of confraternities in the diocese of Michoacán mentions only *mulato* families for Pinzándaro, and these families were described as supportive to authorities in a local rebellion and "extremely affable and obedient" (en extremo afables and obedientes).[23] The late eighteenth-century dominance of mulatos in Pinzándaro is further supported by an extensive case over an inheritance involving the Confraternity of the Solitude. Questions of history and memory again emerge as the many witnesses (at least two-thirds were mulatto) testify, some claiming to be more than one hundred years old.[24] Pinzándaro's long confraternal history, prominent in communal memory, helped these *mulatos* gain their reputation for peacefulness and passivity, making them agreeable colonial subjects. Perhaps in part because of their confraternity, these mulattos' sense of communal cohesiveness more resembled that found in Indian villages than in larger towns such as Celaya or Salvatierra.

As has been observed all over the globe, wherever colonial situations exist, living life as a middle man, trapped between the rulers and the ruled, can be the most difficult position of all. Because of their successful example, those trapped in the middle of racial or social hierarchies are often viewed as those who most support those hierarchies, especially as they distinguish themselves from those who have not been so fortunate. Mulattos in New Spain must have felt this tension in their lives, but they also effectively manipulated it in their dealings with Spanish authorities representing both church and state. Confraternity documents reveal Afro-Mexican understandings of the subtle distinctions of race and class in the colonial world, as well the complexities of Catholicism in the 1600s and 1700s, which often seemed to turn these hierarchies upside down. In the cases described above, mulattos made a point to demarcate the differences between themselves and their enslaved forefathers as well as contemporary Indians. They recognized that they could use the self-deprecating style of Baroque rhetoric by presenting themselves as the most miserable of the king's subjects, although in fact many mulattos were improving their

FIGURE 6.1. Eighteenth-century expression of Mexican religious piety. Courtesy of the Archivo General de la Nación, Mexico City

position in colonial society. Catholics continued to value suffering as the most direct and effective way to show piety and devotion to Jesus and the Christian religion. Therefore, as slaves, freed slaves, or the descendants of slaves, Afro-Mexicans were uniquely well positioned to enthusiastically embrace public penitential displays. In a contradiction typical of Baroque Catholicism, individuals of African descent in New Spain actively chose to celebrate their victimized position in the lowest rungs of society to gain status and respect in their locales, while the rules of their brotherhoods emphasized their dedication to the tenets of Spanish morality, especially humility, peacefulness, and obedience to authority.

Although many cases exist of mulattos rather hopelessly defending their confraternity rights against grasping Spaniards who took full advantage of accepted colonial hierarchies, the above examples show that mulattos also claimed social superiority over other groups. Was there a *mulato* identity in formation? The assumption that mulattos only looked to improve their own lives and those of their families by affiliating more with the Spanish authorities is challenged by the events of the era of Mexican insurgency, when men with African ancestry played a leading role in bringing down Spanish rule. While the ancient imperial truism of divide and conquer was an effective tool in strengthening American race hierarchies and was very well suited to Spanish values and traditions, after a few centuries this system officially disappeared.

✢ NOTES ✢

1. Archivo de la Casa de Morelos, caja 586.

2. See the case of Mateo de Aguilar, a wealthy seventeenth-century testator in Mexico City, described in Nicole von Germeten, *Black Blood Brothers* (Gainesville: University Press of Florida, 2006), chap. 3.

3. John K. Chance, *Race and Class in Colonial Oaxaca* (Stanford: Stanford University Press, 1978), 103.

4. John K. Chance, "The Ecology of Race and Class in Late Colonial Oaxaca," in *Studies in Spanish American Population History*, ed. David J. Robinson, 93–117 (Boulder: Westview Press, 1981).

5. Ben Vinson III, "Bearing Arms for His Majesty: The Free-Colored Militia in Colonial Mexico," Ph.D. diss., Columbia University, 1998, 419.

6. Ibid., 394, 396, 406.
7. For descriptions of penitential confraternities in Rome, see Barbara Wisch, "The Passion of Christ in the Art, Theater and Penitential Rituals of the Roman Confraternity of the Gonfalone," in *Crossing the Boundaries: Christian Piety and the Arts in Italian Medieval and Renaissance Confraternities*, ed. Konrad Eisenbichler, 239–43. (Kalamazoo, MI: Medieval Institute Publications, Western Michigan University, 1991).
8. Frank Graziano's *Wounds of Love: The Mystical Marriage of Saint Rose of Lima* (Oxford: Oxford University Press, 2004) deeply explores this topic. See especially 3, 6, 16, 20–21, 27–30, 134–39, 160–66.
9. For further exploration of Afro-Mexican Baroque Catholicism, see von Germeten, *Black Blood Brothers*, chap. 1.
10. Bancroft Library Special Sets, Microfilm Collection III, Archivo General de Indias , Legajo 98.
11. Archivo General de la Nación (AGN), Bienes Nacionales, vol. 810, exp. 28.
12. AGN, Reales Cedulas Originales, vol. 159, exp. 34, fols. 49–73. Sincere thanks go to Ben Vinson for making an extra effort to track down this citation.
13. Italics mine.
14. AGN, Bienes Nacionales, vol. 444, exp. 3.
15. Archivo de la Casa de Morelos, Cofradías, caja 86, leg. 11, has a case of a widow of a free *negro* complaining about the large donation he made to the cofradía de Tránsito, founded for the poor in the hospital de San Juan de Dios.
16. Ibid., Elecciones, caja 5.
17. AGN, Bienes Nacionales, vol. 1028, exp. 6.
18. Archivo Parroquial de Zacatecas, Libros de la Cofradía de San Juan de la Penitencia. For more information on confraternities in Zacatecas, see Lara Mancuso, *Cofradías mineras: religiosidad popular en México y Brasil, siglo XVIII* (Mexico City: El Colegio de México, 2007), 108.
19. Archivo Histórico de la Arquidiócesis de Oaxaca, caja 18, exp. 486.
20. Cofradía de Rosario pide licencia . . . Morelia, 1679, Archivo de la Casa de Morelos, caja 7, leg. 27, sin fol. "*Esta cofradía siempre se aman tenido y sustentado de limosnas q con licensias de los Señores obispos y illustrusimo cabildo se an pedido fuera desta jurisdicción para q en ella y en esta ciudad no se recojen limosnas bastantes para el ornato y cera de la virgen santisima para sus missas para aniversarios que decimos para las almas de los pobres esclavos nuestros padres para socorro de enfermos que les asistimos y para cera en los entierros de pobres a que acudimos puntual y muy devotamente.*"

21. Casa de Morelos, caja 1267, leg. 1.
22. Ibid., caja 1267, leg. 1.
23. Dagmar Bechtloff, "La formación de una sociedad intercultural: las cofradías en el Michoacán colonial," *Historia Mexicana* XLIII, no. 2 (October–December, 1993): 268–69.
24. Archivo de la Casa de Morelos, caja 591, leg. 418.

Potions and Perils

Love-Magic in Seventeenth-Century Afro-Mexico and Afro-Yucatan

JOAN BRISTOL AND MATTHEW RESTALL

❧

How to Win and Keep a Lover

☧ MARÍA DE CASANOVA WAS BORN IN MÉRIDA EXACTLY A CENTURY after the city was founded as the capital of the new Spanish province of Yucatan. A Spaniard of modest background, she grew up in the city and by the age of thirty was married to a Francisco de los Reyes. In March of 1672—and again in September the same year—Casanova went to see the commissary (head of the regional Inquisitorial court), Dr. Antonio de Horta Barroso, and made a pair of denunciations against María Maldonado (wife of the *Alférez* Joseph Martín de Herrera) and her brother Manuel Maldonado. Until the previous year, Casanova had lived in María Maldonado's house, as a companion (*en compania en cassa*) who helped her around the house (*le asistio*). In other words, Casanova was not a servant, as a Maya or mulatta woman might be, nor was she the social equal of the Maldonados.

María de Casanova's first denunciation laid out the framework of her accusation against Maldonado, while seeking to establish Casanova's own innocence in the matter. Maldonado allegedly "made use of spells and magic, to cast a spell on a certain man." Casanova was told by Maldonado to find and bring to the house a woman named Catalina Álvarez (by 1672, dead two years), "who understood spells and witchcraft." According to this testimony, Maldonado consulted with Álvarez behind closed doors, as she did with Michaela Montejo, a free mulatta (*mulata libre*) who lived in San Cristóbal and was also an expert on witchcraft (see Table 7.1). Montejo visited the house twice and each time she and Maldonado locked themselves in a room so that Casanova could not hear what was happening. Casanova claimed that she knew it was all about a spell "to make a man really love her." Maldonado also consulted a third woman, a mulatta whose name Casanova could not recall ("Ana" was later written in the margin), who provided some enchanted flowers (*unas flores encantadas*). The fourth woman that Maldonado hired was a free black (*negra libre*) named Ursula, a former slave of doña Isabel de Sepúlveda, who "knew something about witchcraft" (*tiene opinion de hechisera*). Ursula brought a jug of water and some flowers and told Maldonado to leave them in the man's doorway. As a result, Ursula claimed, the man would fall in love with her. Casanova also alleged that Maldonado had similarly hired various Maya women.

Finally, Casanova testified that her own sister told her that Sergeant Manuel Maldonado (María's brother) had sought out a Maya woman to put a spell on a woman he was seeing (*con quien el trataba*). Casanova may have borne resentment against both Maldonados, especially María in her role as a former employer, but she also revealed a more immediate motivation for denouncing her: Casanova claimed that on an earlier occasion she was on her way to denounce María Maldonado to the Inquisition when she ran into Maldonado's sister, Isabel, in the street; Isabel threatened to "bear witness" (*lebantar un testimonio*) against Casanova should she tell what she knew about her sister. That night, the threat worked; Casanova went home and kept quiet. But in the long run the threat was counterproductive, helping to convince Casanova to seek out the Holy Office "to absolve herself"; by coming forward on her own, she preempted any future attempts by the Maldonados to implicate her.[1]

Casanova's second denunciation, made six months later, was more detailed. In it, she described the love-magic potion that María Maldonado made with the help of one of the four witches she had hired (Casanova did not specify which one). The recipe and ingredients were pubic hair ("plucked from the shameful parts"), fingernail clippings, a tiny piece of

TABLE 7.1. The Protagonists in the Casanova-Maldonado
Love-Magic Case (Mérida, Yucatan, 1670s)

Accusers	Procurers	Love-magic Witches
María de Casanova; her sister, Isabel	María Maldonado; her brother, Serg. Manuel Maldonado; possibly their sister, Isabel Maldonado	Catalina Álvarez (mulatta?); Michaela Montejo (mulatta); Ana (mulatta); Ursula (negra); Juana Pacheco (mulatta?) and Lucas de Arguello (negro); a Maya woman

Source: AGN, Inquisición, vol. 620, exp. 7, fols. 595–614.

material from her skirt, all burned together. The ashes were then mixed in with a tablet of chocolate, ground, washed, combined with water and whipped up in a chocolate drink, and then given to the man whose deeper affections Maldonado hoped to win. Having stated earlier that the spells were discussed and cast behind locked doors, Casanova now asserted that she saw all this herself, for she lived in the house as a close friend (*comadre*) in whom Maldonado had compete confidence (*toda confiansa*). Furthermore, Casanova claimed that Maldonado often soaked tree bark in water to make *balché*, a drink "much used by the Indians to get drunk and commit idolatries"—balché is an alcoholic drink made from tree bark that has been used in religious rituals by Mayas for centuries—which she gave to "her beau" (*su Galan*) to seduce him more quickly.[2]

Casanova's second testimony also offered inquisitors a little more information about Sergeant Manuel Maldonado's procurement of love-magic services. She claimed to have heard the sergeant discussing with Juana Pacheco her work as a witch (*bruja*) in partnership with Lucas de Arguello, a free black. Casanova claimed to overhear the pair admit to the sergeant that "they flew about together as witches" (*volavan juntos como Brujos*).[3]

The Inquisition moved slowly on Casanova's denunciations. Her first denunciation was not ratified or formally acknowledged by the Inquisition for two years, the second not for two more years (in February 1676). In April that year the commissary sent his report, with a copy of all the interviews, to the senior tribunal of the Inquisition in Mexico City. This report commented that María Maldonado's husband had left her years ago and that she had since resorted to "spells and illicit means to win and retain her lovers." Yet the case's content and evidence did not appear to cause the commissary great concern. Some of the accused were already known to the Inquisition (there were existing files on the free black Lucas de Arguello, the late Catalina Álvarez, and the "ill-reputed" free mulatta Michaela Montejo). Others were insufficiently implicated to warrant action. María Maldonado was not indicted because it had been "years" since her accuser had lived in her house (an ironic judgment in view of the slow pace of the Inquisition's investigation). Nor was her brother Manuel further investigated, as he was "not poorly viewed" and his accuser (Casanova's sister) was not a credible witness.[4]

The Maldonado case is deceptively straightforward. A lonely wife indulges in a little love-magic and is denounced to the Inquisition by her disapproving employee-friend; the Inquisition investigates slowly, turning up love-magic practitioners already known to the Holy Office, and shies away from prosecuting the accused Spanish siblings from an old elite family who had allegedly hired the witches. Yet the case also prompts a number of complex questions, whose answers reveal much about love-magic as a cultural contact point or a site of cultural interaction—and thereby much about the multiracial societies that had developed in Mexico City and Mérida by the middle of the colonial period. In this chapter we examine Inquisition investigations of love-magic witches in Mexico and Yucatan. Our geographical focus is primarily the provincial capital cities of Mexico City and Mérida, where most love-magic was practiced and where all known Inquisition cases were lodged, but the case files also include love-magic incidents from towns and villages scattered across the colonies in Mexico and Yucatan (see map on pp. xvi–xvii). Our temporal focus is the seventeenth century, with most Mexican cases dated 1600–97 and all Yucatec cases dated 1612–80.[5]

We are concerned with the following questions. To what extent did Spaniards, Nahuas, and Mayas, as well as Afro-Mexicans and Afro-Yucatecans, share a common culture of belief in the efficacy of love-magic? What were the materials and rituals used in love-magic practice? Was love-magic practice part of a larger popular culture shared by all residents of Mérida and Mexico City? What was the role of the Inquisition in this culture and its policing of religious belief and cultural practices? Why are love-magic cases concentrated in the seventeenth century? What motivated accusers to denounce others for hiring or working as witches? Were these cases primarily about witchcraft, or were they expressions of other social relations? Did Afro-Mexicans and Afro-Yucatecans use love-magic in particular ways, as distinguished from the rest of the colonial population? Finally, did Afro-Mexicans and Afro-Yucatecans suffer disproportionate attention from the Inquisition over love-magic and related matters?

How Love-Magic was a Crossroads

The story of the many witches hired by María Maldonado in Mérida exemplifies many of the key patterns in the history of love-magic in colonial Mexico and Yucatan. In seventeenth-century central Mexico and Yucatan people of all social groups interacted through the practice of *hechicería amorosa*—love-magic, sexual witchcraft, or erotic medicine. This activity came under the broad category of *hechicería*, or witchcraft, as defined by the Inquisition and by other ecclesiastical authorities. The image of the elite Spaniard María Maldonado sequestered with the free mulatta Michaela Montejo, sharing information about a spell, drives home the point that the practice of love-magic created a forum in which interethnic and interclass relationships developed.[6] Love-magic, like witchcraft in general, was neither gender- nor casta-specific (a person's casta was his or her socioracial rank or status, and castas were people of mixed racial ancestry, often used to include everyone who was neither fully Spanish nor indigenous). Love-magic was inclusive in terms of its origins as well as its protagonists, drawing upon traditions from Spain, West and West Central Africa, and native Mesoamerica (and the Andes). For example, the concept of ligature, or tying objects together to make a spell, was part of witchcraft in Spain before Spaniards settled in the Americas. Likewise in West and West Central Africa before and during the Atlantic slave trade, it was believed that natural substances, when turned into powders and put into food or drink by healers or witches, could cure, poison, enchant, or otherwise affect the targeted person. Other contributions to colonial love-magic—like the ritual use of balché—were obviously native American in origin.[7]

There are many examples in Inquisition records of the interethnic quality of love-magic. As early as 1536 the Spanish wife of a tailor in Mexico City claimed that she had asked a black slave named Marta about how to get a young man to marry a young woman, and Marta had told her that the young woman would have to go to a crossroads and do "certain conjurings" (*ciertos conjuros*) to effect the marriage.[8] Almost a century later, in

Guadalajara in 1620, a Spanish woman claimed that several years earlier she had bought a crow's heart from a mulatta to use to make her sister's husband more tractable. Her sister had also bought some roots from indigenous sellers to put in her husband's drink. These indigenous suppliers told her to wash her genitals in clear water and then give him the water to drink. She later bought yet another herb to tame her husband, this time from a Spanish woman.[9] In 1621 in Celaya, a black slave bought yellow powders from an Otomí woman, to be used to "tame men."[10] In 1626 a Spanish woman in Campeche, Catalina Antonia de Rojas, hired both Maya and mulatta love-magic witches—as María Maldonado later did—to cast spells that would make a certain man come and visit her.[11] Inquisition investigations into witchcraft accusations often produced witness accounts of otherwise-mundane conversations in which men and women (typically the women) of diverse backgrounds discussed love-magic. For example, one afternoon in 1636, three women sat in Melchora de los Reyes's house in Campeche and chatted about love-magic; they were a Spaniard (Melchora), a locally born black woman (a *negra criolla* named Francisca), and a mulatta (Juana Delgada). Three years later Melchora denounced Juana Delgada for love-magic.[12]

Finally, Sergeant Manuel Maldonado's involvement in the case that began this chapter reminds us that love-magic was not only a women's realm. Although women featured more often than men, men also played roles at all stages of the process, most often as objects of the love-magic or as clients hoping to use it (as in the case of Sergeant Maldonado), but occasionally also as dispensers of love-magic.

While people from all ethnic groups associated through the practice of love-magic, all parties did not come to these relationships with the same social power. The Maldonado case, in which María's elite status probably saved her from prosecution, shows that social status was a factor in Inquisitorial investigations. Although the relationship between María and the four witches she worked with may have operated on relatively equal footing behind closed doors, we still see the colonial social hierarchy reflected in these relationships since she had hired Afro-Yucatecan and native witches to do her bidding. Although there were Spanish, indigenous (Nahua, Maya, and others), black and free-colored protagonists, Spaniards tended to appear more often as procurers of witches, perhaps because they could better afford the fees of the practitioners; castas often appeared as dispensers of magic, to Spaniards and to other castas. It is also possible that native and colored men and women in dire romantic straits were able to turn to relatives or close community members for informal, unpaid magical assistance—assistance that by definition was never recorded on paper. These cases show that a great variety of people relied on magic and were familiar with it; it seems likely that techniques originally used by paid healers may have been remembered by their clients and shared among people who did not practice love-magic professionally.

Those castas denounced to Inquisition officials and, in some cases, subsequently prosecuted by the Holy Office for practicing love-magic, were often of African descent. This was not, however, because indigenous people did not practice love-magic; it was primarily because from the 1570s indigenous people in the Spanish American colonies could not be prosecuted at the tribunal (they were placed under the jurisdiction of a separate agency, the *Provisorato de Indios*, sometimes called the Indian Inquisition).[13] Most people accused of practicing love-magic and other forms of witchcraft were not convicted by inquisitors, so that the majority of information we have on these cases consists of incomplete denunciations rather than full cases.

The low rate of conviction is not easily explained, but we suspect it was due to a pair of interrelated factors. First, the Inquisition considered other infractions to be more serious. Sins such as blasphemy, heresy, and bigamy more clearly threatened the authority of the church and thus were more prosecutable—both on ideological and practical grounds (a bigamy case, for example, was far more likely than a love-magic case to result in a conviction leading to the state's seizure of the perpetrator's property). Second, hiring love-magic professionals cost money.[14] Even if fees were low, many castas would not have been able to afford them, meaning that Spaniards were probably more often involved at the hiring end than were castas. As the Maldonado case illustrates, Spaniards' status, especially for elites, was a shield against prosecution when the alleged offense was merely love-magic.

How to Make and Use a Love-Potion

There were two dimensions to the ritual art of love-magic practice: the selection of physical materials used in casting the spell and the ritual or theater of their usage. The materials of magic—the ingredients of love potions or the enchanted items deployed in order to influence someone—were

TABLE 7.2. Love-Potion Ingredients Used in Seventeenth-Century Mexico and Yucatan

Ingredient	Use and Effect	Used in Mexico or Yucatan?
Amulet	Wearer has power to seduce	Both
Chants	Incantations or love prayers taught to, and used by, the person hiring the love-magic professional	Both
Balché	Alcoholic tree-bark beverage given to seductee	Exclusive to Yucatan
Bird organs	Usually the heart, ground and placed in seductee's food or drink	Likely both, but we only found evidence from Mexico
Chocolate	Enchanted chocolate drink (or other food or drink) given to seductee	Both
Flowers	Usually enchanted roses, to be given to the seductee, or placed under the bed, or ground and mixed into a chocolate drink	Both
Herbs and roots	Mixed, often as powder, into chocolate or rubbed on the body (e.g., of a wayward husband); roots also worn in clothing of seducer or chewed by seducer	Both
Water	Water from a special flask or vase, used by the professional to enchant flowers or chocolate	Both
Hair, sweat, and bath water	Seducer places head or pubic hair, water the seducer has bathed in, or sweat from armpits or soles of the feet, in seductee's chocolate drink	Both
Menstrual blood	Placed in chocolate, as above	Likely both, but we only found evidence from Mexico

everyday, mundane objects, not obscure or esoteric ones. These objects fell typically into two categories. One was plants and animals, more commonly the former, such as flowers, roots, herbs, but sometimes the latter (a feather or a piece of a bird's body, such as its heart). The Afro-Yucatecan Juana Delgada allegedly made a living as a love-magic practitioner in the 1630s because "she knows how to enchant or use roses or flowers to attract men."[15] The roots and herbs used for these purposes included *puyomate* and peyote, used by the Nahua for the purposes of attraction and repulsion.[16] As mentioned above, balché was used as a love-magic potion in Yucatan (as Table 7.2 shows, it was the only love-magic ingredient used in Yucatan that was not also used in Mexico). In 1640 a cowboy named Monserrate and, in the 1650s, another cowboy named Nicolas de Mesa asked the devil to give them powers and herbs that would help them attract women.[17] These materials seem to have been ground up into *polvos*, or powders, although the ingredients in these were usually unnamed. Such items were sometimes combined with solutions of water or chocolate to make *bebedizos* or love-potions.

The second category was that of small pieces cut from a person's body, either a snippet of clothing or clippings of pubic hair or finger nails. Sometimes a whole item of clothing belonging to the target of the love-magic was used, such as the man's jacket used in a spell cast in Campeche in 1626.[18] Human secretions such as menstrual blood, and the water used to wash women's *partes bajas* (literally "lower parts," i.e., private parts) or armpits, were also used in love-magic.[19]

The ritual or theatre of love-magic performance can likewise be placed in two categories. One was that of incantations or the uttering of spells,

---

Sources: For Mexico: AGN, Inquisición, vol. 292, exp. 28, fols. 135–39; vol. 296, exp. 3, fol. 18v; vol. 316, exp. 11, fol. 267v, 269v; vol. 339, exp. 26, fol. 245; vol. 339, exp. 89; vol. 341, exp. 1; vol. 339, exp. 89, fols. 669–76; vol. 356, exp. sin enum.a., fol. 126; vol. 356, exp. sin enum.b., fol. 75; vol. 356, exp. 32, fol. 46; vol. 356, exp. 44, fol. 76; vol. 356, exp. 47, fol. 79v; vol. 356, exp. 160, fol. 475; vol. 360, exp. 8, fol. 22–23; vol. 366, exp. 27, fol. 338, 340; vol. 376, exp. 17, 87–90v; vol. 435, exp. sin enum.b., fol. 24–24v; vol. 435, exp. sin enum.c., fol. 1; vol. 435, exp. 131, fol. 222; vol. 478, exp. 18, fols. 162–65; vol. 486, exp. 76, fols. 409–16; vol. 530, exp. 5, fols. 232–37; vol. 536, exp. 22, fols. 146, 150. For Yucatan: AGN-Inquisición vol. 39, exp. 4; vol. 3680, exp. 3; vol. 676, fols. 163, 186, 188, 208v, 423; vol. 627, exp. 6; vol. 919, exp. 26. A Yucatan-only version of this table may be found in Restall (2009), 271, tab. 7.6.

FIGURE 7.1. A black slave or domestic servant preparing chocolate in the kitchen of a Spanish household. In colonial Mexico and Yucatan, as in precolonial times, chocolate was always consumed as a beverage. It was drunk often, typically strong and hot, and was thus an ideal medium for delivering a love potion—with the presence of nail clippings, pubic hair, menstrual blood, or other items disguised by the taste of the chocolate. Detail of José de Páez, *De español y negra, mulato*, 6, ca. 1770–80, Oil on copper, 50.2 × 63.8 cm. Private collection. Reproduced with permission.

FIGURE 7.2. A Spanish-American salamander, likely from South America, similar to that allegedly used by Leonor de Isla to bewitch her lover. From Louis Feuilée, *Journal des observations physiques, mathematiques, et botaniques* (Paris, 1714). Courtesy of the John Carter Brown Library at Brown University, Providence, Rhode Island.

usually chanted or spoken by the witch but sometimes taught to the procurer of love-magic services. Inquisitors usually called these incantations *palabras de hechizo* (magic words) or sometimes *oraçiones* (orations, prayers). In one 1639 case from Campeche, the denouncer was able to recite two love-magic spells in Spanish that she claimed to have learned from a witch. This one, she claimed, recited before a potential suitor's visit, caused him to blush upon seeing her: "On two I see you, on five I take you, I break your heart, I drink your blood, by the peace of the queen of the angels and her precious son, you are with me."[20] This, however, was unusual. More typically, witnesses referred to "certain words that I did not understand." This was the phrase used by Catalina Antonia de Rojas, for example, to describe the incantation used by one of the witches she had hired to induce a man to visit her; the witch, a Maya woman named Catalina Puc, uttered the words while walking slowly around a table, upon which had been placed a jacket owned by the man who was the spell's object. The incantation was probably not simple Maya, as Rojas would have recognized it as such, and Catalina Puc claimed that she had learned the spell from "a mulatta named Antonia" who knew love-magic.[21]

The other ritual involved the placement of enchanted objects near the target of the magic (under a bed, for example, or in a doorway). In 1611 a mulatto man claimed that his lover had placed puyomate under their shared bed. He said that because of this he "couldn't get [his then-lover] out of his memory nor his heart."[22] Ana de Ortega, a mulatta originally from Santo Domingo investigated for witchcraft in 1659 by Inquisition officials in Campeche, instructed clients to use the following spell-casting ritual: acquire a man's handkerchief, sew a button on it, and then rip the button off when he passed by.[23] Spells could also be physically delivered to the victim of the magic (most often in food or drink). In 1695 a Spanish man in Mexico City claimed that his mulatta lover had given him a drink that had made him restless and had given him wet dreams. He explained that six months after he left her he became impotent, and he alleged that this was because his ex-lover had given his cook "potions" to put in his food.[24] At other times the powders and roots were carried, ingested, or otherwise used by the person hoping to effect the attraction.[25] When a Tepeacan man, a Spaniard, was "enamored and trying to obtain a woman" around 1610, his Nahua servant Pedro gave him some powders and a small stick, telling him to put the stick in his mouth when he felt desire for the woman. He also told him to get the powders into her hands.[26] In 1626 Juan de Casa, a mestizo servant, denounced a mulatto named Juan Muñoz for having used love witchcraft "to obtain [a woman] to sin with."[27] According to his denouncer, Muñoz contacted the devil, who told him to rub a certain herb all over his hands and to then wave his hands in the direction of the woman he wanted.

The goals of users of love-magic were similarly twofold. Attracting lovers was a central function, but maintaining a romantic relationship was an equally important use of love-magic. One example of the use of magic to attract is a 1611 case from Puebla, in which a mulatta claimed that she had received an herb from another mulatta that would make her attractive to men.[28] In another example, a mulatta arrested on suspicion of being a witch in Campeche in 1639 was accused of knowing how to use enchanted flowers "to attract men to lascivious love and depraved affection" (*amor lasçibo y deprabada boluntad*).[29] In most cases, women used love-magic to attract men, but the reverse was also true. For example, in 1618 a mulatto named Manuel was said to have bragged that he had a small stick that he used to attract women; the humorous irony of this claim was presumably not lost on many of those who heard of it.[30] In 1650 in Tepozotlan, a Spanish woman claimed that two mulattos took herbs so that women would want them.[31] In 1697 in Guantla, near Cuernavaca, a mulatto was accused of using various materials, including a coin and powders made out of bird parts, to bewitch a Spanish woman to fall in love with him.[32]

Love-magic was also used, particularly by women, to maintain existing relationships and to "tame" targeted lovers and husbands. For example, a Maya woman accused of being a witch in Campeche in 1626 claimed to have learned spells from a mulatta; the mulatta knew how to bewitch a man so that he would visit a woman—or, conversely, never stray from home.[33] In 1612 in Oaxaca a black woman named Catalina gave a woman an unidentified substance to make her husband treat her better.[34] In 1617 a friar wrote an indignant letter claiming that a black man had been dispensing "bebedizos" to women who sought to tame their men.[35]

Love-magic was thus often mundane and predictable in the details of its materials, their use, and their purpose. Everyday objects were typically chosen (from herbs to fingernail clippings), and while their ritual use sometimes required the specialist skill of a love-magician's chants, the application of the spell more often involved an act as simple as drinking a potion or placing an object under a bed. Finally, the purpose of love-magic was not complex; when ordinary powers of seduction or forces of attraction failed, love-magic was deployed to attract lovers or retain their affections.

How to Tame Your Owner

Because men and women of all backgrounds and classes were involved as practitioners, clients, and as objects of love-magic, descriptions of magic and the people who used it provide insight into how power relations operated in colonial society. Denunciations often threw these power dynamics into sharp relief. Motives for denunciation could be rooted in ideological or moral objection, but probably were more often motivated by personal animosities relating to the larger tale of relationships between the protagonists involved. All members of society believed to some degree in the efficacy of witchcraft, but they were also aware that Inquisition officials policed most magic practices during the witch craze's long seventeenth century. While love-magic was almost certainly practiced throughout the colonial period in Mexico and Yucatan,[36] Inquisitorial concern over witchcraft—love-magic included—intensified in New Spain in the late sixteenth and seventeenth centuries before slowly fading in the early eighteenth century.[37] This concern was fed by two related phenomena: the witch craze in the Atlantic world (concentrated in the Protestant north but also felt in Catholic regions); and anti-idolatry campaigns against native communities in many Spanish colonies. Because of these contexts, only in the seventeenth century did Inquisition officials regularly view love-magic as an offense worth investigating. Although there were risks to practicing love-magic, for subordinate groups within the colonies, Inquisition concerns also potentially presented opportunities (offering the non-elite what are sometimes called "weapons of the weak").

In other words, the use of love-magic sometimes amounted to an attempt to invert the existing hierarchy—to make "the world in reverse" by giving normally subordinate people power over their superiors.[38] Scholars of witchcraft in colonial Latin America have tended to focus on the fact that women of all casta categories used love-magic to try to control men's emotions and behavior.[39] When we change the focus from love-magic per se to a focus on Afro-Mexico and Afro-Yucatan, we gain another perspective. Cases in which Afro-Mexicans and Afro-Yucatecans were accused of using love-magic suggest that such practices may have represented an inversion of hierarchies, such as that of slave and slaveowner.[40] In these two provinces, love-magic was related to other kinds of practices, and the blurring of the lines between love-magic and practices used to control owners suggests that love-magic was part of a wider set of witchcraft practices used to manipulate a variety of unequal social relationships.

The magical mediation of hierarchical relations based on casta distinctions is most obvious in cases in which Afro-Mexican slaves used magic on their owners. Although they did not usually call such rituals "love-magic," we see the similarities between the magic used on lovers and the magic used on owners in the 1626 statement of a Spanish woman from Tepeaca. She reported that she had heard that a mulatto slave had used *polvos de bien querer* (love powders) on his owner—not for romantic purposes but in the hope of getting in his good graces.[41] In a 1617 case a woman was denounced for selling both love medicines and materials that slaves could use to make peace with their owners.[42] There were similarities in both the techniques and materials used in love-magic and magic directed at owners. In 1600 a black slave in Mexico City supplied a mulatto slave with a stick to carry in her blouse, telling her that it would influence her owners to treat her better. In Querétero in 1621 another black slave gave a mulatto slave a small black stick, telling her to put it in her own mouth using her left hand when her owner was angry with her.[43] He said that if she chewed it well and spit it out her owner's anger would go away. These applications were similar to love-magic practices in which people carried herbs and sticks in their own clothing to influence others to love them.[44] Other remedies used for both purposes included placing a knife and a bone from a human skeleton under slaveowners' beds to make them oblivious when their slaves sneaked out at night. Placing thumbnails in slaveowners' food supposedly made them better disposed to their slaves,[45] and slaves who carried black hens might also soften up their owners.[46] Likewise in the world of love-magic, women hoping to seduce men or pacify their husbands also placed objects under the beds or in the food of the objects of the magic.[47]

A final example of how love-magic techniques were used by slaves to tame owners is worth describing in more detail. The event took place in Mexico City in 1632, and centered on a pair of African men, both named Francisco. One of them was a black slave of eighteen. Having become frustrated with his owner's mistreatment, this young Francisco turned to an older black man named Francisco for help. The older man's status as slave or free was not noted. Witnesses who testified about the case to inquisitors were divided about whether the younger Francisco wished to make his Spanish owner treat him better or whether he wanted his owner to sell him. The older Francisco may have been an established purveyor of magic, since, according to the testimony of the young slave's owner, the older Francisco claimed that he had sold roots to some black women—marketplace vendors—to help their business.[48]

The older Francisco sold the younger man a root, telling him first to chew it and then put his saliva, mixed with the root, on his face. Unfortunately, this made the younger man extremely ill. His owner, fearing that he was near death, called a priest to confess him. After hearing the story, the owner and other witnesses concluded that the young Francisco had been bewitched. They agreed that the way to cure him was to have the person who bewitched him reverse the process or undo the spell. Rather than blaming the young man's condition on the physical properties of the root, they saw his illness as caused by the way that the older Francisco had used the root. According to witnesses, the older Francisco was thus called back to the young man's bedside. He treated him by putting some white powders in a bowl of water, stirring the solution with his finger, and giving it to young Francisco to drink, saying some words "in his language, which they didn't understand." The older Francisco also put powders in the young man's nose. These cures failed, however, and eventually an indigenous healer, a Nahua woman, was called in. When she was shown the roots and powders used by Francisco she claimed not to recognize them, strengthening the witnesses' suspicions that Francisco's remedies were a dangerous kind of witchcraft—although Francisco had said, when questioned, that he had obtained the materials that he used from "a group of Indians." Oddly enough, during the older Francisco's visit to the younger man's bedside, when doubts about the man's intentions and abilities as a curer were already raised, one of the owner's Spanish friends asked Francisco if he could give him something to make women love him.[49]

This case illustrates not only the connections between love-magic and the magic used on slave-owners, but also several aspects of Afro-Mexican involvement in these magic practices. First, the magic used on owners and on lovers was often the same, as were its practitioners—an assumption clearly made by Francisco's owner's friend. Both kinds of magic were meant to control another person, often to make the person using it appear attractive or pleasing in some sense or another. Second, Afro-Mexican practitioners and clients operated in a multiethnic milieu, in which clients as well as other practitioners were drawn from multiple social groups.

Although, in this case, both practitioner and client were black, the Spanish slaveowner was involved in trying to heal the young man, and a Nahua healer was also called. Finally, the case of the two Franciscos shows that the inhabitants of the colonies took very seriously the magic that was designed to influence people's behaviors and emotions. The Spanish owner as well as the Spanish priest who was at the young man's bedside feared the power of the older Francisco's magic; they wanted it reversed and believed he had the ability to undo the spell.

How Love-Magic Could Be Beneficial—and Dangerous

The case of the two Franciscos also illustrates a further dimension of love-magic practice in Mexico and Yucatan—for practitioners, and even for procurers, love-magic was potentially dangerous. We only know about the two Franciscos, María Maldonado, the witches she hired, and all the love-magic practitioners in the other cases mentioned in this chapter, because they were denounced to the Inquisition. Although most cases were not prosecuted, a denunciation sometimes led to an investigation, which brought the threat of imprisonment. At the very least, rumors and suspicions circulating around practitioners and those who had hired them could damage honor and hurt reputations.

These same cases demonstrate that the risks of love-magic were worth taking, as the practice brought benefits as well as dangers. Fears of Inquisition punishments were offset by the promise of a steady income (for practitioners) or the promise of romantic successes (for procurers). While Afro-Mexican and Afro-Yucatecan slaves used magic to try to control their owners, slaves and free people of African descent joined colonial residents of all groups in using more widespread and conventional forms of love-magic to regulate their romantic relationships.

The case of Leonor de Isla, a free mulatta born in Spain and accused of witchcraft in 1622 in Nueva Veracruz, gives us a sense of what Afro-Mexicans and Afro-Yucatecan practitioners—such as those who acted with María Maldonado in the case that opened this chapter—gained and lost through the use of love-magic. Unlike the young Francisco and other slaves discussed above, the free Leonor seems to have been relatively wealthy. When her belongings were inventoried by inquisitors in 1622 she had one hundred pesos in cash (in the form of small coins called reales, each one-eighth of a peso). Her clothing included four pairs of silk stockings and skirts and jackets (*jubones*) trimmed with silk and velvet. She also owned embroidered pillows and furniture including a cedar buffet, benches, a table and bed, as well as four small pictures (*cuadros*), most likely religious images (although the subjects were not specified). An Angolan slave named Esperanza was also inventoried although she seems to have belonged to Leonor's lover, Francisco de Bonilla, rather than to Leonor herself.[50]

How did Leonor acquire all these possessions? Her lover may have given her some of them, but at least some of her wealth seems to have come from her success in the practice of love-magic. The issue of money came up when Joana Ruíz, a Spanish neighbor, denounced Leonor to the local office of the Inquisition, explaining that Leonor had helped a Spanish woman, Isabel de la Parra, win her straying lover back to her. In her testimony, Isabel referred to herself with the elite title of "doña," reminding us once again of the interclass ties created between clients and practitioners of love magic. After Isabel and her lover were reunited, however, Leonor complained that her client had not paid up. Her insistence on being paid indicates that she relied on the proceeds from her practice of love magic to support herself. Finally, Joana claimed that Leonor bragged about her skills, "she was so proud of her occupation as a witch."[51]

Leonor, therefore, must have had a reputation as a practitioner of love-magic; Isabel herself explained that she had consulted Leonor because she had heard that she knew spells to attract men. But Leonor's activities also caused suspicions among neighbors, as Joana Ruíz's testimony indicates. Joana Ruíz had lived in the same house as Leonor for a short period two years before she denounced her and continued contacts with her after that. She explained that Leonor used a number of methods, many of which we have seen already, to help her clients win back errant lovers. She said that Leonor and Isabel had gone out at midnight to stand in the crossroads where they did spells (*conjuros*) and invoked demons in order to induce Isabel's lover to return. Joana reported that Leonor used "an [image of] Santa Marta conjured in paper or engraved" that she carried with her. According to Joana, Leonor lit candles and prayed to the image as part of a series of efforts to get the man to return to Isabel.[52]

Joana Ruíz also passed on another tale that Leonor had told her. Apparently, while Leonor lived in Cádiz (Spain) her lover had traveled to Tierra Firme in Panama. Leonor, wanting to learn his fate, had said the prayer for souls in purgatory (*oración de las ánimas*) and then offered up her baby to the *ánima*, or spirit. A great duck then appeared to her while she was in bed. The duck carried the spirit of her lover, now dead, and told her to stop looking for him. Once Leonor was in Veracruz, the spirit came looking for Leonor's daughter as payment and the girl died. Thus according to Joana's testimony, Leonor's magic was dangerous for her as well as for others.[53]

Joana also described how Leonor used love-magic to manage her own relationship with her lover, Francisco de Bonilla. According to Juana, Leonor had bewitched every stitch of Francisco's clothing so that he would not leave her, and Joana's slave had told her that Leonor had also mixed water and her menstrual blood with chocolate and given it to him, to further strengthen her hold over him. She also cooked and ground jonquil (*junquillo*, a Spanish plant that is a variety of narcissus) to use in his chocolate. Another of Leonor's rituals involved feeding her lover's leftover food to salamanders, after which she ground the salamanders into a paste to put in his next meal. It seems, however, that Leonor also used magic to tame Bonilla, not just to keep him tied to her. After an episode in which Bonilla took her clothes and hit her, Joana witnessed Leonor chewing something and saying orations "different than those that are used here in the church" (*oraciones diferentes de las que aca usa en la iglesia*), a technique reminiscent of that used in the case of the two Franciscos above.[54]

We may speculate about Joana's reasons for denouncing Leonor, but we cannot be sure why she turned in a woman who was a friend, neighbor, and one-time housemate. We might be tempted to imagine that casta identity played a role (Joana was Spanish, Leonor a mulatta), but there is no evidence of socioracial prejudice as a motive. Furthermore, in our first case, María de Casanova denounced María Maldonado, likewise an old friend and one-time housemate, and both women were Spanish. In fact, the close relationships between these two pairs of women may explain why they ended up under Inquisition scrutiny. Ultimately, these are intensely personal stories of friends who shared tales of past experiences and swapped secrets—secrets that were exposed when friendship went sour and mutual affection turned to resentment and antagonism.

Both María de Casanova and Joana appear to have had reasons to denounce their old friends that are barely hinted at in investigation records. For example, Joana claimed to be disgusted by Leonor's use of menstrual blood to make a love-magic potion and frightened (*espantada*) by Leonor's activities. She claimed that she asked Leonor to confess her activities but that Leonor had refused. While Joana's testimony may have been designed to make her seem more devout in the eyes of inquisitors, Joana may well have been genuinely worried about the possibility of being complicit in Leonor's blasphemy. María de Casanova was likewise afraid of being implicated in an Inquisition investigation and chose therefore to prompt one by being the first to denounce her old friend. The fact that her first denunciation caused little stir and that she went back to talk to inquisitors six months later, suggests an element of spite. Indeed, personal antagonisms were so often a part of accusers' motives that in Yucatan a disclaimer was part of the formulaic phrasing of a love-magic investigation; the denouncer made her accusations "not out of hate but to unburden her conscience."[55]

Practitioners' motives seem clearer. For example, take Leonor's motives for continuing her love-magic business, despite her old friend's newfound objections. Besides the power she would gain in her own household if she brought Francisco de Bonilla under her power, her use of love-magic brought her income and even some status. If Joana's testimony is to be believed, Leonor was proud of her work and boasted about her successes. Whatever Joana's reasons for denouncing, her testimony as well as that of doña Isabel's indicates that Leonor's knowledge of love-magic gave her a certain importance and a central role in her neighborhood in Nueva Veracruz. She provided an important service to doña Isabel and other women who were having romantic problems.

In conclusion, looking at the larger picture of Afro-Mexican and Afro-Yucatecan involvement in love-magic gives us a sense of how blacks and mulattoes were in some ways integrated into colonial society and in other ways marginalized. On the one hand, they were integral members of the colonial societies of Mexico City and Mérida, called upon by members of all social groups for their expertise in magical practices. As we saw in some of the cases above, Spaniards tended to hire love-magic specialists of African descent before turning to local indigenous practitioners. On the other hand, black slaves had specific uses for love medicines that were based on their bonded status and on the subservient conditions under which they lived and worked. Love-magic by black and mulatto witches inspired fear, as well as respect, among clients and witnesses. Love-magic practitioners were sought after in times of trouble, but they were also vulnerable to suspicions of witchcraft and denunciations before the Inquisition.

Still, practitioners of African descent were no more vulnerable to prosecution than were Nahuas and Mayas accused of witchcraft. Love-magic was a certainly an important part of Afro-Mexican and Afro-Yucatecan life and culture in the seventeenth century, but it was by no means an exclusively or even primarily black and mulatto phenomenon. On the contrary, it was one of the ways in which people of African descent were tied economically, socially, and culturally to their indigenous and Spanish neighbors.

✥ NOTES ✥

1. Archivo General de la Nación (AGN), Inquisición, vol. 620, exp. 7, fols. 595–614 (quotes from fol. 598; long phrases quoted are *"se balia de encantos, y hechisos, para echisar, y encantar a çierto hombre," "que entendia de hechissos, y encantasiones,"* and *"a un hombre, para que la quisiesse mucho"*).

2. The long phrases quoted above are *"se rapava los pelos de las partes vergonsosas"* and *"que usan mucho los indios para embriagarse, y idolatrar."* Balché (or *baalche'*), the Maya term meaning "wild animal," is also the name used for several trees of the genus *Lonchocarpus* and for the alcoholic beverage made from the tree's bark; the bark is placed in a honey-water mixture and left to ferment for three days. See Anderson et al., *Those Who Bring The Flowers: Maya Ethnobotany in Quintana Roo, Mexico* (San Cristóbal de las Casas, Chiapas: ECOSUR, 2003), 110; Anderson and Medina Tzuc, *Animals and the Maya in Southeast Mexico* (Tucson: University of Arizona Press, 2005), 104. The accusation that Maldonado made and used balché was a potentially dangerous one, as possession of the beverage was illegal in colonial Yucatan. John Chuchiak, in "It is Their Drinking That Hinders Them: *Balché* and the Use of Ritual Intoxicants among the Colonial Yucatec Maya, 1550–1780," in *Estudios de Cultura Maya* XXIV (2003): 137–71, recently documented 138 cases of balché usage prosecuted by church officials between 1560 and 1813 (three-quarters of them between 1590 and 1696), almost all resulting in sentences against Mayas of whippings and forced labor. Afro-Yucatecan participants in balché-drinking rituals were referred to—and some prosecuted by—the Inquisition.

3. AGN, Inquisición, vol. 620, exp. 7, fols. 599v–600v. Arguello seems to be implying not only that the pair were companions about town, but that they literally flew (as witches were rumored to do).

4. Ibid., fol. 596r. The quoted phrases are *"encantos y medios ilicitos para conservar a sus amantes," "de mala fama,"* and *"no es mal opinado."*

5. All cases are archived in AGN, Inquisición, with the exception of one that is housed in the Huntington Library (HL), San Marino, California. We have made thorough but not exhaustive searches through the Inquisition files of the AGN for love-magic cases. This means that while there are surely other cases not found by us, we have probably found a representative (possibly majority) sample, and thus our temporal focus reflects that of the Inquisition's seventeenth-century preoccupation with love-magic (see note 36 below).

6. See Ruth Behar, "Sexual Witchcraft, Colonialism, and Women's Powers: Views from the Mexican Inquisition," in *Sexuality and Marriage in Colonial Latin America*, ed. Asunción Lavrin (Lincoln: University of Nebraska Press, 1989) and Maria Emma Mannarelli, *Hechiceras, Beatas y Expósitas: Mujeres y poder inquisitorial en Lima* (Lima: Ediciones del Congreso de la República del Perú, 1998), 21–42, for discussions of the interethnic character of networks that women formed to use erotic medicines in Spanish America.

7. Susan Kellogg, *Weaving the Past: A History of Latin America's Indigenous Women from the Prehispanic Period to the Present* (New York: Oxford University Press, 2005), 80; Martha Few, *Women Who Live Evil Lives: Gender, Religion, and the Politics of Power in Colonial Guatemala* (Austin: University of Texas Press, 2002), 74–75; Noemi Quezada, *Sexualidad, Amor y Eroticismo. México Prehispánico y México Colonial* (Mexico City: Universidad Nacional Autónoma de México, Plaza y Valdés, 1996), 46–70.

8. AGN, Inquisición, vol. 38, exp. 2, fol. 50v. This may also reflect Marta's African background; although she was not identified as African, she must have either been African or have been only one generation removed, given the date. Crossroads are sacred places, where ancestors and other deities are invoked, in West and West Central African cosmologies.

9. Ibid., vol. 339, exp. 89, fols. 669–76.

10. Ibid., vol. 486, exp. 76, fols. 409–16.

11. Ibid., vol. 360, fols. 275–76.

12. Ibid., vol. 388, fol. 412r.

13. Laura Lewis, *Hall of Mirrors: Power, Witchcraft, and Caste in Colonial Mexico* (Durham: Duke University Press, 2003), 153–58, has argued that witchcraft cases show that Afro-Mexicans were often intermediaries between the indigenous people who controlled the magic and the Spaniards who used it. Whatever the origins of the magical knowledge, however, Afro-Mexicans used magic for their own purposes and they also made money and gained reputations as curers and as ritual practitioners. The origins of the magic and the way it was used are not the same, and by disentangling these factors we can gain insight into how Afro-Mexicans functioned in colonial society

and how they understood it. For an argument that people of African descent played multiple intermediary roles in the Spanish colonies, see Matthew Restall, *The Black Middle: Africans, Mayas, and Spaniards in Colonial Yucatan* (Stanford: Stanford University Press, 2009).

14. Although we could not find evidence of how much love-magic practitioners charged, there is evidence that other "witches"—those who specialized as healers in colonial Yucatan—earned between four and twelve pesos a month (Restall, *The Black Middle*, tab. 4.1). This was more than most non-Spaniards earned, suggesting that Spaniards were primarily the market for such professionals, especially in the city.

15. AGN, Inquisición, vol. 388, fol. 412r (the quoted phrase is *"que ella sabia encantar o disponer rosas o flores para atraer a los honbres"*).

16. Gonzalo Aguirre Beltrán, *Medicina y magia* (Mexico City: Fondo de Cultura Económica, 1992 [1963]), 162–63. Aguirre Beltrán suggests that people found it appropriate for sexual uses because of its strong smell and because the color, shape, and folds made the root look like genitals.

17. AGN, Inquisición, vol. 429, exp. 9, fols. 368–71v; HL, 35129, sin enum.

18. Ibid., vol. 360, fol. 275.

19. Ibid., vol. 435, sin enum (a Mexican example); vol. 388, fol. 419v; vol. 443, fol. 503r (Yucatec examples).

20. Ibid., vol. 388, fols. 419–20r.

21. Ibid., vol. 360, fol. 276r. Puc's claim may have been disingenuous, based on her assumption that inquisitors readily believed mulattas to be witches.

22. Ibid., vol. 292, exp. 28, fols. 135–39.

23. Ibid., vol. 443, fols. 491–503. Witnesses also mentioned that to cast the spell one had also to pluck hair from one's armpits and private parts, presumably before the button-plucking ritual—so that the latter, done in public, invoked the magic power of the former, done in private.

24. Ibid., vol. 530, exp. 5, fols. 232–37.

25. Aguirre Beltrán, *Medicina y magia*, 163. Also see this for Aguirre Beltrán's discussion of how materials were used.

26. AGN, Inquisición, vol. 356, exp. 41, fol. 206.

27. Ibid., vol. 356, exp. 25, fol. 170.

28. Ibid., vol. 292, exp. 28, fols. 135–39.

29. Ibid., vol. 388, fol. 412r

30. Ibid., vol. 317, exp. 40: sin enum.

31. Ibid., vol. 435, exp. 11, fol. 21.
32. Ibid., vol. 536, exp. 22, fols. 144–50v.
33. Ibid., vol. 360, fol. 276r.
34. Ibid., vol. 478, exp. 18, fols. 162–65.
35. AGN-Inquisición 316, sin enum: fols. 590–91v (the phrase is "*las que desean la mansedumbre*").
36. It is, after all, still practiced in parts of Latin America; for example, see Raquel Romberg, *Witchcraft and Welfare: Spiritual Capital and the Business of Magic in Modern Puerto Rico* (Austin: University of Texas Press, 2003) on Puerto Rico.
37. The seventeenth-century curve was slightly different in each colony: in Mexico, love-magic cases peaked in the 1610s–20s and in the 1650s; in Yucatan they peaked in the 1620s–30s and again in the 1670s. The rise and fall of Inquisition attention to love-magic in Yucatan can be linked to specific church officials, who (like Dr. Antonio de Horta Barroso, mentioned in the first paragraph of this chapter) brought their zeal with them—and took it when they died or left. The total number of complete cases (from denunciation through trial to judgment) is only a handful for each region, but there are dozens of denunciations.
38. The quoted phrase is Ruth Behar's. See: Ruth Behar, "Sexual Witchcraft, Colonialism, and Women's Powers: Views from the Mexican Inquisition," in *Sexuality and Marriage in Colonial Latin America*, ed. Asunción Lavrin, 179 (Lincoln: University of Nebraska Press, 1989).
39. Behar, "Sexual Witchcraft"; Mannarelli, *Hechiceras, Beatas y Expósitas*, 21–42; Noemi Quezada, *Amor y magia amorosa entre los aztecas: supervivencia en el México colonial* (Mexico City: Universidad Nacional Autónoma de México, Instituto de Investigaciones Antropológicas, 1975); Quezada, *Sexualidad, Amor y Eroticismo*; Few, *Women Who Live Evil Lives*; Restall, *The Black Middle*, chap. 7. Solange Alberro also discusses magic and witchcraft as a way of manipulating the social structure, focusing on the fears generated by people thought to be practicing witchcraft. See his *Inquisición y sociedad en México, 1571–1700* (Mexico City: Fondo de Cultura Económica, 1988).
40. Joan Cameron Bristol, *Christians, Blasphemers, and Witches: Afro-Mexican Ritual Practice in the Seventeenth Century* (Albuquerque: University of New Mexico Press, 2007), chap. 5.
41. AGN, Inquisición, vol. 356, exp. 47, fol. 79.
42. Ibid., vol. 316, exp. 11, fols. 266–70r.
43. Ibid., vol. 254, exp. 103, fols. 248v–49r; and vol. 486, exp. 79, fol. 422.

44. Ibid., vol. 292, exp. 28, fols. 135–39.
45. Ibid., vol. 360, exp. 8, fols. 40–42v.
46. Ibid., vol. 316, exp. 11, fols. 266–70r.
47. For example, see AGN, Inquisición, vol. 292, exp. 28, fols. 135–39; vol. 316, exp. 11, fols. 266–70r; vol. 339, exp. 89, fols. 669–76.
48. Ibid., vol. 376, exp. 17, fols. 87, 89.
49. Ibid., fols. 89–90.
50. AGN, Inquisición, vol. 341, exp. 1, fols. 9–12v.
51. Ibid., fol. 26 (quoted passage is "*se precia tanto de este oficio de hechicera*"). Although she was referred to as "doña Isabel" in the document, the fact that she was so open about her nonlegalized union with her lover indicates that she may not have been particularly elite—she would probably have taken more pains to hide her relationship if she were trying to protect her elite honor.
52. Ibid., fols. 27, 25v.
53. Ibid., fol. 26.
54. Ibid., fols. 27v, 24v–25v (the quoted phrase is "*oraciones diferentes de las que aca usa en la iglesia*").
55. The phrase appears in almost every love-magic case from Yucatan, but examples are the 1626 Rojas and 1672 Maldonado cases, AGN, Inquisición, vol. 360, fols. 275–76; and vol. 620, exp. 7, fols. 595–614. The phrase is "*no por odio sino por descargo de su consiensia*." The allegation by Rojas that the love-magic failed to work suggests an additional motive for denunciation—an ironic one, in view of the fact that inquisitors took allegedly successful love-magic witches more seriously than those who appeared to lack the requisite skills or powers.

Section II

Engaging Modernity

"Afro" Mexico in Black, White, and Indian
An Anthropologist Reflects on Fieldwork

LAURA A. LEWIS

For my friend, the late Miguel Angel Gutiérrez Avila

"Why should we be Afro-Mexicans? That's something outsiders say. White people don't refer to themselves as Spaniards, do they?"

—don Domingo,[1] eighty-four years old,
San Nicolás Tolentino, Guerrero

Introduction

✢ DON DOMINGO'S WIFE, DOÑA ANA, RECENTLY DIED OF A STROKE in San Nicolás. She was in her mid-eighties and I had known both her and don Domingo for many years. I was not in San Nicolás at the time, but one of my *comadres* there let me know of doña Ana's condition.[2] San Nicolás is one of what are often referred to as the "black villages" (*pueblos negros*) of the Costa Chica (the "small coast"), a region that runs along Mexico's Pacific coast from Acapulco in Guerrero to southern Oaxaca. San Nicolás, which is not far from the Oaxacan state line, is the largest town pertaining to Cuajinicuilapa, its municipal seat, and is referred to by locals as Cuaji. Cuajinicuilapa is a Nahuatl term meaning "place of the Cuajiniquipil trees." Nahuatl terms reflect the history of the region, where Nahuas are no longer the indigenous majority but were during the pre-Columbian and early colonial periods. Other terms, such as those for flora and fauna, are also derived from Nahuatl. Many of these are, of course, used all over Mexico. But some words deemed particular to Africa-descent populations on the coast, such as *cuculuste* for very kinky hair, *cuita* for excrement, and *chocoyote* for a family's youngest son or daughter are also derived from Nahuatl.[3] Spanish-derived Mixtec words, such as *paño* (*rebozo* or shawl) can also be found in African descent communities in Oaxaca, such as in Collantes in a text written by a former mayor about local dance, hand copied by me in 1992.[4]

Most San Nicoladenses are families of small farmers and most are partially descended from black (*negro*, in the colonial vernacular) and mulatto (*mulato*) slaves and servants brought to the coast by Spanish cattle ranchers toward the end of the sixteenth century. These slaves and servants might have been joined by maroons, or runaway slaves, who established small communities (palenques) up and down the relatively inaccessible coast.[5] A lush region, the Costa Chica is still a cattle-owner's paradise. Although San Nicolás gained community land ownership during Agrarian Reform in the mid-1930s, land disputes with neighboring communities continue to exist.[6]

I began ethnographic fieldwork in San Nicolás in the 1990s, my curiosity piqued by research into Mexico's colonial "caste" system and the place of African-descent populations within that system.[7] A cultural anthropologist becoming bored with archives and longing to talk to actual people, I searched for Mexico's contemporary African-descent peoples. Although questions about "race" and identity informed my early research, after years of fieldwork in San Nicolás I am all too aware that economic class is a more compelling local concern than is race. There is no money (*no hay dinero*) to get ahead[8] and out-migration has become the norm. Mexican government policies opening borders to trade, lowering tariffs on imports, and even "modernizing" agricultural production have only exacerbated San Nicoladenses' struggles to get by as these policies accelerate migration, especially to Winston-Salem, North Carolina.

I have often heard San Nicolás referred to as the "cradle" (*cuña*) of "Afro-Mexican" culture, although Afro-Mexican is a label largely rejected by San Nicoladenses themselves, as the epigraph to this chapter suggests.

"Afro" Mexico in Black, White, and Indian 185

FIGURE 8.1. San Nicolás, central plaza. Photograph taken by author.

FIGURE 8.2. Many migrant San Nicoladenses live in this apartment complex in Winston-Salem. Photograph taken by author.

Indeed, don Domingo's reference to "outsiders" also hints that Afro-Mexican (and Afromestizo) was invented by what I call culture workers, who include politicians, artists, anthropologists, and government cultural promoters. Peter Wade consolidates two important points when he notes that terms such as Afro-descendant and Afro-Latin "obey[s] a *U.S. logic* of putting everyone who has some African descent . . . in the same ethnic-racial category [while] also responding to a growing interest, especially among black social movements, with an African cultural heritage."[9]

Such movements on the coast began in the 1980s, in the context of the government sponsored "Third Root Project."[10] The head of that Project, Luz Maria Martínez Montiel, once told me that "Afromestizo 'culture' does not exist," that "anthropologists are sentimental" about it, and that there was no "black diaspora in Latin America." Yet the "Africa thesis," as another scholar calls it,[11] generated a surge in outside visits to local Costa Chican communities; government-sponsored recuperation projects, particularly around the reconstruction of what some claim to be African-styled wattle-and-daub round houses (*redondos*) built by African-descent Mexicans from the colonial period until the 1960s; a revival of what some claim to be the African-inspired music known as *sones de artesa*; and Cuaji's museum of Afromestizo history and culture inaugurated by Guerrero's governor in 1999. San Nicolás's musicians will play sones de artesa if requested, and one can still see the shell of a redondo on the outskirts of town. Although both cultural forms were once vital parts of daily life, the redondo is actually a replica built at the urging of the late anthropologist Miguel Angel Gutiérrez Avila in the 1980s, while he revived sones de artesa, traditional wedding music long replaced by *cumbia* and techno-pop, at the same time. Neither artifact has been proven to be African at all, and one of the sones de artesa musicians is don Domingo.[12]

San Nicoladenses generally reject the label "black" as well as Afro-Mexican or Afromestizo. Well aware of racist ideologies and everyday discourses that in the past have marginalized African-descent Mexicans and continue to do so, in their view Afro or black Mexican identities do nothing to help them achieve their economic goals.[13] Instead, being black or Afro-Mexican conflicts with their national identities by making them something "other than" Mexican. As my comadre Rosa once said to me, "we're Mexican, we don't want to be from Africa."[14] She and other San Nicoladenses typically reserve the term "black" for some of their ancestors, for *other* people from the coast's black communities, including Santiago

Tepextla and Collantes in Oaxaca, for African Americans, for how outsiders refer to them, and for particularly dark-skinned local people. In most everyday discourse black is offensive and anti-black racism can inform local social relations.[15]

A sector of the coast's urban and more highly educated African descent population, along with outside politicians and cultural promoters, many of whom are white, have spearheaded a social movement that includes the Meetings of Black Villages (*Encuentros de Pueblos Negros*), which have taken place since 1997 in Guerreran and Oaxacan locales; few San Nicoladenses are involved. In 1997, when the first meeting was held in Ciruelo, Oaxaca, only the sones de artesa musicians attended.[16] In 1999, the third meeting was held in Cuaji, but no one from San Nicolás was there. Indeed, one of my comadres passed by the venue in Cuaji as she was shopping, bumped into me, and said she "didn't have time" to attend, the kind of comment I often heard. Yet even in 2002, when the meeting was held in San Nicolás itself, only one local woman attended, and she went with me.[17] During that meeting a farmer from another community stood up to say that he did not understand the goals of the meeting's organizers. A discussion then ensued that underscored the gulf between the concerns of intellectuals and rural farmers, even those from the same region of the country. George Reid Andrews makes this point more generally for the early 1990s: "Throughout Afro-Latin America . . . black activists tended to be either of middle-class background . . . or upwardly mobile individuals who had acquired high school and, in some cases, university educations. Their target constituencies were overwhelmingly poor and working-class. The prejudice and discrimination that middle-class activists felt . . . were much less salient in the lives of lower-class blacks and browns, for whom immediate issues of survival . . . were far more pressing."[18]

While the history of African-descent Mexicans needs to become a part of the consciousness of both local people and outsiders, in many respects that history is deeply entwined with Indians (indios) and whites (blancos) (as San Nicoladenses refer to indigenous people and mestizos on the coast and as I, therefore, generally refer to them here). Local identity formation cannot be understood without reference especially to the ties many African-descent Mexicans, including San Nicoladenses, have with Indians. San Nicolás's African-descent residents self-identify as morenos, a term that indicates their black-Indian "mixture," often couched in terms of "blood" (sangre).[19] Morenos share genealogical ties, agrarian and religious experiences, as well as a general coastal history with Indians, whom they also consider to be lighter-skinned than themselves. Today there is a neighborhood of morenos who identify as Indian in San Nicolás. They came from the area around Ayutla, a northwestern part of the Costa Chica in the mid-1960s, when federal highway 200, the only paved road down the coast, was completed. They were given land, which was plentiful at the time, in part to protect San Nicolás's land from whites, and the Indians stayed on. Most now have legal titles to that land.[20] While morenos do not see themselves *as* Indian, their genealogical stories are replete with Indian and some white "mixture," they claim Indian blood, and they liken their own economic predicament to that of Indians, who have similar histories of land struggles and deception by the Mexican government and large landowners, both of which morenos identify as "white." Thus, in some sense moreno can be seen as a political challenge to Mexican national ideologies of mestizaje or race-mixing between Indians and Spaniards/whites.[21]

As is the case for many Mexicans, the intense nationalism of San Nicolás morenos is deeply entwined with their connection to Indianness. Locally, this is notable and symbolically revealed in the yearly festivities commemorating Mexican Independence through a two-day dance/performance known as La América or Los Apaches. During the performance, San Nicoladenses dress up as "Indians" (Apaches) in feathered headdresses and red, white, and green clothing to match the Mexican flag and as *gachupines* (a derogatory colonial term for Spaniards). The Indians and gachupines do mock battle in the village streets with firecrackers and blunted arrows. The Indians always win; the gachupines are symbolically jailed in San Nicolás's only cell, and the Indian La América, typically played by a young woman who looks neither "too" black nor "too" Indian, waves the Mexican flag for a crowd that through speeches link San Nicolás to the nation and its independence leaders (see fig. 8.3).

In addition to La América, narratives of the whereabouts of San Nicolás's patron saint, Saint Nicholas of Tolentino, place his "authentic" self, a dark-skinned moreno statue, in a church in Zitlala, a Nahua community in the Montaña region of Guerrero, about three hundred kilometers north of San Nicolás. According to local lore, the statue was taken away by a white priest and planted itself in Zitlala, refusing to move. Every year San Nicoladenses travel to Zitlala, whose local residents venerate the saint and his powers of fertility, to accompany him "home" for his saint's day. It is said that when he is in San Nicolás the doors to the church in Zitlala will

FIGURE 8.3. La América and Los Apaches. Photograph taken by author.

not open, and that when he returns he has sand on his feet from visiting the coast. If one interprets this narrative together with an Independence Day battle won by Indians and another tale about a coastal shipwreck and the slaves who escaped it to a "free" Mexico, Indian "ownership" of Mexico and, by extension, of the village of San Nicolás, becomes clear.[22] Indeed, during La América the "Indians" of San Nicolás symbolically break the "chains of slavery" (crepe paper streamers hanging from the ceiling) as they usher in an independent and free Mexico.

"Black" Mexico in the United States

When Rosa told me that she did not want to be from Africa, she also asked me where it was and whether there was work there. At the time, her seventeen-year-old son Ismael had just left for the United States to find a job. Now she has not seen Ismael for more than ten years and has never met his children, who were born in Winston-Salem. Ismael is not unusual, for on any given day about one-third of San Nicolás's residents—both "Indians" and "morenos"—are in Winston-Salem or in nearby U.S. communities. They labor in construction, service, and light manufacturing, often for years, in order to save money to get ahead in San Nicolás, a place to which many San Nicoladenses, even younger people, remain deeply attached. Indeed, migration motives are usually couched in terms of "building my house" in San Nicolás. By this people mean a cinder-block house, a sturdy house to cement their ties to their home community and to replace what they denigrate as the "mud" out of which wattle-and-daub (including redondos) and adobe houses are or were made. They also send remittances to start small businesses in San Nicolás to bring them a steady income, to buy enough head of cattle to prosper there, to support family left behind, and to build the tombs where they one day expect to rest.[23]

The day before doña Ana died, I spent the late morning and afternoon in a small town outside of Richmond, Virginia, a few hours from where I live. I was visiting other ritual kin from San Nicolás, Margarita and her husband Maximino. Their family, which is a fluid unit depending on who is coming and going, had recently left Winston-Salem, which they were finding overcrowded with other Mexicans and increasingly dangerous.[24] They also had relatives in Virginia and wanted a quieter and less expensive place to live. Their Virginia location is not far from Winston-Salem, so they typically travel back and forth, in part because their eldest daughter,

FIGURE 8.4. Young extended (joint) "Indian-moreno" family from San Nicolás in Winston-Salem. Photograph taken by author.

a grandchild, and one of their sons live in Winston-Salem, as do some of their own siblings, nieces, nephews, and other kin.

I was a *madrina* (godmother) at their eldest son's wedding in San Nicolás in 2004, which Margarita asked me to attend as she could not, given her undocumented status and the problems she would have re-crossing the border. Her son had previously spent time in North Carolina before returning home to rest for a few months and to find a bride.[25] His wife recently gave birth to a daughter in the United States right after they crossed the border to rejoin the family.[26] Margarita and Maximino's younger children had already moved to the United States over the years. Now the whole family, including many of its lateral extensions, is in North Carolina and Virginia.

Margarita and Maximino's move to the United States was meant to last only a few years—long enough to build their house in San Nicolás. But the house is mostly built (I stay in it when I am in San Nicolás) and their sojourn has turned into seven years as their youngest daughter, Jenny, the only family member who speaks English, grows to hardly remember San

Nicolás at all.²⁷ Margarita first spoke of returning home when Jenny finished high school, but Margarita now talks about college.

During this visit, Margarita, Maximino, and Jenny wanted to go shopping, which is usual after Margarita serves an *almuerzo* or mid-morning meal of mole, tamales, or one of the other traditional dishes from the Costa Chica, which she continues to make even after years in the United States. We went to the upscale Short Pump Mall, where I had never been but where they had gone on several occasions. Jenny wanted to exchange a pair of sunglasses her parents had bought her.

As we wandered around, Maximino, without any apparent irony, pointed out a statue set in front of the Nordstrom's department store that anchors the mall. It was a monument to Chief Powhatan, a leader of Virginia's former Native American tribes, who died shortly after Jamestown was "settled." Maximino asked me about "Indians" in the United States, where they all were, and whether they looked like Mexico's Indians. He was also people watching, and he commented on a couple—a white man with an African-American woman. "You almost never see that here," he said. "It's usually a black man (negro) with a white woman (*gabacha*)."²⁸ I responded with a comment about the similarities to San Nicolás, where one almost always sees a lighter-skinned Indian woman with a moreno man rather than the other way around. One reason for this might be that on the Costa Chica African-descent women are considered too aggressive (*brava*) for Indian men, as a white woman from Collantes once told me and which San Nicoladenses themselves have confirmed.²⁹ Morenos also tend to be taller than Indians. Because husbands are supposed to be taller than their wives, an Indian man might find himself shorter than his moreno wife. However, I believe that the principal reason for the typical pairings is economic: Indians on the coast, including those who live in San Nicolás, are generally poorer than and have a lower status than morenos, even if Indianness does symbolize the nation and the glorious Mexican past.³⁰ Sirina confirmed this understanding. While more Indian men marry morena women than was the case a decade ago (see, for instance, fig. 8.4),³¹ she said, morena women do like nice clothes and gold jewelry, specifically necklaces and earrings, which are often used as collateral for loans. Indian men are not often in a position to buy these luxuries.

Like other morenos from San Nicolás, Maximino rejects the "Afro" Mexican label. Nor does he identify with African Americans as might also be the case in other places where African-descent Costa Chicans live in the United States.³² Instead, he contrasts himself to African Americans by referring to himself, again like other San Nicoladenses, as a moreno, and to African Americans as black. Once he rubbed his inner arm to point out his lighter skin as he talked about his mixed black-Indian blood. In some contexts San Nicoladenses like Margarita and Maximino also refer to themselves as hispanos, which references the ways in which U.S. categories identify "Latinos" by language and alleged ethnic unity. Recently, San Nicoladenses have started referring to themselves as *mexicanos* (Mexicans) and to African Americans as morenos. When I asked about this shift I was told by several people that San Nicoladenses were morenos in Mexico, but that African Americans were "moreno moreno." This double emphasis on morenoness, or "reduplication," as a linguist termed it,³³ is similar to the reduplication San Nicoladenses in Mexico use for some Indians by referring to them as *"indios indios"* or *indios naturales* ("native" Indians). These "double" Indians are even *more* Indian than "regular" Indians. The latter might look Indian but unlike the former they do not speak indigenous languages (at least in public) or wear indigenous dress. They also tend to come from mountainous, rural indigenous communities. Thus, moreno moreno indicates the extreme morenoness of African Americans in comparison to San Nicolás's own morenos who are, quite simply, "less black."

As I conversed with Maximino about morenoness, we were sitting in the kitchen of the two-bedroom apartment that seven members of his family, including the baby, shared in a rundown complex outside of Richmond. Most of the complex's other residents were African American. Maximino and Margarita recently moved out and then moved back in as their economic circumstances deteriorated. They do not consider themselves to have much in common with their neighbors, whom they have claimed are "lazy," and unwilling to work. They express resentment of African Americans who, unlike undocumented and even some documented Latinos, are eligible for social services. San Nicoladenses also do not see many African-American men supporting their families the way "hispanos" do. "They even ask for handouts from poor immigrants like us," Maximino once commented to me of his male neighbors in the apartment complex. When Jenny was younger, Margarita would pick her up after school and bring her back to work with her because she did not want to leave her home alone. One she told me that blacks should just "get over" the fact that they were enslaved over a hundred years ago. "So much time has passed. Why are they still caught up in this?" During my frequent visits

I have never witnessed either them or their African-American neighbors so much as acknowledge each other.[34] Nor does my goddaughter in Winston-Salem speak to her African-American neighbors. As Bobby Vaughn has noted, Afro-Mexicans "subscribe, at least in part" to prevailing stereotypes that categorize African Americans as "violent, drug-addicted, and generally undesirable."[35] While my fieldwork has shown that some African Americans in Winston-Salem are resentful of Mexican immigrants, some also try to reach out, only to be rebuffed, in part because most do not speak Spanish and in part because at least middle-aged San Nicoladenses, and even sixteen- to thirty-year-olds who arrived unschooled and immediately went to work, do not find common ground with African Americans.

It is ironic, of course, that on the Costa Chica and elsewhere in Mexico "blacks" like Margarita and Maximino are subject to racist comments about their own "laziness" and unwillingness to work.[36] But in the United States, morenos like Margarita and Maximino quite possibly bring similar racial prejudices from Mexico with them, quickly learning dominant U.S. sociracial discourses and a political economy that continues to favor whiteness while demeaning blackness.[37] Ongoing and perhaps escalating tensions between African Americans and Latinos have been documented by other scholars as well as in the popular press.[38] Such tension is not surprising given the language barriers and the struggles for upward mobility both groups have faced in a society riven by race and class.[39] But rather than identifying with others who face similar predicaments, the San Nicoladenses that I know distance themselves from those they see—mainly working class and unemployed African Americans—occupying the bottom rung.

One afternoon, I tried to explain to Maximino and Margarita segregation, the U.S. civil rights movement, ongoing structural inequalities, racism, and the problems of urban poverty (which they see as temporary for themselves). But San Nicoladenses know little about the history and legacies of African slavery in their own country, much less in the United States. Indeed, when they do refer to some of their ancestors as slaves their comments are almost always prefaced with "'they' say that" (*dicen que* or *se dice que*). Although they are aware of anti-black racism from both whites and Indians in Mexico, they themselves can be racist toward Indians and do not see racism as a major impediment given their rural lives and the fact that discrimination has not been institutionalized since the colonial era.[40]

This does not mean that blackness is nothing to them. It is more that blackness is a part of something that is complicated (for us) by a particularly Mexican combination of politics, genealogical ties, and agrarian history. While San Nicoladenses do not interact a great deal with either whites or African Americans in the United States, they understand that it is through whites—who control geopolitical borders, create immigration policies, are usually their bosses, and, in general, hold the most power (as they do in Mexico itself)—that they will have to make it. Some, interestingly enough, model their aspirations not after whites, African Americans, or even other hispanos. Instead, they admire entrepreneurial immigrants they see building businesses and wealth, such as the Chinese and Asian Indians.

"White" United States in Mexico

The day I returned home from my visit to the mall with Margarita and Maximino, I received a call from North Carolina from a godson, Oscar. His mother, my comadre Angela, had asked him to call me to tell me of doña Ana's stroke. Angela and her son are Indians according to categories used in San Nicolás, and Angela lives among other Indians from the group that came to San Nicolás from the Ayutla region in the 1960s. While San Nicolás's Indians and morenos have a somewhat ambivalent relationship, and San Nicolás's morenos denigrate "Indian Indians," the town's Indian residents try to learn local customs. Morenos and Indians intermarry, and many morenos, even elderly ones, claim Indian ancestry. As don Margarito, who was over ninety years old when I first met him in 1997, told me, "my grandmother was a black-Indian; my family is black-Indian." And don Domingo says that he is an Indian as his mother was, even though everyone says he is moreno.

When I was in San Nicolás in 2006 I had asked Angela to call if anything happened to my elderly friends because I knew I would not be back for a while. The call from Oscar, and my own call the next morning to Angela, were highly emotional. Angela was going to send someone to call don Domingo to the phone, but as I was speaking to her he walked by her house and she passed the phone to him. He thought that if doña Ana knew that I had called she would hold on for a few more days, yet she died that night and was buried less than twenty-four hours later. The next day I cried on my way to Western Union to send Domingo money, which I knew he would need for funeral arrangements and for his own sustenance.

Unlike most San Nicoladenses, doña Ana and don Domingo had little family in Mexico and none in the United States; they have no children or grandchildren, and therefore no one to send remittances when emergencies arise. They built their single room cinder-block house with a dirt floor over a number of years as they painstakingly saved small sums of money from harvests. I spent many afternoons lying in a hammock as we talked in their breezeway. When I first met them, they lived out in the countryside in a house made of sticks during the planting and harvest seasons and otherwise stayed with a nephew in town. I remember doña Ana showing me the chickens that lived with them, the *comal* (baked clay griddle) for tortillas, how she did the wash, the kind of bed she and Domingo slept in. During a visit in 2006 she made me fresh chicken soup and an embroidered border for a pillowcase.

In addition to being an artesa musician, don Domingo is a storyteller and one of San Nicolás's local intellectuals. Whenever outsiders interested in local culture pass through, they are directed to him. That was the case for me the very first time I went to San Nicolás, back in 1992. On this first trip, two music producers I knew in Mexico City had suggested I go there because they had recorded traditional songs in San Nicolás and thought that I would be well received. I remember listening, on the long bus trip from Mexico City, to a tape one of them had made of don Domingo narrating a story of the first slaves and the ways in which the white men who enslaved blacks later betrayed their mixed offspring.[41] It was clear from this story that in the minds of the people I would soon understand as morenos, whites had no affection for them. Indeed, San Nicoladenses have a local history with whites, including a late nineteenth-century U.S. estate owner. San Nicoladenses remember him fondly: they produced cotton for him and he provided for them, even as he amassed hundreds of thousands of hectares, out of which San Nicolás's *ejido* (collectively held land) was carved during Agrarian Reform in the 1930s. But one of his Mexican sons fought for the land into the 1970s.

San Nicoladenses are hostile to the memory of this son, as well as to the memory of the last white businesspeople to live in the village who, before they were run out of town, told "blacks" to "shut up" and "turn down the music," which for some San Nicoladenses is ironic given the current interest in reviving sones de artesa. But there are no longer any white people living there, except for a few schoolteachers, a few cultural promoters (some also schoolteachers) who periodically work to make San

Nicolás a place outsiders want to visit in part by resurrecting the music whites used to hate, and, until recently, a group of Chilean evangelicals. As several San Nicoladenses have told me, "in his heart" the white has no love for blacks.

I had heard from various sources both on and off the coast that the Costa Chica was a violent place and that San Nicolás was particularly inhospitable. But this was a part of the racist discourse endemic both to the coast and within Mexico and, in 1997, I began a long stint of fieldwork in San Nicolás with my family, including my then-four-year-old son. He attended kindergarten there and I was known as "Laura, *la mamá de Lukas*" (Laura, Lukas's mom) because no one knew how to pronounce my last name.

My own "ethnic" and "racial" identities are ambiguous and changeable. In the United States, I often feel like an ethnic minority but I also pass for "white" due to my pale skin and the particular and peculiar history of race/ethnicity and assimilation in the United States. In San Nicolás, I am just white. Beyond San Nicolás, people know me as the *gringa* (the white U.S. American woman), as I am the only one within hundreds of square miles consistently present over the past ten years. Even people I have never met know me. But while I am "white" I am also a U.S. American, female, and a mother; I began fieldwork with my family in tow, and I am of an age when many of my contemporaries in San Nicolás are already grandparents. Thus, my interactions with people are constituted in and around a number of different axes.

During my years of fieldwork I have become close to many San Nicoladenses. I brought copies of documents pertaining to San Nicolás I had found in the National Archives in Mexico City to the community (a white municipal president had burned those once held in Cuaji, don Domingo told me[42]), became part of the chain of reciprocity to which *compadrazgo* or ritual kinship is so central, and gave the community funds to repair a road, to buy sports equipment for local children and books for the schools—monies written into my grant budgets. Although most of what I had to give came from money and what money can buy, San Nicoladenses also help each other with money. I have been "repaid" many times over as my ritual kinship ties grow, as people I know in Mexico and the United States trust me, and as I move back and forth between my home in Virginia and San Nicoladenses' homes, weddings, and other celebrations in Winston-Salem in southeastern Virginia, and between the United

States and San Nicolás bringing with me food, medicines, video tapes of events that take place on both sides of the border, and even children.

But when I first arrived, people suspected I was from *la cultura*, the term San Nicoladenses use to refer to Mexican outsiders who come to study and to promote them.[43] I was also asked if I was a *halelujah*, the term they use for the evangelical Christians who have a presence in the village but who have not been able to displace the Catholic traditions most see as central to village unity because the majority of fiestas and weddings revolve around the Catholic Church and involve the whole community. When it became clear that I was not from la cultura, not an evangelical, and also not Mexican, suspicions eased. It has occurred to me that while people perceived me as white and relatively wealthy, they also saw that I was not a white Mexican. I could go on to say that although my skin is pale, my eyes are brown, and my hair is dark and wavy; these characteristics make me much less "strange" to San Nicoladenses than the *güera* blonde-haired, blue-eyed, and freckled students I occasionally bring with me. And, indeed, they do not consider me a güera or a "white white" person. My nationality, sex, general decorum, and the fact that I have a family San Nicoladenses know, have as much to do with my fieldwork as my "race" and my economic class. I cannot say which part of me is most reflected in my fieldwork, but I have never experienced any direct hostility because of my color. I am embarrassed to say that don Domingo once flattered me by proclaiming that I was the only white person they trusted, because every other white came in, took what they wanted, and was never heard from again.

Although I am aware of the advantages that I might have as a white U.S. academic, it is the U.S. part that perhaps for San Nicoladenses demarcates my "difference." Most of them are undocumented while my papers are in order and I can travel freely and in relative comfort. This was brought home to me after one arduous nonstop trip to the coast in 2002, which took some eighteen hours from my home in Virginia to San Nicolás. I arrived exhausted, hungry, sweaty, dirty, and in need of sympathy. But I was quickly reminded that at least I did not have to wait for days or weeks for a chance to cross the border, and I did not have to do any part of the journey on foot. The border crossing issue is sometimes conflated with nationality and sometimes with whiteness. It can be a source of bitterness. As one woman said to me, "we love you, but you don't love us." She did not mean me personally. Rather, she used *ustedes* (you, plural) to refer to the U.S. border guards who make life difficult for these rural people, who often get by on tortillas and chile and go to the United States only to "better" themselves.

So now I am left thinking about doña Ana and my ties to the people of San Nicolás. Right after doña Ana died, Angela's niece was killed by a neighbor's boy playing with a gun that his father had purchased with money sent from the United States. Her daughter-in-law has now joined her son in North Carolina, and I just received pictures of their baby, as well as of her daughter's two children, only the oldest of whom I had known in San Nicolás. Issues of life and death—guns, subsistence, health, crossing the border—are more on people's minds than race, which they usually comment on only when they are asked questions by outsiders, making jokes, hurling insults, or comparing themselves to other people. Moreover, women, especially, talk to me mostly about "women things": husbands' affairs with other women, domestic violence, money problems, the difficulties so-and-so is having getting pregnant, the sons and daughters who skip out and leave them to raise grandchildren. It is thus clear to me that my femaleness and my age give me access to and insight into a variety of issues.

In addition, while in some ways my "whiteness" and my class position set me apart from San Nicoladenses, they can also draw me closer. They have, for instance, given me insight into the conflation of "white" and "the rich" on the Costa Chica, and I become more central to San Nicoladenses' own transmigration precisely *because* I have a passport and money, do not need a visa, can go back and forth with ease, and speak English as well as Spanish. My cultural capital has enabled me to carry things back and forth across the border, make phone calls to Verizon and U.S. insurance companies, pick out medications and have prescriptions filled at Wal-Mart, interpret during visits to the doctor and the landlord, communicate with public schools, and the like. In short, I help San Nicoladenses to navigate their lives in the United States, while they help me to navigate mine in San Nicolás by instructing me on how to get scorpions out of the house, by letting me know when the water tap will be on, by offering me companionship, food, and a hammock, and by sharing with me what life means to them.

My ritual kin relationships and many personal ties to San Nicoladenses both in Mexico and in the United States are just as important as questions of race, which in San Nicolás as everywhere are complicated by issues of history, class, gender, sex, and national belonging. This is not to say that race does not matter to San Nicoladenses. Certainly it does matter, just as sex, gender, age, family, and class do. I am still learning, but as my ritual kin and other ties with both "moreno" and "Indian" San Nicoladenses expand and I feel it when people I know die, I am convinced that my efforts to get to know San Nicoladenses and to see the world through their eyes have not been in vain. When my goddaughter in Winston-Salem became pregnant, I was the first person she called after her own mother in San Nicolás; she recently asked me to be her own daughter's godmother. Margarita phoned to ask if I would *be madrina de anillos*, godmother of the rings, at her sister-in-law's wedding in Virginia. Thus she, her husband, her son, her daughter-in-law, her sister-in-law, and her sister-in-law's husband will all be my ritual kin.

It might be the case that, as the coast opens up to outsiders and as local people leave the coast, younger people especially will learn about the history of slavery in Mexico and their African heritage. Indeed, this is already a development in the Costa Chica's local schools and social movements and among some young Costa Chicans who live in the United States and are attending college. Yet I am still struck by the Mexican answers to the questions raised here, answers which come from a history and a way of thinking that is quite different from our own and answers that are in large part informed by a lack of knowledge, especially about the history and legacy of slavery in Latin America. But then, to put this in perspective, most of my public university students in Virginia are unaware that until 1967 a person socially classified as "white" could not legally marry one socially classified as "black" in their own state.

Mostly I have a heightened awareness of another issue, which did not, I confess, hit me with full force until I was already deeply involved in my fieldwork. This is that San Nicoladenses' experiences and aspirations are now so tied up with globalization and migration and what these processes mean for families, for the community, and for identities, that it is hard to say in which direction the winds of race are blowing.

✣ NOTES ✣

1. All local names in this chapter are pseudonyms.
2. Comadre literally means co-mother. It is embedded in a system of godparenthood (compadrazgo) entered into when an individual helps sponsor the ceremonies surrounding another's rite of passage, thereby becoming a godparent. Although its origins are Catholic, in San Nicolás the relationship does not have to be a religious one. While a child's baptismal godparents (padrinos) are the most important, people often become ritual kin through the sponsorship of wedding components, school graduations, and the like.
3. I thank Dr. Jonathan Amith for identifying Nahuatl terms and providing their equivalents. According to him, cuculuste is probably derived from the Náhuatl *xokolochitl*; cuita from the Náhuatl *kwitlatl*; and chocoyote from the Náhuatl *xokoyotl*, all of which have the same meanings as the terms used by morenos. For a list of Costa Chican vocabulary, see Francisca Aparicio Prudente, Maria Cristina Díaz Pérez, and Adela García Casarrubías, *Choco, chirundo y chando: Vocabulario Afromestizo* (Chilpancingo, Mexico: Dirección General de Culturas Populares, Unidad Regional Guerrero, n.d.).
4. On "Afromixtecos" in Collantes see Gutierre Tibón, *Pinotepa Nacional. Mixtecos, negros y triques*, 2nd ed. (Mexico: Editorial Posada, 1981 [1961]), 39–54.
5. Most maroon communities were located on Mexico's eastern coast, in and around Veracruz. But the Guerreran/Oaxacan coast is also mentioned in the following sources: Gonzalo Aguirre Beltrán, *Cuijla: Esobozo etnográfico de un pueblo negro* (Mexico City: Fondo de Cultura Ecónomica, 1985 [1958]), 48, 59–60; Patrick Carroll, "Mandinga: The Evolution of a Mexican Runaway Slave Community, 1735–1827," *Comparative Studies in Society and History* 19, no. 4 (October, 1977): 493; Peter Gerhard, *A Guide to the Historical Geography of New Spain*, rev. ed. (Norman: University of Oklahoma Press, 1993 [first edition, Cambridge: Cambridge University Press, 1972]), 381; J. Arturo Motta Sánchez, "Tras la heteroidentificación. El 'movimiento negro' costa chiquense y la selección marbetes étnicos," *Dimension Antropológica* 13, no. 38 (September/December, 2006): 115–50; Rolf Widmer, *Conquista y despertar de las costas de la Mar del Sur (1521–1684)* (Mexico City: Consejo Nacional para la Cultura y las Artes, 1990), 135–40.
6. On the history of these disputes from the colonial period to the present, in indigenous areas of the Costa Chica as well as in African-descent ones, see Veronique Flanet, *Viviré si Díos quiere: un estudio de la violencia en la mixteca de la costa* (Mexico City: Instituto Nacional Indigenista, 1977); Maria de los Angeles Manzano, *Cuajinicuilapa, Guerrero: Historia Oral (1900–1940)*

(Mexico City: Ediciones Artesa, 1991); Norberto Valdez, *Ethnicity, Class and the Indigenous Struggle for Land in Guerrero, Mexico* (New York: Garland Publishing, 1998); Widmer, *Conquista y despertar*.

7. Laura A. Lewis, *Hall of Mirrors: Power, Witchcraft, and Caste in Colonial Mexico* (Durham: Duke University Press, 2003).

8. See the broader discussion in George Reid Andrews, *Afro-Latin America, 1800–2000* (Oxford and New York: Oxford University Press, 2004), esp. chaps. 5 and 6.

9. Peter Wade, "Afro-Latin Studies: Reflections on the Field," *Latin American and Caribbean Ethnic Studies* 1, no. 1 (April, 2006): 107–8, my emphasis. Also Odile Hoffmann, "Reseña de *Afroméxico, el pulso de la población en México: Una historica recordada y olvidada y vuelta a recordar* de Ben Vinson III y Bobby Vaughn," *Desacatos* 20 (January–April 2004): 175–78.

10. Miguel Angel Gutiérrez Avila, *La conjura de los negros: Cuentas de la tradición Afromestiza de la Costa Chica de Guerrero y Oaxaca* (Chilpancingo, Guerrero: Universidad Autónoma de Guerrero, 1993); Malinali Meza Herrera, *Presentación. Jamás fandango al cielo: narrativa afromestiza* (Mexico City: Dirección general de culturas populares, 1993); Luz María Martínez Montiel, "Nuestra tercera raíz," *Nuestra Palabra* 2, no. 11 (November 29, 1991); Luz María Martínez Montiel, *Presencia africana en Centroamérica* (Mexico City: Consejo Nacional para la Cultura y las Artes, 1993).

11. The term "the Africa thesis" is from John McDowell, *Violence and Poetry: The Ballad Tradition of Mexico's Costa Chica* (Urbana: University of Illinois Press, 2000), 9.

12. See Gutiérrez Avila, *La conjura de los negros*, 22, on the replica of the round house; Richard Thompson, *Flash of the Spirit* (New York: Random House, 1984), 197–206; Aguirre Beltrán, *Cuijla*, 89–100; Tibón, *Pinotepa Nacional*, 49; and Laura A. Lewis, "Home Is Where the Heart Is: North Carolina, Afro-Latino Migration, and Houses on Mexico's Costa Chica," in *The Last Frontier? The Contemporary Configuration of the U.S.-Mexico Border (South Atlantic Quarterly)*, ed. Jane Juffer, 801–29 (Durham, NC: Duke University Press, 2006) for perspectives regarding the origins of such houses; Frederick Starr, *In Indian Mexico* (Chicago: Forbes and Company, 1908), 122, 128, 134, 138, for early twentieth-century photographs of round houses in indigenous communities in the higher elevations of Oaxaca, where there was no contact with blacks; Archivo General de la Nación (AGN), Tierras, vol. 48, exp. 6, for a map depicting round houses in the context of an indigenous/Spanish land dispute on the coast; and Moisés Ochoa Campos, *La chilena guerrerense* (Chilpancingo, México: Gobierno del Estado de Guerrero, 1987) and

Carlos Ruíz Rodríguez, *Sones de artesa de San Nicolás Tolentino, Guerrero*, Ethnomusicology thesis, Universidad Nacional Autónoma de México, Escuela Nacional de Música. Mexico City, 2001, and Carlos Ruíz Rodriguez, *Versos: música y baile de Artesa de la Costa Chica: San Nicolás, Guerrero y Ciruelo, Oaxaca* (Mexico City: El Colegio de México, Centro de Estudios Lingüísticos y Literarios, Consejo Nacional para la Cultura y las Artes, Seminario de Tradiciones Culturales, 2004) on traditional music.

13. As Anani Dzidzienyo points out, interest in African cultural remnants does not translate into sensitivity toward blacks in Mexico; see his "Coming to Terms with the African Connection in Latino Studies," in *Latino Studies* 1 (2003): 161. Indeed, the recent controversy over the reissuance of the comic book character Memín Pinguín, whom Marco Polo Hernández describes as a "little pickaninny" and who was recently commemorated on postage stamps in a nostalgic gesture, has been derided by both U.S. Americans and Mexicans as racist. See Marco Polo Hernández, "Memín Pinguín: uno de los cómicos mexicanos más populares como instrumento para codificar al negro," *Afro-Hispanic Review* 22, no. 1 (spring 2003): 52–59. Wal-Mart recently removed the comic book from its shelves in Texas stores after complaints from U.S. Americans.

14. On the denigration of blackness in Mexican national discourse see Gonzalo Aguirre Beltrán, *El negro esclavo en Nueva España y otros ensayos* (Mexico City: Fundo de Cultura Económica, 1994); Hernández Cuevas, "Memín Pinguín"; Marco Polo Hernández Cuevas and Richard Jackson, *African Mexicans and the Discourse on the Modern Nation* (Dallas: University Press of America, 2004); Laura A. Lewis, "Blacks, Black Indians, Afromexicans: The Dynamics of Race, Nation, and Identity in a Mexican Moreno Community (Guerrero)," *American Ethnologist* 27, no. 4 (2000): 898–926; Laura A. Lewis, "Modesty and Modernity: Photography, Blackness and Representation on the Costa Chica (Guerrero)," *Identities: Global Studies in Culture and Power* 11, no. 4 (October–December 2004): 471–99; Nancy Leys Stepan, *"The Hour of Eugenics": Race, Gender and Nation in Latin America* (Ithaca: Cornell University Press, 1991), 145–49; José Vasconcelos, *La raza cósmica: Misión de la raza iberoamericana* (Paris: Agencia mundial de librería, 1924), 30–31.

15. One young morena woman from San Nicolás was almost disowned by her relatively wealthy parents when she married against their wishes a man they deemed too dark-skinned (*prieto*). An older morena woman, with two dark-skinned daughters herself, was pleased when her son married an Indian woman and their children were lighter skinned; and since Rosa and Sirina have been in a feud for years, Rosa has insulted Sirina by commenting that she is so black she is almost "purple." See also Lewis, "Modesty and Modernity."

16. However much the musicians enjoyed performing, they also complained bitterly that they were not adequately compensated. Moreover, as I had a car and lived in San Nicolás, I organized their transportation to and from Ciruelo at the request of Father Glyn Jemott, Ciruelo's Trinidadian priest who has been instrumental in organizing the meetings.

17. The organizers did provide an evening's entertainment well attended by San Nicoladenses. This included an emcee's jokes about "La India María," a buffoon from rural Mexico who goes to the big city, urinates in the street, and does not know how to survive. It struck me as more than ironic that La India María was attractive not just to local people, who share dominant Mexican cultural reference points, but also to the meeting organizers, who offered La India María up as a kind of sacrificial victim for anti-black racism, a point I made to them the following day.

18. Andrews, *Afro-Latin America, 1800–2000*, 189; also G. Reginald Daniel, "Multiracial Identity in Global Perspective: The United States, Brazil and South Africa," in *New Faces in a Changing America: Multiracial Identity in the 21st Century*, ed. Loretta Winters and Herman DeBose, 260 (Thousand Oaks, CA: Sage, 2002).

19. Latin Americans and indeed U.S. Americans who have identified as "mixed" black-Indians are not unusual. On this issue and on the politics of black/Indian multiculturalism in Latin America see Mark Anderson, "When Afro Becomes (like) Indigenous: Garifuna and Afro-Indigenous Politics in Honduras," *Journal of Latin American and Caribbean Anthropology* 12, no. 2 (2007): 384–413; Rebecca Bateman, "Africans and Indians: A Comparative Study of the Black Carib and Black Seminole," *Ethnohistory* 37, no. 1 (winter 1990): 1–24; James Brooks, ed., *Confounding the Color Line: The Indian-Black Experience in North America* (Lincoln: University of Nebraska Press, 2002); Juliet Hooker, "Indigenous Inclusion/Black Exclusion: Race, Ethnicity and Multicultural Citizenship in Latin America," *Journal of Latin American Studies* (JLAS) 37, no. 2 (2005): 285–310; Baron Pineda, *Shipwrecked Identities: Navigating Race on Nicaragua's Mosquito Coast* (New Brunswick: Rutgers University Press, 2006); Peter Wade, *Race and Ethnicity in Latin America* (London and Chicago: Pluto Press, 1997); Wade, "Afro-Latin Studies," 105–24; Norman Whitten and Rachel Corr, "Imagery of 'Blackness' in Indigenous Myth, Discourse, and Ritual," in *Representations of Blackness and the Performance of Identities*, ed. Jean Muteba Rahier, 213–33 (Westport, CT: Bergin & Garvey, 1999). As these authors additionally point out, identities are "made" as they shift with politics, class and history.

20. Lewis, "Blacks, Black Indians, Afromexicans"; Laura A. Lewis, "Of Ships and Saints: History, Memory and Place in the Making of Moreno Mexican

Identity," *Cultural Anthropology* 16, no. 1 (February 2001): 62–82. See Rolf Widmer, *Conquista y despertar de las costas de la Mar del Sur (1521–1684)* (Mexico City: Consejo Nacional para la Cultura y las Artes, 1990), 131, on the speed with which some indigenous communities on the coast became *pardizado* (mixed black-Indian) during the colonial period.

21. On this point see Wade, "Afro-Latin Studies," 115.
22. See Lewis, "Of Ships and Saints," for an initial analysis of these connections.
23. Lewis, "Home Is Where the Heart Is," 801–29.
24. Much of that danger has fallen on the shoulders of San Nicolas's younger people due to the general problems that U.S. culture spawns—such as drug use, which has become an issue in San Nicolás itself—gang violence, the breakdown of extended family ties, and a reliance on cars.
25. San Nicolás is highly endogamous at the community level. Its young people usually marry each other, meeting either in Mexico or in the United States, and San Nicoladenses typically migrate to the same places. The largest immigrant communities are in Winston-Salem and nearby cities such as Greensboro and Charlotte; a much smaller one, principally made up of an extended family, is in southeastern Virginia. Some San Nicoladenses also live in Santa Ana, California, which was the initial receiving community until it became too expensive. At the same time, the southern United States became a magnet for retirees and businesses, its economy grew and, with it, a demand for largely unskilled labor, and Latino immigration greatly increased; on this, see Murphy, Blanchard, and Hill, eds., *Latino Workers in the Contemporary South* (Athens: University of Georgia Press, 2001); McClain et al., "Racial Distancing in a Southern City: Latino Immigrants' Views of Black Americans," *The Journal of Politics* 68, no. 3 (2006): 571–85. Indeed, the Winston-Salem/Greensboro region of North Carolina saw a more than 800 percent increase in its Latino population between 1990 and 2000 (McClain et al., 572). New immigrant San Nicoladenses began to leave southern California largely because the cost of living rose. More established families have stayed there and many San Nicoladenses still cross the border there even if their final destination is North Carolina. A community college student from Santa Ana, whose family is from San Nicolás, recently contacted me to request my articles. When he received them he replied: "I want to thank you for sending me your wonderful articles. I read your articles and they are the best articles I have read about the Costa Chica. All your information is accurate and interesting. I am amazed at everything you know about San Nicolás. I wish my grandmother still lived because she told me stories similar

to don Domingo's of how she lived in San Nicolás in the early 1900s. I told my mother about all the people you mention" (September 2005).

26. Postmarital residence patterns in San Nicolás are patrilocal. These patterns carry over to the United States, where wives also live with their husbands' families unless the couple is in a different city or unless the parents have not migrated.

27. Many younger members of the community, like Jenny, have anglicized names picked up in the United States or from Mexican television.

28. *Gabacho/a* and *gringo/a* refer to white people. They are slightly derogatory terms though not as derogatory as *mollo/a*, a term San Nicoladenses often use for African Americans, or *macuano/a*, a term they reserve for the Costa Chica's Indians. The origins of all of these terms are unknown, but mollo and macuano are likely derived from Náhuatl (Jonathan Amith, personal communication) and *macuache* is a general Mexican term for an Indian.

29. Lewis, "Blacks, Black Indians, Afromexicans," 905.

30. For more on *indigenismo*, or the elevation of indigenousness in Mexican nationalism, see Alan Knight, "Racism, Revolution and Indigenismo: Mexico, 1910–1940," in *The Idea of Race in Latin America, 1870–1940*, ed. Richard Graham, 71–114 (Texas: University of Texas Press, 1990); Judith Friedlander, *Being Indian in Hueyapan* (New York: Palgrave Macmillan, 2005 [1975]).

31. In Figure 8.4, for instance, the young moreno woman is married to and has a child with the Indian man on the right; one of her brothers is partnered with the Indian man's sister-in-law, with whom he has several children.

32. A recent *Los Angeles Times* article about a Pasadena, California, soccer team called "Costa Chica" noted "the unique racial and cultural identities" of Costa Chicans and that "Afro-Mexicans in Southern California have little interaction with African Americans." See www.latimes.com/news/local/la-me-afromex13apr13,0,7656217.story?page=1 (accessed April 15, 2008).

33. On this point I would like to thank Dr. Amy Paugh (personal communication).

34. One exception is an elderly African-American woman who now sits outside admonishing African-American children for picking on Mexican ones as the children play in the complex. The African-American woman, known as Mama Mae, does not speak Spanish.

35. Bobby Vaughn, "Afro-Mexico: Blacks, Indígenas, Politics, and the Greater Diaspora," in *Neither Enemies Nor Friends: Latinos, Blacks and Afro-Latinos*, ed. Anani Dzidzienyo and Suzanne Oboler, 132 (New York: Palgrave, 2005). Although Vaughn works in Collantes, Oaxaca, he extends his observations to all coastal African-descent people and thus finds it difficult to engage

my assessment of San Nicoladenses' "mixed" identity formations, which developed in a different geographical space and over a different history (e.g., see Bobby Vaughn, "Los Negros, los indígenas y la diáspora. Una perspectiva etnográfica de la Costa Chica," in *Afroméxico*, ed. Ben Vinson III and Bobby Vaughn, 82, n. 11 (Mexico City: Fondo de Cultura Económica, 2004). My own work over the years in Collantes, as well as my familiarity with the work of Gutierre Tibón (*Pinotepa Nacional*) suggest to me that the patterns in many Oaxacan villages might not be that different from those in San Nicolás. See also Adela L. Amaral, "Morenos, Negros, and Afromestizos: Debating Race and Identity on Mexico's Costa Chica," B.A. thesis, UCLA, 2005; and John McDowell, "Soy el Negro de la Costa: Visions of Blackness on Mexico's Costa Chica," paper presented at the conference *Blackness in Latin America and the Caribbean*, Indiana University, Bloomington, 2008. McDowell interviews the Oaxacan "El Cobarde" about an identity that combines El Cobarde's African and Spanish heritage in his music.

36. Lewis, "Blacks, Black Indians, Afromexicans," 905.

37. On the possibility that Latinos in general, and Mexicans in particular, bring anti-black racism to the United States with them, see McClain et al., "Racial Distancing in a Southern City," 581.

38. Randal C. Archibold, "In Los Angeles' Effort to Stem Violence, Antigang Officer Reads Streets," *New York Times*, January 29, 2007; Kimberly M. Grimes, *Crossing Borders: Changing Social Identities in Southern Mexico* (Tucson: University of Arizona Press, 1998), 85–86; Dzidzienyo, "Coming to Terms with the African Connection," 160–67; Tanya Katerí Hernández, "'Too Black to be Latino/a:' Blackness and Blacks as Foreigners in Latino Studies," *Latino Studies* 1 (2003): 152–59; Sarah Mahler, *American Dreaming: Immigrant Life on the Margins* (Princeton: Princeton University Press, 1999), 229–31; McClain et al., "Racial Distancing in a Southern City," 571–85; "Blacks, Latinos, and the Immigration Debate," National Public Radio, March 31, 2006, available at www.npr.org/templates/story/story.php?storyId=5314594.

39. For a recent discussion of the struggles faced by undocumented Mexicans for upward mobility in the United States, see Anthony DePalma, "Fifteen Years on the Bottom Rung," *New York Times*, May 26, 2005.

40. On Costa Chican racism among whites, Indians, and morenos see Lewis, "Blacks, Black Indians, Afromexicans," 905–6; Lewis, "Of Ships and Saints," 68; Lewis, "Modesty and Modernity"; In Mexico a federal law to prevent and eliminate discrimination was passed on April 29, 2003, although Afro-Mexicans are not specifically named (Jean-Philibert Mobwa-Mobwa Ndjoli,

personal communication; www.conapred.org.mx/acerca/docs/ley.pdf (accessed April 16, 2009).

41. For two versions of this story, both told by don Domingo, see Lewis, "Blacks, Black Indians, Afromexicans," 906; Gutiérrez Ávila, *La conjura de los negros*, 153–60. As an elderly, local intellectual who has had a lot of contact with cultural promoters and other outsiders, don Domingo is much more familiar with the history of slavery in Mexico than are most San Nicoladenses and, indeed, more so than most Mexicans.

42. Also see Eduardo Añorve Zapata, "Crónica municipal e historia en el municipio de Cuajinicuilapa," *El Sur*, June 28, 1999, 13.

43. Arlene Torres and Norman Whitten note that pairing the article *la* (the) with "culture" among Afro–Latin Americans has the effect of elevating culture to a level of "refinement" and "civilization" that contrasts with "low" culture; see Torres and Whitten, "General Introduction: To Forge the Future in the Fires of the Past: An Interpretive Essay on Racism, Domination, Resistance and Liberation," in *Blackness in Latin America and the Caribbean*, ed. Arlene Torres and Norman E. Whitten, 4 (Bloomington: Indiana University Press, 1998). That local people in San Nicolás collectively refer to cultural promoters in this way underscores the distance they perceive between themselves and those who have come to study them.

My Blackness and Theirs
Viewing Mexican Blackness Up Close

BOBBY VAUGHN

❧

❦ THIS ESSAY GIVES ME AN OPPORTUNITY TO STEP BACK AND REFLECT upon what I have learned over the many years that I've been involved in ethnographic fieldwork in southern Mexico. My first trip to the Costa Chica was in 1992—a brief number of days as part of a bus trip throughout southern Mexico. Having lived in the megalopolis of Mexico City for four months, it was time for a breath of fresh air. I knew almost nothing about the black experience in Mexico and was scarcely aware that one existed. The study of Spanish brought me to Mexico City. Had my interest in Latin America's African diaspora been more developed, I would not have chosen to study in Mexico, but would likely have chosen a decidedly Afro-Latin country like the Dominican Republic, Cuba, or perhaps Colombia to be the site of my first international travel. However, in 1992, I (then a young black male undergraduate) was attracted to Spanish both as a marketable skill as well as a tool that might allow me to engage with my home state of California's growing Latino community through grassroots activism, community-based politics, and so forth.

My brief 1992 visit to the Costa Chica, motivated by some word-of-mouth tips that I might "find" Black Mexicans there, forever altered the way I looked at Mexico. The fact that I was standing in the midst of Mexicans who in many ways looked like me and who also appeared to live a social reality so different from mine was the hook that captured my imagination, curiosity, and empathy. A one-year study abroad experience became a personal and academic journey that has continued. The exploration of questions of racial formation in general and Mexican blackness in particular became the focus of my doctoral work and subsequent teaching and writing. In the following pages I intend to share some of my fieldwork experiences and reflections as a way of approaching the question of Mexican blackness by taking a somewhat less than academic approach.

Over the years I worked in and visited many Costa Chican towns in both Guerrero and Oaxaca. During those first trips in the early 1990s, I studied in Cuajinicuilapa and Cerro del Indio, both communities lying on the Guerrero side of the state line. Most of my work, however, was centered principally on the Oaxaca side in the communities of Collantes, Cerro de la Esperanza, and Pinotepa Nacional (see map on pp. xvi–xvii). What strikes me most about the state line is that, with respect to the Costa Chica region, it means less than one might expect. In most situations, people identify more regularly as Costeños than as Guerrerenses or Oaxaqueños and some people joked with me that it would make more sense for the Costa Chica to form its own state, with Acapulco as its capital. Many families have ties that extend across the state line, such as that of the elderly Afro-Mexican woman in Cuajinicuilapa who first described Collantes to me—she was born there and had a vague recollection of its location on the banks of the river.

In the years that I've been involved in studying Afro-Mexico I have often heard two views of Mexican blackness. One is the idea that blackness in Mexico is really little more than a variant of being a mixed-race mestizo or even an *indígeno*. An extreme version of this view—a kind of "blackness means nothing" notion—would argue that the experience of Mexicans of African descent has next to nothing in common with the experiences of blacks in the greater diaspora. The experience of Mexicans of African descent, then, would be evaluated solely on its own terms, with the broader African diaspora bringing little to the table. On the other hand, the other view that I often encounter is almost the inverse: "blackness is everything." When the Afro-Mexican experience is considered from this perspective, blackness and African heritage trump all other identities and lenses of

My Blackness and Theirs

FIGURE 9.1. Replica of traditional Costa Chica *redondo* dwelling. Photograph taken by author.

analysis. Indeed, I attended a public event in the United States in 1996 in which the African-American speaker stated very forcefully that blacks in Mexico were not to be seen as "Afro-Mexicans," but rather, were "Africans in Mexico."

My experiences in the Costa Chica have convinced me that neither view is particularly descriptive of life on the ground as I've come to know it. The racism to which Black Mexicans have been subjected, the ubiquitous stigmatization of blackness in the Costa Chica, and the strong social boundaries that separate blacks, Indians, and mestizos from one another suggest that although Mexican identity has important meaning for people, it cannot be characterized as essentially consistent with the popular refrain and national slogan of unity, "todos somos mestizos" (we are all mestizos).[1]

Doña Juana Mariche, a dark-skinned black woman who estimates her own age to be about sixty-five, tried to explain to me why she rarely went into "town," preferring to stay close to her home in the mostly black village of Cerro de la Esperanza. "Well, it's obvious, isn't it?" she explained. "You know very well that blacks (*la gente negra*) don't get along well with whites (*la gente blanca*).² I even have family who ask why I never visit them over in the town (*rancho*) where they live; it's just too uncomfortable. I'm happy right where I am! I imagine it's the same in your country?"

"Yes, we have some of that where I live, too," I explained. "There are a lot of places where we don't feel comfortable going, but is there anything in particular that happens when you go there? What makes you uncomfortable?"

"You know, it depends on where you are," doña Mariche continued. "In the stores, they don't want to help you or they ask you questions that you don't know the answers to. That's why I send my children to town for me, because they know how to deal with it better than I can. Sometimes whites will take advantage of you, especially if you don't know how to take care of yourself (*defenderte*), right?"

"You got that right," I answered. "But don't you think it's important to go wherever you want to go, even if people don't want you there or it feels uncomfortable? I mean, how will things change?"

"Well, it's not up to me to change all of this!" She responds with a chuckle. "I'm too old for all of that! Maybe things are changing for the young people today [but] I'm still too reluctant (*me da pena*) to be around white people very much."

This short excerpt from one of countless conversations I've had with people in the Costa Chica highlights what I think has been an important element of my research—both asking *and answering* questions. I have found that many Afro-Mexicans are almost as interested in what being black is like for me as I am interested in their life experiences. I used to be more hesitant to engage in such discussions with my "informants" out of the misguided belief that I was there to collect data that would be unadulterated by ideas that I might introduce. Sustained, meaningful relationships with people over the years have weakened those quasi-colonial pretensions. My interactions with many Afro-Mexicans, indígenas, and mestizos have enlightened me on many levels. So, too, should my friends in the Costa Chica have the benefit of learning from, accepting, challenging, or otherwise pondering my perspectives. They are as interested in my experience of blackness in my country, and they are quick to point out the similarities *and the many differences* in our experiences.

My collaboration with México Negro is an important example of an active, ongoing exchange of ideas that has characterized an increasing part

FIGURE 9.2 Mother and youngest child, Costa Chica region, Oaxaca. Photograph taken by author.

FIGURE 9.3. Teenager, Costa Chica region, Oaxaca. Photograph taken by author.

of my day-to-day activities in these communities.[3] The grassroots movement has attempted to create spaces for local people to come together and reflect on their shared ethnic history and, inspired by the sense of ethnic solidarity, to create an organizational mechanism that would allow them to address their economic and educational needs. This effort at ethnic organizing, which started in the mid-1990s, was unprecedented in Afro-Mexican communities.

In 1998 I was drawn to and supported the efforts of what was—and continues to be—a small core of community leaders.[4] It always seemed perfectly sensible to me that Afro-Mexicans—long marginalized and exploited by local entrenched élites and ignored by national leaders—might experiment with an overt and positive assertion of their ethnic identity. My conversations with organizers and my involvement in helping them think through some of their goals provided important insights. One such conversation in 2000 involved four members of México Negro and myself discussing whether to use the word *afromestizo, afromexicano'* or *negro* in some of their promotional literature. They eventually settled upon "afromestizo," but the conversations that led up to that consensus involved an import negotiation of understanding "who are we?" They decided that, at least for now, "afromestizo" best satisfies their desire to differentiate themselves from other groups, such as the indigenous population, while also recognizing the fact that their work has been concerned with addressing the broader definition of being black, one which includes all shades and colors (keep in mind that being "afromestizo" acknowledges racial mixture, while being "negro" can be confused with just signifying dark-skinned people). I was the one who thought afromexicano sounded perfectly reasonable, but I was overruled summarily. It is heartening to me that we were able to have a productive discussion about these issues and that I, as a collaborator, ethnographer, and a friend, was invited to participate.[5]

My involvement in the growing interest in the lives of blacks in Mexico has had one foot in the Costa Chica and the other in cyberspace. One of the most rewarding activities that I have been involved in over the years has been introducing people to the Costa Chica via the connections I have made online. My personal website at www.afromexico.com has provided information for general audiences since 1997, and through this electronic medium I've communicated with hundreds of people who've expressed interest in learning more about Mexico's black population. I often provide travel information to those interested in exploring the region on their own, and I have, on occasion, accompanied travelers there. The people that I've introduced to the experience of Afro Mexico—including a mix of students, artists, community activists, and reporters—are a small part of a larger wave of interest in Afro-Mexico.

Over the years, I have witnessed the arrival of some African Americans who, having misunderstood the complexities of Mexican blackness, have touted a sort of Pan-Africanism that rings hollow in the Costa Chica. In 1998, at the annual community meeting sponsored by México Negro, one African-American visitor proceeded to explain to the local citizens how México Negro (and other groups and individuals) might profit from her civil rights organizing experience with the Student Non-Violent Coordinating Committee (SNCC) in the 1960s. "We have to learn how to organize and engage in civil disobedience in order to achieve our goals," she went on to explain in well-intentioned remarks that fell quite flat with the audience of *campesinos* (peasants). Another speaker addressed the audience by discussing the heritage of the kings and queens of ancient Africa. However, the uniqueness of the black experience in the Costa Chica, combined with

FIGURE 9.3. Teenager, Costa Chica region, Oaxaca. Photograph taken by author.

the way race is understood in Mexico more generally, makes such overt appeals to the African diaspora's "Black is beautiful" discourses or politicized black mass movement dialogues difficult to grasp for the majority of blacks in the Costa Chica.[6]

Yet I do think that Costeños will inevitably continue to be exposed to such diverse ways of thinking about blackness. As more "outsiders" visit the region and, more importantly, as more Costeños travel outside of the region and continue to consume an ever-increasing number of channels on satellite television systems, their perspectives will broaden. Not only is this an inevitability but, in my view, it is a welcome development. While, on the one hand, I can respect the ubiquitous origin narrative that Afro-Mexicans relate of themselves, of having escaped from modern ships that ran aground on any number of beaches along the coast, on the other hand there is a kind of blissful ignorance that tends to captivate the researcher at the expense of informing the people whose lives we study. Surely, basic facts about the Mexican slave trade and the diverse historical experiences of blacks, both slave and free throughout Mexican

FIGURE 9.5. Woman and a neighborhood child, Costa Chica region, Oaxaca. Photograph taken by author.

history, *should* be shared with all Mexicans, but especially with Mexicans of African descent.[7]

During my first visits to the Costa Chica, my friends in Collantes and in other communities wondered why an anthropologist such as myself would want to study their culture. The scholarly role of anthropology in contemporary Mexico has privileged indigenous communities. Blacks have not been traditionally seen as offering anything of "cultural" interest. Over the last ten years, however, I have witnessed greater receptivity among people to celebrate their culture. The attention of scholars, combined with Mexican government-sponsored festivals, the annual Encuentros de Pueblos Negros (Gathering of Black Villages), the Afro-Mestizo Museum in Cuajinicuilapa, and the efforts of local radio programs and community newsletters has created a kind of common discourse surrounding the common elements of Afro-Mexican culture. These very recent events have created a kind of consciousness, at least at the level of expressive culture, so that now a range of cultural elements are commonly celebrated by people as expressions of Afro-Mexican culture—expressions that have gained strength, interestingly, through their validation by people from outside the region.[8] I remember the joy with which one of the members of Collantes' Danza de los Diablos (Devil Dancers) group recounted their participation in a dance festival in Mexico City in 2003. "We were invited to go and we all went and had a great time . . . And the audience loved it, and after all of the other groups—you know, the ones from other regions—after they had finished, the audience called us back on stage and we danced some more, because they enjoyed it so much!"[9]

It is my hope that, in the coming years, Afro Mexicans of the Costa Chica will continue to collaborate with others *on their own terms*. I am personally gratified to have been able to work and share my experiences with this very diverse range of Afro-Mexican people and communities, engaging the potentialities and pitfalls inherent in the dynamics of racial formation in a complex world.

⁕ NOTES ⁕

1. The boundaries I draw attention to here manifest themselves in the fact that in the region nearly all small towns are identified by locals as black towns, indigenous towns, or mestizo towns. Certainly before the recent increased mobility that came with improved roads in the last thirty years, the ethnic segregation in terms of settlement patterns was stark and such lack of black-indigenous race mixing has been noted in the late eighteenth century. See Ben Vinson III, "The Racial Profile of a Rural Mexican Province in the 'Costa Chica': Igualapa in 1791," *The Americas* 57, no. 2 (October 2000): 269–82.

2. In the Costa Chica, Afro-Mexicans typically use the word blanco (white) to describe people who in most other parts of Mexico would be described as mestizo. In casual conversation people talk about blacks, whites, and Indians, and hardly ever use the word mestizo.

3. México Negro began in El Ciruelo, Oaxaca, under the direction of Trinidadian-born parish priest Glyn Jemmott, who has been living in the Afro-Mexican town since 1984. The annual meetings (Encuentro de Pueblos Negros) began in 1997 and continue to be held every spring. For more on political organizing and México Negro see Bobby Vaughn, "Afro-Mexico: Blacks, Indigenas, Politics, and the Greater Diaspora," in *Neither Enemies nor Friends: Latinos, Blacks and Afro-Latinos*, ed. Anani Dzidzienyo and Suzanne Oboler, 117–36

(New York: Palgrave, 2005); and Laura Castellanos, "Buscan volver etnia a los afromexicanos," *La Reforma* (Mexico City), June 8, 2005, 3C.

4. I was not alone among those outsiders who have supported the effort. Others include Daniel Widener (Los Angeles), Lilly Alcántara (Xalapa, Veracruz), Janein Chávez (Los Angeles), Cristina Díaz (Mexico City), and Ron Wilkins (Los Angeles).

5. Please note that for the purpose of maintaining stylistic consistency throughout this volume we have chosen to adopt the hyphenated spelling Afro-Mexico and Afro-Mexican in each chapter. We fully realize that the terms Afromexico and Afromexicans are also commonly used, particularly in Latin America.

6. A strong sense of black identity in the absence of overtly political mass movements is not uncommon in Latin America, as Robin Sherrif discusses in the Brazilian case. Robin Sherrif, *Dreaming Equality: Color, Race, and Racism in Urban Brazil* (New Brunswick: Rutgers University Press, 2001).

7. While both North American and Mexican historians have been shedding much-needed light on the Afro-Mexican experience and the quality of their research is impressive, rural Afro-Mexicans have had little access to such scholarly work and I have yet to see how it might be informing their experience with racial formation.

8. Examples of cultural practices commonly associated with Afro-Mexicans of the Costa Chica include: music and dance such as Son de Artesa, Danza de los Diablos, and Danza del Toro de Petate; the *redondo* (round house); and the burial rite known as *levantamiento de sombra*.

9. The pride with which Dago recounted his participation with the *diablos* echoes the excitement of the same group of dancers who participated in 1999 at the internationally acclaimed Guelaguetza cultural festival in Oaxaca. It was the first time that an Afro-Mexican group participated in the indigenous-centered event that purports to showcase the diverse cultures of the state.

The Thorntons
Saga of an Afro-Mexican Family

ALVA MOORE STEVENSON

❧ FROM COMPTON TO NEWARK, WITH FREQUENT HEADLINES screeching about violence between Mexican and Black youth, one could easily be convinced that relations between the two groups have always been brimming with hostility. The media's embrace of sensationalism blots out an important aspect of history and a very different kind of relationship: the Afro-Mexican family dating back a century.

I am Afro-Mexican. Stories like those of my family and those of entire Afro-Mexican communities in the United States have been ignored for too long. In this society where racial and ethnic identity is narrowly defined, we haven't fit into anyone's box.

How does a person of African-American and Mexican heritage self-identify? What were the experiences of our forebears who embraced each other across national and ethnic lines? I hope to answer these questions by sharing the story of my family.

The root of the Afro-Mexican Thornton family can be traced back to nineteenth-century Versailles, Kentucky. It was there that James Thornton, reportedly of African, European, and Choctaw ancestry, was born a slave in 1835.

He was mustered into the U.S. Colored Troops' 12th Heavy Artillery regiment during the Civil War. James was court marshaled and tried on charges of mutiny for supposed offenses against a white officer. His original sentence to be shot by musketry was commuted to hard labor on the Dry Tortugas islands off the Florida coast. But the war ended before he could serve his sentence and he left Kentucky for Kerr County, Texas.

Believed to be the first black landowner in that county, James married Adeline Joiner in 1870 and they had twelve children. One of them was my grandfather, Daniel.

My great grandparents told their children they would never be treated fairly in the United States and should either go to Canada or Mexico. Daniel chose Mexico and migrated there around the turn of the century. Arriving in Guadalajara, he quickly became fluent in Spanish and secured a position as a foreman helping to build the Mexican railroad. He was the liaison between English-speaking white management and Spanish-speaking Mexican workers.

Tráncito Pérez de Ruíz, my grandmother, was born in San José de Grácia, Sinaloa, a mining town. Tráncito had fled the ranch where she lived during the Mexican Revolution because many girls were kidnapped and raped. She worked in the army of General Elias Plutarco Calles as a cook and nursemaid. One of her most memorable moments was serving breakfast to Calles, Pancho Villa, and General Alvaro Obregón. Daniel met Tráncito and they married in 1914.

My grandparents were provided a caboose to live in until work on the railroad was completed. Then they migrated to Nogales, Arizona. The Thorntons joined a small, tightly-knit enclave of Afro-Mexican families living in that border town between the 1920s and 1950s. Many were black soldiers, from nearby Camp Stephen D. Little and later Fort Huachuca, who married Mexican women from across the line.

Daniel spent time as caretaker at the Nogales City Cemetery, as a mail carrier, as a worker at the Tovrea meat-packing plant, and as the owner of a shoeshine parlor. Tráncito owned a restaurant for a short time, but gave it up to raise her family. They had eight children, including my mother, Lydia Esther. My grandmother was also ordained as a minister in the El Mesías United Mexican Methodist Church in 1947.

My mother and her siblings were native Spanish speakers who learned English only upon attending school. Nogales's segregated Grand Avenue School was a one-room building with African-American teachers. In many Afro-Mexican families there were children born to the women during previous marriages to Mexican men; one such child was my Aunt Soledad, who we called "Sally." By virtue of having black stepfathers, they, too, were mandated to attend the segregated school.

There was a unique syncretism expressed between these children—Afro-Mexican, African American and Mexican—as friends and classmates. Language and culture was shared. Afro-Mexican and Mexican children taught their African-American classmates Spanish. At the first annual reunion of the Grand Avenue/Frank Reed School in Nogales in 1994, I observed that many of the African-American students had remained fluent.

My mother was one of the first Nogalians to enlist in World War II. She was given a choice to join either a white or black regiment. She chose the black regiment—the 6888th Central Postal Directory, otherwise known as the black WACS. Like others of this second generation of Afro-Mexican families, she left Nogales after World War II for Los Angeles, where she married and became a bilingual schoolteacher.

Much has been written about biracials who are black and white, but not about those who are of two marginalized groups. In the Thornton family, my mother and her siblings saw themselves as African American, as Mexican, or fluidly, able to shift between two identities. Key for them was to self-identify in ways they perceived would give them the best quality of life.

To varying degrees, the self-identity of second generation Thorntons was tied to their ability to speak Spanish. This comes into much sharper focus in the third generation. My sister, my cousins, and I carved out a self-identity largely based on language. Those who did not speak Spanish generally identified as black. Others, such as some older cousins, who became fluent at a Spanish-speaking convent, gravitated toward a Mexican identity.

I view my family's history in a much larger context. It is important to look at the history of the southwest United States, Mexico, and the Spanish-speaking Americas. You will find African peoples brought into Mexico, for instance, both as slaves and free people as early as the beginning of the sixteenth century. One of them, Juan Garrído, came with the party of Hernán Cortes and was the first person to sow wheat in the western hemisphere.¹

Some Afro-Mexicans traveled north into the southwest United States—then part of the Spanish Crown and later Mexico—such as the family of Pío Píco, a businessman, military leader, and the last Mexican governor of California.² Conversely, African Americans such as James Hughes, the father of writer Langston Hughes, fled south to escape virulent racism. He migrated to Mexico in 1909 to work for the Sultepec Electric Light and Power Company.³

Afro-Mexicans in Mexico and the United States exist. We may be left out of the history books, but that doesn't make our contributions to the development of both cultures and both countries any less significant.

✣ NOTES ✣

1. Matthew Restall, "Black Conquistadors: Armed Africans in Early Spanish America," *The Americas* 57, no. 2 (2000): 171–205.
2. William Ellsworth Smythe, *History of San Diego, 1542–1908: An Account of the Rise and Progress of the Pioneer Settlement on the West Coast* (San Diego: Kessinger Publishing, 2007).
3. Arnold Rampersad, *The Life of Langston Hughes*, Vol. I: 1902–1941, *I, Too, Sing America*, 2 vols. (New York: Oxford University Press, 1986).

The Need to Recognize Afro-Mexicans as an Ethnic Group

JEAN-PHILIBERT MOBWA MOBWA N'DJOLI

❧ DEFENDERS OF FUNDAMENTAL HUMAN RIGHTS ARE TODAY CRYING out for Afro-Mexicans to be recognized as a minority ethnic group.[1] The cultural uniqueness of this group is shown in their ways of thinking, speaking, dressing, and beliefs—among other elements they hold in common. The lack of their ethnographic recognition is part of the widespread denial of the African contribution to Mexican national culture and constitutes one of the thousands of indirect forms of discrimination against Afro-Mexicans.

There are several ways Afro-Mexicans are being rendered invisible, or *invisibilized*.[2] The first form of invisibilization is to erroneously include them in the category of Mexican indigenous people. Although native peoples are also clearly discriminated against—as demonstrated in the 2005 First National Survey on Discrimination, which revealed that 43 percent of Mexicans believe that natives will always be socially subordinated simply because of their racial characteristics—it is also obvious that Afro-Mexicans and indigenous Mexicans are not ethnically the same.[3] Furthermore, Afro-Mexicans face greater discrimination and less protection because they are not an officially recognized ethnic group; there is thus no specific legal basis on which to defend or protect their fundamental human rights.

A second factor that hinders the recognition of Afro-Mexicans as an ethnic group is based on the rejection of difference. This is rooted in the nineteenth-century notion that

> to make a nation it was necessary to civilize those who were different, share the Catholic religion, promote principles of personal property, speak the national language, be Spanish, Creole, or racially mixed, and to whiten the Indians. That meant dissolving cultural and phenotypical difference, and its bases of reproduction, but also separating out supposed cultural incompatibilities.[4]

Mexican thinkers at the time appropriated various similar ideas from Europe. For example:

> Taking as paradigmatic the criteria of European physical beauty and ideas of moral decency, typical for the bourgeoisie and the middle class (order, harmony, moderation, moral behavior, the work ethic), Mexican scientists resisted the physical characteristics that made it possible to visually identify the inferiority and the threat posed by the Indian race; [thus] the indigenous race appeared problematic because of their physical and moral characteristics. Amen! to their communitarian forms of organization, which contradicted the ideal of the homogeneity of the national culture.[5]

It is important to emphasize that in these attempts to vindicate—but not rehabilitate—the image of natives as constituent elements of national culture, no mention is made of Afro-Mexicans, neither as a minority nor as part of Mexico's original multiculturalism.

A third factor that hinders the recognition of Afro-Mexicans as an ethnic group is Mexico's social inequality. This generally refers to levels of family income and consumption, but in Mexico:

> social inequality means not only differences in income and family consumption, but, as an immediate consequence, unequal standards of living stemming from limited opportunities of

development, levels of participation and, importantly, the exercise of rights and liberties.[6]

It is therefore possible to construe social inequality in Mexico as a key phenomenon. In particular, it has created a situation of marginalization and discrimination toward Afro-Mexican minorities, by virtue of which they are excluded from work opportunities, education, access to justice, health, and political participation.

The inclusion of Afro-Mexican minorities within the indigenous populations of the country, the rejection of difference through prejudice and negative stereotypes, and social inequality: these are only three elements among many that continue to foster the marginalization and exclusion of Afro-Mexican minorities.

The *Nuestra Tercera Raíz* (Our Third Root) National Program

In spite of all the attempts by intellectuals and politicians to eradicate the presence of Afro-Mexicans from the history of Mexico, the existence of African-descended people in Mexico is an historical fact that speaks for itself. It is necessary to recognize that there has always been an interest in Afro-Mexico from some national citizens and foreigners. Likewise, there have been some state initiatives, most notably the creation in 1989 of the *Nuestra Tercera Raíz* National Program, by the National Council for Culture and the Arts (CONACULTA).

This program was designed to combine efforts to uncover and recount the Afro-Mexican experience and, at the same time, to recognize Afro-Mexican ethnic groups as part of the multiculturalism of the United States of Mexico. An initial phase of the effort was to recognize the history and legacy of slavery (streaming into Mexico from Veracruz, among other points). In this sense, the initiative was built upon the influential writings of Gonzalo Aguirre Beltrán, and academic research remained key to *Nuestra Tercera Raíz*. The program was then strengthened in the 1990s by the activities of civil associations promoting "Afro-Mexicanness." One example is that of *México Negro, A.C.* (Black Mexico, Inc.), founded in 1996.

The *Nuestra Tercera Raíz* National Program continues to promote the recognition of African contributions to national culture, helping to preserve those typically Afro-Mexican cultural expressions that have been passed down through the generations. Nevertheless, there remains much to do. The Afro-Mexican situation deserves the implementation of affirmative action, compensatory measures, and public policies to place black identity and inclusion at the heart of national culture.

On the subject of affirmative action, Jesús Rodríguez Zepeda recently said:

> affirmative action has been almost invisible for social jurists, scientists or political philosophers in Mexico. It seems that many consider it as an exclusive phenomenon of North American society, without relevance for our country. Nevertheless, nowadays it is difficult to conceive of a society that is able to offer its citizens true equal opportunities without making reference to some type of preferential treatment towards discriminated and traditionally excluded groups . . . Affirmative action, in this sense, supposes a preferential treatment in favor of a specific social group that has undergone discrimination and fundamental limitation of its rights and opportunities. Arguments for affirmative action maintain that since the real social conditions under which discriminated people live suppose all the weight of a series of undeserved disadvantages (constituting a barrier to accessing fundamental rights and to improving opportunities regularly available to the rest of the population), the value of the equality will only be able to be reached if it includes the idea of compensatory measures to these groups, promoted, supervised, and/or stimulated by the State.

In the Mexican case, affirmative action measures are most abundant in their general form. They are found, at the highest legal level, in Article 2 of the Political Constitution of the Mexican United States, whose intention is to guarantee the fundamental rights, the preservation of identity and the possibilities of development for indigenous communities. This article establishes compensation measures to promote the equality of opportunities for the natives and to eliminate any discriminatory practice against them.

Let us consider the possibility that taking advantage of the rights and opportunities offered in a society is not equal for all. For certain groups, negative prejudices and stigmas cultivated over time constitute a real disadvantage in securing access to rights and opportunities; this is why their members live in a state of inequality for which they are not morally responsible, and that can seldom be overcome by themselves, given that their inequality is rooted in the customs, laws, institutions, culture, success models, beauty standards and other elements of public life that define the relations among social groups.

Considering the world in this way, and not as an ideal world where everyone has equal opportunities, the historical disadvantage of disenfranchised groups demands a "compensation" that allows them to balance the situation of competitive weakness that they have long suffered. This compensation must consist of a strategy in favor of equality in its constituent sense, which would imply the acceptance of preferential treatments, temporarily, in favor of those who belong to historically discriminated groups.[7]

It is within this perspective that we demand that affirmative action, compensatory measures, and public policies be taken in favor of Afro-Mexican minorities. The Mexican State must assume a particularly urgent responsibility for this, in response to public requests by Afro-Mexican civil organizations, such as México Negro,[8] currently operating in the Costa Chica. For this civil association, affirmative action enacted by the Mexican State must include at least the following three elements:

1. That by means of the Secretariat of Government (SEGOB), the National Institute of Statistics, Geography and Informatics (INEGI) be instructed to initiate a process in which African-descended people in Mexico are taken into consideration (included) in the next National Census of Population during year 2010.
2. That the legislative organs of the federation and the states where there are a significant number of African-descended people speed up the political and administrative processes whereby recognition is given to different ethnic groups of African-descended Mexicans.
3. That the National Council to Prevent Discrimination (CONAPRED) and the Commission for the Development of Indigenous People (CDI), as control systems of the government, be able to create the mechanisms needed to diagnose the real situation of African-descended Mexicans.

It is significant that some of these proposals were presented before the Mexican Senate (as can be seen in its parliamentary newspaper, no. 11, July 2004). In 2005, the proposals reappeared in a letter that México Negro sent to the president of the republic,[9] CONAPRED, and the CDI. These proposals were taken before the Senate by Deputy Ángel Heladio Aguirre Rivero, who presented them in the following manner:

> Points of Agreement
> First. We exhort the holder of the Federal Executive authority to grant to the Afro-Mexican population, as the third cultural root of Mexico, the recognition status of an ethnic group, so that they can receive the same benefits as indigenous peoples, and can be included within the programs that the National Commission for the Development of the Indigenous people handles.
> Second. We exhort the Commission of Budget and Public Accounting that within the Budget of Debits in the Federation for the following fiscal year, the resources destined to the National Commission for the Development of the Indigenous People be increased, so that Afro-Mexican people can be allowed to share the benefits that the indigenous people receive.
> Third. We exhort the Secretariat of Public Education that in the interests of the historical recognition of the contribution from Afro-Mexican people, the corresponding programs can be orchestrated by means of which the Afro-Mexican culture is promoted.
> Fourth. We exhort the National Institute of Statistics, Geography and Informatics to apply the criterion of Afro-Mexican origin, to release the necessary statistics that will make public the official number of Afro-Mexican inhabitants, as well as the places where they are mainly settled in the country.

As one can see, the issue of Afro-Mexican minorities continues to crop up in different arenas of civil society and government. Nevertheless, a true conscience check, change of mentality, and political will is needed in order to create and develop affirmative action, compensatory measures, and public policies to identify Afro-Mexican minorities and defend their fundamental human rights.

Conclusion

From the perspective of our national culture: "In Mexico, the concept of culture is strongly tied to language and dress. Black Mexicans, the majority of whom speak only Spanish and who now dress in typical mestizo clothes, and thus do not share typical 'ethnic' markers, do not see themselves as an 'ethnic' group (*grupo étnico*) distinct from mestizos . . . [It is] not that blacks do not see themselves as ethnically distinct from natives; the difference lies not in the *different* ethnicity of blacks, but rather, in their *lack* of ethnicity. The indigenous population is considered ethnic and the blacks are not. In the Costa Chica, then, since Afro-Mexicans are not readily considered to be part of the discourse on indigenismo, ethnicity, and culture, they have not been able to tap into the ideological power with which these concepts are imbued in Mexico."[10]

This outlook of our national culture must be overcome, since in Mexico there are nowadays certain legal bases and precedents that allow us to speak of multiculturalism. In this sense, one should consider that: "What it means to be black in Mexico is inextricably linked with what it means to be indigenous and, likewise, to what it means to be mestizo . . . [But] the Afro-Mexican experience, while perhaps sharing parallels with other Afro-Latin American communities, is a unique experience whose particularities stem from a range of ethnohistorical and demographic phenomena that give rise to characteristically Mexican racialized discourses. Along with nationalist discourses of mestizaje [race-mixing] which pervade Mexican society, indigenismo—a generalized preoccupation with the 'Indian question'—likewise dominates contemporary contemplations of race in Mexico."[11]

It is not this essay's goal to take from, or diminish, the gains made by Mexico's indigenous population for their causes—gains made through significant advances in research and hard-won victories earned through debates and discourse at the national level. Rather, the point is that if we do not assign the same importance and priority to Afro-Mexican communities, in terms of understanding their specific contributions to our broader national culture, we will fall once again into one of the dangerous traps of the colonial period. We will not consider Afro-Mexicans as a distinct people who are worthy of receiving equal treatment, and worthy of possessing respect for their fundamental human rights. The lack of equal treatment encountered for the Afro-Mexican population is a situation that can be found not only at the regional level, but for blacks internationally.

Particularly for Latin America and the Caribbean, there is a lack of explicit legal bases to promote and defend the fundamental human rights of the minorities of African descent throughout the region.

✢ NOTES ✢

1. I use the term African-Mexican minorities in my paper "The human rights of African-Mexicans," presented to the Congress titled "Diaspora, Nation & Difference: Populations of African Descent in Mexico and Central America," Veracruz, Mexico, June 2008.
2. From the Spanish *invisibilizar*, "to make invisible."
3. See the findings at the websites for the Secretaría de Desarrollo Social (Mexico): www.sedesol.gob.mx/index/index.php and for the Consejo Nacional Para Prevenir la Discriminación (Mexico): www.conapred.org.mx.
4. José Jorge Gómez Izquierdo, ed., *Caminos del racismo en México* (Mexico City: Plazas y Valdés Editores, 2005), 93.
5. Ibid., 124.
6. Carlos De la Torre Martínez, *El derecho a la no discriminación en México* (Mexico City: Porrúa, 2006), 263, 265.
7. Jesús Rodríguez Zepeda, "Affirmative Action in Mexico," *Voices of Mexico* 71, *CISAN-UNAM*, June 2005, 15–18.
8. Consejo Nacional para Prevenir la Discriminación, *Plan Nacional para Prevenir y Eliminar la Discriminación* (Mexico City: Impresora y Encuadernadora Progreso, S.A. de C.V., 2006), 42.
9. Senado de la República, *Gaceta Parlamentaria*, no. 11, *1er año de Ejercicio, Segundo Período Permanente* (Mexico City: Senado de la República, Julio de 2004, México, D.F.)
10. Ben Vinson III and Bobby Vaughn, *Afroméxico: El pulso de la poblacion negra en México, una historia recordada, olvidada y vuelta a recordar* (Mexico City: Fondo de Cultura Económica, 2004), 79.
11. Ibid., 77.

Glossary

Except where otherwise noted, all foreign language terms listed below are Spanish.

Afromestizo, -za (adjective). A term used to describe persons with some degree of African ancestry; the term "mestizo" suggests a mixture of backgrounds, not just African.

Afro-Mexicano, -na (adjective). A term used, occasionally, to describe Mexicans possessing some African ancestry

agregado, -da (noun; masculine and feminine). An appended or incorporated household member; a member of a household beyond those comprising the nuclear family

alcalde mayor (noun; masculine). A district magistrate or justice of the peace

alférez (noun; masculine). A lieutenant in a local militia

almuerzo (noun; masculine). Lunch or a mid-morning meal of mole, tamales, or another traditional dish

arriero, -ra (noun; masculine and feminine). A muleteer; one in charge of a group of pack animals

arroba (noun; feminine). Unit of weight measure, frequently used in cotton transactions

audiencia (noun; feminine). A royal court oftentimes charged with executive and legislative powers along with judicial authority

bajareque (noun; masculine). A small wooden hut or simple cabin

balché (noun; masculine). An alcoholic drink of Mayan origin, commonly drunk in southeastern Mexico

baquero (also spelled vaquero, from *vaca*, meaning "cow") (noun; masculine). A cowherd or cowboy

barrio (noun; masculine). An area, district, or neighborhood of a city

bebedizo (noun; masculine). An elixir or love-potion

benta (noun; feminine). An inn

blanco, -ca (noun; masculine and feminine). A white man or woman; a man or woman of European descent

bolero, -ra (noun; masculine and feminine). A professional shoe shiner

bozal (adjective). Term used to describe someone who is Africa-born, but removed from the land of his/her birth

bruja (noun; feminine). A witch or sorceress

cabecera (noun; feminine). An administrative term to describe the chief provincial town of a particular region

cabildo (noun; masculine). An administrative body in the Spanish colonies, similar to a town or city council

cacica/cacique (noun; feminine and masculine). An Indian chieftain or boss, female or male

campesino, -na (noun; masculine and feminine). A peasant or country person

casta (noun; feminine). Caste, descent, lineage; a colonial resident of mixed ancestry; type or category of person in colonial Latin America, often associated with racial markers

castizo, -za (noun; masculine and feminine). In the Spanish colonies, this term referred to a light-skinned mestizo—technically, the mixture of a white and a mestizo

chino, -na (noun; masculine and feminine). Literally, Chinese; more generally, a term used in colonial New Spain to describe Asians (of any background) and their descendants

cimarrón, -ona (noun; masculine and feminine). A renegade, or runaway slave

cimarronaje (noun; masculine). Flight, an attempt to seek one's freedom *cochero, -ra* (noun; masculine and feminine). A coachman; a driver of a horse-drawn coach

cofradía (sometimes *confradía*) (noun; feminine). A religious confraternity or lay brotherhood

color aindiado (adjective). Bronze or coffee colored; Indian-like or Indian-looking

comadre (noun; feminine). A godmother; also a very close friend or neighbor to whom one might feel closer than to one's own family

compadrazgo (noun; masculine). Godparentage or another form of ritual kinship

compadre (noun; masculine). A godfather or guardian; can also mean a very close friend, buddy

conjuro (noun; masculine). A spell

corral (noun; masculine). In a residential context, a multifamily residence that had adjoining farming plots

coyote (noun; masculine). A coyote, but used in colonial Latin America as a race label to describe nonwhites, especially with Indian ancestry

criado, -da (noun; masculine and feminine). A servant

criollo, -lla (adjective and noun; masculine and feminine). An individual of non-Amerindian descent (i.e., European, African, or mixed) born in the Spanish colonies of the Americas; initially the term was primarily applied to individuals of European descent born in the Americas; this is the origin of the English term "creole"

cuadro (noun; masculine). A picture, painting, work of art

cuartel (noun; masculine). Quadrants, or quarter of a city; a term used for the administrative districts of Mexico City

cuña (noun; feminine). A cradle; can also be used figuratively to describe the birthplace or point of origin of a people or a movement

dama de compañia (noun; feminine). A female attendant or lady-in-waiting

encomendero, -ra (noun; masculine and feminine). In the context of the colonial Americas, a high-ranking person who was given land to be worked by a group of Indians (see *encomienda* below), with the understanding that the encomendero, in return, would offer protection and Catholic evangelization

encomienda (noun; feminine). An institution employed in the Spanish colonization of the Americas, whereby a colonizer (*encomendero*) was "given" land and a group of Indians to work the land, in exchange for which labor the colonizer was expected to offer protection and Catholic evangelization

esclavos esclavo, -va (adjective and noun; masculine and feminine). A slave

estancia (noun; feminine). A ranch or a farm; a commercial ranching enterprise with mixed farming plots

gabacho, -cha (noun; masculine and feminine). In Mexico, this is a slightly derogatory term that refers to white people; connotation similar to that of *gringo, -ga* (see below).

gachupín, -na (noun; masculine and feminine). A term used during the colonial period to describe a Spaniard living in the Americas; the connotation is somewhat derogatory

gañán (noun; masculine). A farmhand or laborer; a hired hand

gente de razón (noun; feminine). Literally, "people of reason," this term was used during the colonial period in a hierarchical sense to differentiate between people perceived to possess the ability to reason and those perceived not to

gringo, -ga (adjective; masculine and feminine). In Mexico, this term generally refers to people from the United States, particularly Anglos or people of fair complexion; the term can sometimes have a derogatory overtone

grupo étnico (noun; masculine). Ethnic group

hacendado, -da (noun; masculine and feminine). A landowner, planter, or rancher; owner of a *hacienda* (see below)

hacienda (noun; feminine). Large landed estate or ranch, usually used for agricultural activities and raising livestock

halelujah (noun; masculine and feminine). A term used in Mexico to describe evangelical Christians

hechicería amorosa (noun; feminine). Witchcraft with amorous objectives; love-magic

hispano, -na (adjective). A Spanish term meaning "Hispanic" or "Spanish American"; a category of racial and/or ethnic identification

indigenismo (noun; masculine). The study and celebration of the Indian peoples of Ibero-America; the elevation of indigenousness in Mexican nationalism

indígena (adjective and noun; masculine and feminine). Indigenous, or native to a particular locale; in the context of Mexico, used to refer to the Indian peoples of that country *indio, -a* (adjective and noun; masculine and feminine). Amer-Indian; Native American; the indigenous peoples of the Americas

indios naturales (noun; masculine). "Native" Indians, sometimes referred to as "indios indios." The implication is that indios naturales are in some way strongly Indian, or more Indian than "regular" Indians.

ingenio (de azúcar) (noun; masculine). An ingenio is a machine or device; commonly used in the Spanish-speaking Americas to refer to a sugar mill

invisibilizar (verb). To make or render invisible

jacal (noun; masculine). A hut or single household shack

jubón (noun; masculine). A type of waist-length jacket

junquillo (noun; masculine). Jonquil, a Spanish plant that is a variety of narcissus

justicia mayor (noun; masculine and feminine). An appeals judge

labrador, -dora (noun; masculine and feminine). A farm worker, sometimes a landholder of means, sometimes not

ladino, -na (adjective). A term used to describe someone not ethnically Spanish, but who adopted the Spanish language and some elements of Iberian culture; a non-European (a black African or an indigenous person) who adopted Hispanic culture; Central American term for a person of Spanish and Indian ancestry or mixed culture; also an enslaved person of African ancestry born in Europe.

libre (adjective and noun; masculine and feminine). A free person; often used to describe a free person of African descent

limpieza de sangre (noun; feminine). Literally "cleanliness of blood"; an early modern Iberian conception of racial purity dependent on the quality of not having non-Christian and non-white ancestors

lobo, -ba (adjective; masculine and feminine). Used to describe persons of mixed African and American Indian ancestry; the precise connotation could imply someone who appeared of primarily black and secondarily indigenous American phenotype

madrina (noun; feminine). A godmother; in a figurative sense it can also mean a protectress or benefactress

majordomo (noun; masculine) (also spelled *mayordomo*). The leader of a confraternity, or cofradía (see above)

Maya (noun; masculine and feminine). Someone from the indigenous Indian cultural zone covering the Yucatán Peninsula, Guatemala, and other parts of Central America

mayordomo (noun; masculine). A foreman or manager on a ranch or estate

mestizaje (noun; masculine). Miscegenation; racial and cultural mixing between Spaniards and Indians

mestizo, -za (adjective and noun; masculine and feminine). Person of mixed race, especially of combined Spanish and Indian heritage

metate (noun; masculine). A curved stone on which maize is ground

milpa (noun; feminine). A plot dedicated to the cultivation of maize and other grains

mollo, -lla (adjective; masculine and feminine). A derogatory term used in parts of Mexico to describe people of African ancestry

macuano, -na (adjective; masculine and feminine). A derogatory term used in the Costa Chica area to describe the region's Indian population

moreno, -na (noun; masculine and feminine). Literally, someone of dark complexion; in the context of Latin America, this usually refers to blacks or people of African ancestry and little to no admixture

morisco, -ca (adjective and noun; masculine and feminine). In colonial New Spain (modern Mexico and a large part of the Southwestern United States), morisco designated an individual of mixed Spanish and African ancestry, who exhibited more qualities of the former than did a *mulato*

mozo (noun; masculine). A young male attendant

mulato, -ta (adjective and noun; masculine and feminine). Typically used to describe the human offspring of African and European unions; in the early colonial period, it was often applied to African intermarriage with a person of any other "race"

nación (noun; feminine). Literally, nation; the term was often used in the colonial era to refer to what we now might call an ethnic group; a group of people sharing a language and other cultural traditions

Nahua (adjective and noun; masculine and feminine). Describes the indigenous peoples who occupied the interior highlands of what is now Mexico prior to the sixteenth-century Spanish conquest; the language spoken by these people is called *Nahuatl*

natural (noun; masculine and feminine). A native of a particular place

negro, -a (adjective and noun; masculine and feminine). Used to refer to individuals of sub-Saharan African ancestry, generally those born in the Americas (as opposed to *bozales*, born in Africa)

obraje (noun; masculine). A primitive workshop, producing items such as textiles

operario, -ria (noun; masculine and feminine). A worker, laborer

oración (noun; feminine). Prayer or oration; for instance, the *oración de las ánimas*—the prayer for souls in purgatory

Otomí (adjective and noun; masculine and feminine). An ethnic group of Indians in Mexico, inhabiting the region in and around Celaya

palabras de hechizo (noun; feminine). Literally, magic words, the words comprising a spell or charm

palenque (noun; masculine). An isolated or well-hidden hamlet or settlement; the term was frequently used to describe settlements of escaped slaves

panadería (noun; feminine). A bakery

panadero, -ra (noun; masculine and feminine). A breadmaker, baker

pardizado, -da (adjective; masculine and feminine). Term used to describe someone of mixed African and European ancestry (see *pardo*, below)

pardo, da (adjective and noun; masculine and feminine). A person with any combined degree of African and European heritage, which was not necessarily limited to someone with one black and one white parent

pesos de oro de minas (noun; masculine plural). A Spanish-American unit of currency

petate (noun; masculine). Woven straw used for packaging

polvo (noun; masculine). A powder or love potion

Provisorato de Indios (noun; masculine). A tribunal; sometimes called the Indian Inquisition

pueblo (noun; masculine). A small community or village

pueblos de indios. Indian peasant communities

pulque (noun; masculine). An intoxicating beverage made from the juice of the agave cactus

puyomate (noun; masculine). A root or herb used in love-magic potions

quebrado, -da (adjective; masculine and feminine). Literally, broken or fractured; in mathematics it refers to fractions; when used in the context of *color quebrado*, this refers to someone possessing a multiplicity of ethnic backgrounds

ranchería (noun; feminine). A collection of small farms or ranches that, together, form a community

rancho (noun; masculine). A small farm or agricultural community

reales (noun; masculine). A unit of currency

recamerera (noun; feminine). A female house cleaner, maid

redondo (noun; masculine). An African-style wattle-and-daub round house

regidor, -ora (noun; masculine and feminine). A town alderman, municipal official

República de Indios (noun; feminine). A Spanish administrative term for an Indian village or settlement, implying a degree of political autonomy

sangre (noun; feminine). Blood

sastre (noun; masculine and feminine). A tailor

sirviente, -a (noun; masculine and feminine). A servant

sistema de castas (noun; masculine). The system of social hierarchy, based on castes, which governed society in Colonial New Spain

tejedor, -ora (noun; masculine and feminine). A weaver; *tejedor de ancho*—broadcloth weaver

teniente de justicia (noun; masculine). A deputy judge

terrateniente (noun; masculine and feminine). A landowner, estate owner

tierra caliente. Literally, the "hot lands," a region of coastal lowlands on Mexico's Pacific Coast, in the states of Michoacán and Guerrero

tocinero, -ra (noun; masculine and feminine). A tanner

trapichero, -ra (noun; masculine and feminine). A textile worker who operated independent cottage industries; people who ran small family-style operations consisting of one or two looms

vecindad (noun; feminine). Citizenry

virrey (noun; masculine). A viceroy; a person who governed a territory in the name of the king

visita (noun; feminine). An official visit of investigation; royal inspection

zapatero, -ra (noun; masculine and feminine). A shoemaker, cobbler

Bibliography

Archival Sources

Mexico:

ARCHIVO DE LA CASA DE MORELOS (MORELIA, MICHOACÁN, MEXICO)
    Cofradías
    Elecciones

ARCHIVO GENERAL DE LA NACIÓN (AGN) (MEXICO CITY)
    Acordada
    Alcaldes Mayores
    Bienes Nacionales
    Criminal
    General de parte
    Indiferentes de Guerra
    Indios
    Inquisición
    Ordenanzas
    Padrones
    Reales Cedulas Originales
    Tierras
    Tributos

ARCHIVO HISTÓRICO DE LA ARQUIDIÓCESIS DE OAXACA

ARCHIVO JUDICIAL DE PUEBLA
   Tributos

ARCHIVO MUNICIPAL DE CÓRDOBA

ARCHIVO PARROQUIAL DE JALAPA (APJ) (JALAPA, MEXICO)
   División del curato de Jalapa

ARCHIVO PARROQUIAL DE SAN PEDRO CHOLULA

ARCHIVO PARROQUIAL DE ZACATECAS
   Libros de la Cofradía de San Juan de la Penitencia

ARCHIVO DEL PODER JUDICIAL (PUEBLA, MEXICO)
   Fondo Real de Cholula, Instituto Cultural Poblano

NOTARIA ECLESIÁSTICA DE LA PARROQUIA DEL SAGRADA CORAZÓN
(NEPSC) (JALAPA, MEXICO)
   Registros de Bautizos, Entierros, y Matrimonios

Spain:
ARCHIVO GENERAL DE INDIAS (AGI) (SEVILLE, SPAIN)
   México

United States of America:
BANCROFT LIBRARY SPECIAL SETS
   Microfilm Collection III, Archivo General de Indias (Seville, Spain), Legajo 98

NETTIE LEE BENSON LATIN AMERICAN COLLECTION OF THE UNIVERSITY OF TEXAS AT AUSTIN
   W. B. Stevens Collection

GENEALOGICAL SOCIETY OF UTAH (GSU)
   Microfilmed archival material from the Archivo de la Casa de Morelos (Morelia, Michoacán, Mexico)

HUNTINGTON LIBRARY (HL) (SAN MARINO, CALIFORNIA)

Published Primary Sources

Acuña, René, ed. "Relación de Ajuchitlan." In *Relaciones Geográficas del siglo XVI: Michoacán*, 29–45. Mexico City: Universidad Nacional Autónoma de México, 1987.

———, ed. "Relación de Sirandaro y Guayameo." In *Relaciones Geográficas del siglo XVI: Michoacán*, vol. 9, 261–67. Mexico City: Universidad Nacional Autónoma de México, 1987.

Ajofrín, Francisco de. *Diario del viaje que hizo a la América en el siglo XVIII el padre fray Francisco de Ajofrín*. Mexico City, Instituto Cultural Hispano Mexicano, 1965.

Alegre, Francisco Javier. *Historia de la Compañía de Jesús en Nueva-España*. 2 vols. Mexico City, 1842.

Cabeza de Vaca, Alvar Núñez. *La relación; o Naufragios*. Potomac, MD: Scripta Humanistica, 1986.

Consejo Nacional para Prevenir la Discriminación. *Plan Nacional para Prevenir y Eliminar la Discriminación*. Mexico City: Impresora y Encuadernadora Progreso, S.A. de C.V., 2006. (El Consejo is accessible at www.conapred.org.mx)

Díaz del Castillo, Bernal. *Historia verdadera de la conquista de la Nueva España*. Introducción y notas de Joaquín Ramiírez Cabañas. Mexico City: Editorial Porrúa, 1983.

Durán, Fray Diego. *The History of the Indies of New Spain*, edited by Doris Heyden. Norman: University of Oklahoma Press, 1994.

Gage, Thomas. *Nuevo reconocimiento de las Indias Occidentales*. Mexico City: Fondo de Cultura Económica, 1982.

———. *Travels in the New World*, edited by J. Eric Thompson. Norman: University of Oklahoma Press, 1958.

Gemelli Carreri, Juan F. *Viaje a la Nueva España, México a fines del siglo XVII*. Mexico City: Ediciones Libro-Mex, 1995.

López de Gómara, Francisco. *Cortés, the Life of the Conqueror by His Secretary*. Berkeley: University of California Press, 1964.

Paredes Martínez, Carlos, ed. *"Y por mí visto . . .": Mandamientos, ordenanzas, licencias y otras disposiciones virreinales del siglo XVI*. Mexico City and Morelia: CIESAS and Universidad Michoacana de San Nicolás de Hidalgo, 1994.

Pérez de Ribas, Andrés. *Corónica y historia religiosa de la provincia de la Compañía de Jesús de México en Nueva España*. 2 vols. Mexico City, 1896.

Relaciones geográficas de Indias (contenidas en el Archivo General de Indias de Sevilla). La Hispanoamérica del siglo XVI: Virreinato de Nueva España. (México. Censos de población), 4 (4), Coleccion y publicacion hecha por Germán LaTorre. 1920.

Ruiz de Alarcón, Hernando. *Treatise on the Heathen Superstitions that Today Live among the Indians Native to this New Spain, 1629*, translated by J. Richard Andrews and Ross Hassig. Norman: University of Oklahoma Press, 1984.

Secretaría de Desarrollo Social (Mexico): www.sedesol.gob.mx/index/index.php.

Seijas y Lobera, Francisco. *Gobierno militar y político del reino imperial de la Nueva España*, transcribed and edited by Pablo Emilio Pérez-Mallaína Bueno. Mexico City: Universidad Nacional Autónoma de México, 1986.

Senado de la República. *Gaceta Parlamentaria*, No. 11, *1er año de Ejercicio, Segundo Período Permanente*. Mexico City: Senado de la República, July 2004.

Sigüenza y Gongora, Carlos. *Alboroto y motín de México del 8 de junio de 1692*. Mexico City: Talleres Gráficos del Museo Nacional de Arqueologóa, Historia y Etnografía, 1932.

Torquemada, Juan de. *Monarquía Indiana*. 3 vols. Mexico City: Editorial Porrúa, 1969.

Vázquez de Espinosa, Antonio. *Compendio y descripción de la Indias Occidentales*, edited by Charles Clark. Washington, D.C.: Smithsonian Institute, 1948.

Vetancourt, Augustín. *Teatro Mexicano*. México: Editorial Porrúa, 1971.

Villaseñor y Sánchez, José Antonio de. *Theatro Americano, descripción general de los reynos, y provincias de la Nueva España, y sus jurisdicciones*. Mexico City: Editora Nacional, 1952 [1746].

Secondary Sources

Arrom, Silvia. *The Women of Mexico City, 1790–1857*. Stanford: Stanford University Press, 1985.

Aguirre Beltrán, Gonzalo. *Cuijla: Esobozo etnográfico de un pueblo negro*. Mexico City: Fondo de Cultura Ecónomica, 1985 [1958].

———. *Medicina y magia*. Mexico City: Fondo de Cultura Económica, 1992 [1963].

———. *El negro esclavo en Nueva España y otros ensayos*. Mexico City: Fondo de Cultura Económica, 1994.

———. *La Población Negra de México: Estudio etnohistórico*. Mexico City: Fondo de Cultura Económica, 1963 [1946].

———. *Regiones de refugio: el desarrollo de la comunidad y el proceso dominical en mestizamérica*. Mexico City: Instituto Nacional Indigenista, 1987.

Aguirre, Carlos. *Agentes de su propia libertad: Los esclavos de Lima y la desintegración de la esclavitud: 1821–1854*. Lima: Fondo Editorial de la Pontificia Universidad Católica del Perú, 1993.

Alberro, Solange. *Inquisición y sociedad en México, 1571–1700*. Mexico City: Fondo de Cultura Económica, 1988.

Althouse, Aaron P. "Contested Mestizos, Alleged Mulattos: Racial Identity and Caste Hierarchy in Eighteenth-Century Pátzcuaro, Mexico." *The Americas* 62, no. 2 (2005): 151–75.

Amaral, Adela L. "Morenos, Negros, and Afromestizos: Debating Race and Identity on Mexico's Costa Chica." B.A. thesis, UCLA, 2005.

Amith, Jonathan D. *The Möbius Strip: A Spatial History of Colonial Society in Guerrero, Mexico*. Stanford: Stanford University Press, 2005.

Anderson, E. N., et al. *Those Who Bring the Flowers: Maya Ethnobotany in Quintana Roo, Mexico*. San Cristóbal de las Casas, Chiapas: ECOSUR, 2003.

Anderson, E. N., and Felix Medina Tzuc. *Animals and the Maya in Southeast Mexico*. Tucson: University of Arizona Press, 2005.

Anderson, Rodney D. "Race and Social Stratification: A Comparison of Working-Class Spaniards, Indians and Castas in Guadalajara, Mexico in 1821." *Hispanic American Historical Review* 68, no. 2 (1988): 209–43.

Andrade Torres, Juan. *El comercio de esclavos en la provincia de Tabasco (siglos XVI–XIX)*. Villahermosa: Universidad Juarez Autónoma de Tabasco, 1994.

Andrews, George Reid. *Afro-Latin America, 1800–2000*. Oxford and New York: Oxford University Press, 2004.

Andrews, Norah. "I Could not Determine the Truth:" Ambiguity and Afromexican Royal Tribute." Master's thesis, Johns Hopkins University, 2009, 23.

Aparicio Prudente, Francisca, Maria Cristina Díaz Pérez, and Adela García Casarrubías. *Choco, chirundo y chando: Vocabulario Afromestizo*. Chilpancingo, Mexico: Dirección General de Culturas Populares, Unidad Regional Guerrero, n.d.

Archibold, Randal C., "In Los Angeles' Effort to Stem Violence, Antigang Officer Reads Streets." *The New York Times*, January 28, 2007.

Ares Queija, Berta, and Alessandro Stella. *Negros, mulatos, zambaigos: derroteros africanos en los mundos ibéricos*. Seville: EEHA/CSIC, 2000.

Barrett, Elinore M. *La cuenca de Tepalcatepec: Su colonización y tenencia de la tierra*, translated by Roberto Gómez Ciriza. Mexico City: Secretaría de Educación Pública, 1975.

Basauri, Carlos. *Breves notas etnográficas sobre la población negra del distrito Jamiltepec, Oaxaca*. Mexico City: Consejo Editorial del Primer Congreso Demográfico, 1943.

Bateman, Rebecca. "Africans and Indians: A Comparative Study of the Black Carib and Black Seminole." *Ethnohistory* 37, no. 1 (winter 1990): 1–24.

Bechtloff, Dagmar. "La formación de una sociedad intercultural: las cofradías en el Michoacán colonial." *Historia Mexicana* XLIII, no. 2 (October–December 1993): 251–69.

Beckles, Hilary McD. *Black Rebellion in Barbados: The Struggle Against Slavery, 1627–1838*. Bridgetown, Barbados: Antilles Publications, 1984.

Behar, Ruth. "Sexual Witchcraft, Colonialism, and Women's Powers: Views from the Mexican Inquisition." In *Sexuality and Marriage in Colonial Latin America*, edited by Asunción Lavrin, 218–46. Lincoln: University of Nebraska Press, 1989.

Bennett, Herman L. *Africans in Colonial Mexico: Absolutism, Christianity, and Afro-Creole Consciousness, 1570–1640*. Bloomington: Indiana University Press, 2003.

———. *Colonial Blackness, Sin, Sex, and Emergent Private Lives in New Spain, 1622–1778*. Bloomington: University of Indiana Press, forthcoming.

Birrichaga Gardida, Diana. "Distribución del espacio urbano en la ciudad de México en 1790." In *La población de la ciudad de México en 1790: Estructura social, alimentación y vivienda*, edited by Manuel Miño Grijalva and Sonia Pérez Toledo, 311–41. Mexico City: UAMI, 2004.

Blanchard, Peter. "The Language of Liberation: Slave Voices in the Wars of Independence." *HAHR* 82, no. 3 (2002): 499–523.

———. *Slavery and Abolition in Early Republican Peru*. Wilmington, DE: Scholarly Resources, 1992.

———. *Under the Flags of Freedom: Slave Soldiers and the Wars of Independence in Spanish South America*. Pittsburgh: University of Pittsburgh Press, 2008.

Borah, Woodrow. *El juzgado general de indios en la Nueva España, traducido por Juan Utrilla*. México: Fondo de Cultura Económica, 1985.

Borah, Woodrow, and Sherburne F. Cook. "Sobre las posibilidades de hacer el estudio histórico del mestizaje sobre una base demográfica." *Revista de historia de América* 53/54 (1962): 181–90.

Boruchoff, Judith A. "Creating Community Across Borders: Reconfiguring the Spaces of Community, State and Culture in Guerrero, Mexico and Chicago." Ph.D. diss., University of Chicago, 1999.

Bowser, Frederick P. "The African in Colonial Spanish America: Reflections on Research Achievements and Priorities." *Latin American Research Review (LARR)* 7, no. 2 (1972): 77–94.

Boyd-Bowman, Peter. "Negro Slaves in Early Colonial México." *The Americas* 26, no. 2 (1969): 134–51.

Brading, David A. "Grupos étnicos; Clases y estructura ocupacional en Guanajuato (1792)." In *Historia y población en México (Siglos XVI–XIX)*, edited by Thomas Calvo. Mexico City: El Colegio de México, 1994.

———. *Miners and Merchants in Bourbon Mexico, 1763–1810*. Cambridge: Cambridge University Press, 1971.

Brady, Robert LaDon. "The Domestic Slave Trade in Sixteenth Century México." *The Americas* 24, no. 3 (1968): 281–89.

Bristol, Joan Cameron. *Christians, Blasphemers, and Witches: Afro-Mexican Ritual Practice in the Seventeenth Century*. Albuquerque: University of New Mexico Press, 2007.

———. "Negotiating Authority in New Spain: Blacks, Mulattos, and Religious Practice in Seventeenth-Century Mexico." Ph.D. diss., University of Pennsylvania, 2001).

Brooks, James, ed. *Confounding the Color Line: The Indian-Black Experience in North America*. Lincoln: University of Nebraska Press, 2002.

Butler, Kim D. *Freedoms Given, Freedoms Won: Afro-Brazilians in Post-Abolition São Paulo and Salvador*. New Brunswick: Rutgers University Press, 1998.

Cáceres, Rina. *Negros, mulatos, esclavos y libertos en la Costa Rica del siglo XVII*. Mexico City: Instituto Panamericano de Geografía e Historia, 2000.

———. *Rutas de la esclavitud en Africa y América Latina*. Costa Rica: Universidad de Costa Rica, 2001.

Carrera Stampa, Manuel. *Los gremios Mexicanos: La organización gremial en Nueva España, 1521–1861*. Mexico City: EDIAPSA, 1954.

Carrillo Cázares, Alberto, ed. *Michoacán en el otoño del siglo XVII*. Mexico: El Colegio de Michoacán, Gobierno del Estado de Michoacán, 1993.

———, ed. *Partidos y padrones del obispo de Michoacán, 1680–1685*. Morelia: Gobierno del Estado de Michoacán, El Colegio de Michoacán, 1996.

Carroll, Patrick J. "Black-Native Relations and the Historical Record in Colonial Mexico." In *Beyond Black and Red*, edited by Matthew Restall, 245–67. Albuquerque: University of New Mexico Press, 2005.

———. *Blacks in Colonial Veracruz: Race, Ethnicity, and Regional Development*. Austin: University of Texas Press, 1991.

———. "Estudio sociodemográfico de personas de sangre negra en Jalapa, 1791." *Historia Mexicana* 23, no. 1 (1973): 111–25.

———. "Mandinga: The Evolution of a Mexican Runaway Slave Community, 1735–1827." *Comparative Studies in Society and History* 19, no. 4 (October 1977): 488–505.

———. "Los mexicanos negros: El mestizaje y los fundamentos olvidados de la 'raza cósmica,' una perspectiva regional." *Historia Mexicana* 44, no. 3 (1995): 403–48.

Carroll, Patrick J., and Adriana Naveda Chávez-Hita. "Familia esclava y Resistencia en Veracruz colonial." *Anuario* IX (diciembre 1994), cuadro 2.

Carroll, Patrick J., and Aurelio de los Reyes. "Amapa, Oaxaca. Pueblo de cimarrones (Noticias Históricas)." *Boletín del Instituto Nacional de Antropología e Historia de México, época II*, 4, (1973): 43–50.

Castellanos, Laura. "Buscan volver etnia a los afromexicanos." *La Reforma* (Mexico City), June 8, 2005, 3C.

Castro Gutiérrez, Felipe. *La extinción de la artesanía gremial*. Mexico City: UNAM, 1986.

———. "Indeseables e indispensables: Los vecinos españoles, mestizos y mulatos en los pueblos de indios de Michoacán." *Estudios de Historia Novohispana* 25 (2001): 59–80.

Cervantes, Fernando. *The Devil in the New World: The Impact of Diabolism in New Spain*. New Haven: Yale University Press, 1994.

Chance, John K. "The Ecology of Race and Class in Late Colonial Oaxaca." In *Studies in Spanish American Population History*, edited by David J. Robinson, 93–117. Boulder: Westview Press, 1981.

———. *Race and Class in Colonial Oaxaca*. Stanford: Stanford University Press, 1978.

Chance, John K., and William B. Taylor. "Estate and Class in a Colonial City, Oaxaca in 1792." *Comparative Studies in Society and History* 19 (1977): 454–87.

Chasteen, John Charles. *National Rhythms, African Roots: The Deep History of Latin American Popular Dance*. Albuquerque: University of New Mexico Press, 2004.

Chaves, María Eugenia. *María Chiquinquirá Díaz: Una esclava del siglo XVIII: acerca de las identidades de amo y esclavo en el puerto colonial de Guayaquil.* Guayaquil: Archivo Histórico del Guayas, 1998.

Chávez Carbajal, Maria Guadalupe. *Propietarios y esclavos negros en Michoacán (1600–1650).* Morelia: Universidad Michoacana de San Nicolás de Hidalgo, 1994.

Chuchiak, John F. "It is Their Drinking That Hinders Them: *Balché* and the Use of Ritual Intoxicants among the Colonial Yucatec Maya, 1550–1780." *Estudios de Cultura Maya* XXIV (2003): 137–71.

Cook, Sherburne F., and Woodrow Borah. *Essays in Population History.* 3 vols. Berkeley: University of California Press, 1963.

Contreras Cruz, Carlos, Francisco Téllez Guerrero, Claudia Pardo Hernández, and Melitón Mirto Tlalpa. "La población parroquial en la Puebla de los Ángeles hacia 1777. El caso del Sagrario, San Marcos, y San José, análisis preliminar." In *Población y estructura urbana en México, siglos XVIII y XIX*, edited by Carmen Blázquez Domínguez, Carlos Contreras Cruz, and Sonia Pérez Toledo, 17–35. Xalapa, Veracruz: Universidad Veracruzana, 1996.

Cope, R. Douglas. *The Limits of Racial Domination: Plebeian society in Colonial Mexico City, 1660–1720.* Madison: University of Wisconsin Press, 1994.

Corro, Octaviano. *Los Cimarrones y la fundación de Amapa.* Mexico City, 1951.

Craton, Michael. *Testing the Chains: Resistance to Slavery in the British West Indies.* Ithaca: Cornell University Press, 1982.

Crosby, Alfred. *Columbian Exchange.* Westport, CT: Greenwood, 1972.

Curtin, Phillip D. *The Atlantic Slave Trade, A Census.* Madison: University of Wisconsin Press, 1969.

Daniel, G. Reginald. "Multiracial Identity in Global Perspective: The United States, Brazil and South Africa." In *New Faces in a Changing America: Multiracial Identity in the 21st Century*, edited by Loretta Winters and Herman DeBose, 260. Thousand Oaks, CA: Sage, 2002.

Davidson, David M. "Negro Slave Control and Resistance in Colonial Mexico, 1519–1650." *Hispanic American Historical Review* XLVI, no. 3 (August 1966): 235–53.

Davies, Keith. "Tendencias demográficas urbanas durante el siglo XIX en México." In *Historia y población en México (Siglos XVI–XIX)*, edited by Thomas Calvo, 261–304. Mexico City: El Colegio de México, 1994.

Davis, Darién J., ed. *Beyond Slavery: The Multilayered Legacy of Africans in Latin America and the Caribbean.* New York: Rowman and Littlefield, 2007.

Deans-Smith, Susan. *Bureaucrats, Planters, and Workers: The Making of the Tobacco Monopoly in Bourbon Mexico*. Austin: University of Texas Press, 1992.

Degler, Carl N. *Neither Black Nor White*. New York: Macmillan, 1971.

Dehouve, Danièle. *Entre el caimán y el jaguar: Los pueblos de indios de Guerrero*. Mexico City: Centro de Investigaciones y Estudios Superiores en Antropología Social, 1994.

———. "El pueblo de indios y el Mercado: Tlapa en el siglo XVIII." In *Empresarios, indios y estado. Perfil de la economía mexicana (siglo XVIII)*, edited by Arij Ouweneel and Cristina Torales Pacheco, 86–102. Amsterdam: Centrum voor Studie en Documtatie van Latijns Amerika, 1988.

De la Fuente, Alejandro. *A Nation For All: Race, Inequality, and Politics in Twentieth-Century Cuba*. Chapel Hill: University of North Carolina Press, 2001.

De la Serna Herrera, Juan Manuel. *Pautas de convivencia étnica en la América Latina colonial (indios, negros, mulatos, pardos y esclavos)*. Mexico City: Universidad Autónoma de México, 2005.

De la Torre Martínez, Carlos. *El derecho a la no discriminación en México*. Mexico City: Porrúa, 2006.

DePalma, Anthony. "Fifteen Years on the Bottom Rung." *The New York Times*, May 26, 2005.

Dubois, Laurent. *A Colony of Citizens: Revolution and Slave Emancipation in the French Caribbean, 1787–1804*. Chapel Hill: University of North Carolina Press, 2006.

Duncan, Quince. "Existen las razas?" In *Poblaciones y culturas de origen africano en México*, edited by María Elisa Velázquez and Ethel Correa, 217–25. Mexico City: Instituto Nacional de Antropología e Historia, 2005.

Dusenberry, William H. "Discriminatory Aspects of Legislation in Colonial Mexico." *The Journal of Negro History* XXXIII, no. 3 (1948): 284–302.

Dzidzienyo, Anani. "Coming to Terms with the African Connection in Latino Studies." *Latino Studies* 1 (2003): 160–67.

Dzidzienyo, Anani, and Suzanne Oboler, eds. *Neither Enemies Nor Friends: Latinos, Blacks, Afro-Latinos*. New York: Palgrave Macmillan, 2005.

Eltis, David. *The Rise of African Slavery in the Americas*. New York: Cambridge University Press, 1999.

Fernández Repetto, Francisco, and Genny Negroe Sierra. *Una población perdida en la memoria: Los negros de Yucatán*. Mérida: Universidad Autónoma de Yucatán, 1995.

Few, Martha. *Women Who Live Evil Lives: Gender, Religion, and the Politics of Power in Colonial Guatemala*. Austin: University of Texas Press, 2002.

Fisher, Andrew B. "Creating and Contesting Community: Indians and Afromestizos in the Late-Colonial Tierra Caliente of Guerrero, Mexico." *Journal of Colonialism and Colonial History* 7, no. 1 (2006), available at http://muse.jhu.edu/journals/journal_of_colonialism_and_colonial_history.

———. "Marketing Community: State Reform of Indian Village Property and Expenditure in Colonial Mexico, 1775–1810." In *Commodifying Everything: Relationships of the Market*, edited by Susan Strasser, 215–34. New York: Routledge, 2003.

———. "Worlds in Flux, Identities in Motion: A History of the Tierra Caliente of Guerrero, Mexico, 1521–1821." Ph.D. diss., University of California, San Diego, 2002.

Flanet, Veronique. *Viviré si Díos quiere: un estudio de la violencia en la mixteca de la costa*. Mexico City: Instituto Nacional Indigenista, 1977.

Forbes, Jack. *Africans and Native Americans: The Language of Race and the Evolution of Red-Black Peoples*. Urbana: University of Illinois Press, 1993.

Fra Molinero, Baltasar. "Ser mulato en España y América: discursos legales y otros discursos literarios." In *Negros, mulatos, zambaigos, derroteros africanos en los mundos ibéricos*, edited by Berta Ares Queija and Alessandro Stella, 123–47. Seville: Escuela de Estudios Hispano-Americanos, 2001.

Freyre, Gilberto. *Casa grande y senzala*. Rio de Janeiro: José Olympio, 1933.

———. *The Masters and the Slaves: A Study in the Development of Brazilian Civilization*, translated by Samuel Putnam. New York: Alfred A. Knopf, 1946.

Friedlander, Judith. *Being Indian in Hueyapan*. New York: Palgrave Macmillan, 2005 [1975].

Gálvez Jiménez, Mónica Leticia. *Celaya: sus raíces africanas*. Guanajuato: Ediciones la Rana, 1995.

García Martínez, Bernardo. "Pueblos de Indios, Pueblos de Castas: New Settlements and Traditional Corporate Organization in Eighteenth-Century New Spain." In *The Indian Community of Colonial Mexico: Fifteen Essays on Land Tenure, Corporate Organizations, Ideology and Village Politics*, edited by Arij Ouweneel and Simon Miller, 103–16. Amsterdam: CEDLA, 1990.

Gaspar, David Barry. *Bondmen and Rebels: A Study of Master-Slave Relations in Antigua, with Implications for Colonial British America*. Baltimore: John Hopkins University Press, 1985.

Gerhard, Peter. "A Black Conquistador in Mexico." *Hispanic American Historical Review* 58, no. 3 (1978): 451–59.

———. *A Guide to the Historical Geography of New Spain*. Rev. ed. Norman: University of Oklahoma Press, 1993 [first edition, Cambridge: Cambridge University Press, 1972].

Gilroy, Paul. *The Black Atlantic: Modernity and Double Consciousness*. Cambridge: Harvard University Press, 1993.

Gómez Izquierdo, José Jorge, ed. *Caminos del racismo en México*. México: Plazas y Valdés Editores, 2005.

González Navarro, Moisés. *Los Extranjeros en México y los Mexicanos en el extranjero, 1821–1970*. 3 vols. Mexico City: COLMEX, 1994.

González Sánchez, Isabel. "Sistemas de trabajo, salaries y situación de los trabajadores agrícoloas, 1750–1810." In *La Clase Obrera en la Historia de México*, edited by Enrique Florescano, Isabel González Sánchez, Jorge González Angulo, Roberto Sandoval Zarauz, Cuauhtémoc Velasco A., and Alejandra Moreno Toscazo, 125–72. Mexico City: Siglo XXI, 1980.

Gordon, Edmund T. *Disparate Diasporas: Identity and Politics in an African Nicaraguan Community*. Austin: University of Texas Press, 1998.

Graziano, Frank. *Wounds of Love: The Mystical Marriage of Saint Rose of Lima*. Oxford: Oxford University Press, 2004.

Grimes, Kimberly M. *Crossing Borders: Changing Social Identities in Southern Mexico*. Tucson: University of Arizona Press, 1998.

Guardino, Peter F. *Peasants, Politics, and the Formation of Mexico's National State: Guerrero, 1800–1857*. Stanford: Stanford University Press, 1996.

Gudmundson, Lowell. "Negotiating Rights Under Slavery: The Slaves of San Geronimo (Baja Verapaz, Guatemala) Confront Their Dominican Masters in 1810." *The Americas* 60, no. 1 (2003): 109–14.

Gutiérrez Avila, Miguel Angel. *La conjura de los negros: Cuentas de la tradición Afromestiza de la Costa Chica de Guerrero y Oaxaca*. Chilpancingo, Guerrero: Universidad Autónoma de Guerrero, 1993.

Helg, Aline. *Liberty and Equality in Colombia, 1770–1835*. Chapel Hill: University of North Carolina Press, 2003.

———. *Our Rightful Share: The Afro-Cuban Struggle for Equality, 1886–1912*. Chapel Hill: University of North Carolina Press, 1995.

Hernández Cuevas, Marco Polo. "Memín Pinguín: uno de los cómicos mexicanos más populares como instrumento para codificar al negro." *Afro-Hispanic Review* 22, no. 1 (spring 2003): 52–59.

Hernández Cuevas, Marco Polo, and Richard L. Jackson. *African Mexicans and the Discourse on the Modern Nation*. Dallas: University Press of America, 2004.

Hernández Jaimes, Jesús. "El comercio de algodón en las cordilleras y costas de la mar del sur de Nueva España en la segunda mitad del siglo XVIII." In *Mercaderes, comercio y consulados de Nueva España en el siglo XVIII*, edited by Guillermina del Valle Pavón, 224–56. Mexico City: Instituto Mora, 2003.

Herrera, Robinson A. *Natives, Europeans, and Africans in Sixteenth-Century Santiago de Guatemala*. Austin: University of Texas Press, 2003.

Herrera Moreno, Enrique. *El Cantón de Córdoba*. 2 vols. Tacubaya, México: Editorial Citlatépel, 1959.

Hoffmann, Odile. "Reseña de *Afroméxico, el pulso de la población en México: Una historica recordada y olvidada y vuelata a recordar* de Ben Vinson III y Bobby Vaughn." *Desacatos* 20 (January–April 2004): 175–78.

Hooker, Juliet. "Indigenous Inclusion/Black Exclusion: Race, Ethnicity and Multicultural Citizenship in Latin America." *Journal of Latin American Studies* 37, no. 2 (2005): 285–310.

Horne, Gerald. *Black and Brown: African-Americans and the Mexican Revolution*. New York: New York University Press, 2005.

Howard, David. *Coloring the Nation: Race and Ethnicity in the Dominican Republic*. Boulder: Lynne Rienner, 2001.

Humboldt, Alexander von. *Ensayo Político sobre el reino de la Nueva España*, translated by Vicente González Arnao. 4 vols. Paris: Rosa, 1822; Available in English as: *Political Essay on the Kingdom of New Spain*, translated by John Black. 2 vols. New York: I. Riley, 1811.

Hünefeldt, Christine. *Paying the Price of Freedom: Family and Labor Among Lima's Slaves, 1800–1854*. Berkeley: University of California Press, 1994.

Johnson, Lyman L. "Artisans." In *Cities and Society in Colonial Latin America*, edited by Louisa Schell Hoberman, and Susan M. Socolow, 227–50. Albuquerque: University of New Mexico Press, 1986.

Johnson, Lyman L., and Sonya Lipsett-Rivera, eds. *The Faces of Honor: Sex, Shame and Violence in Colonial Latin America*. Albuquerque: University of New Mexico Press, 1998.

Katerí Hernández, Tanya. "'Too Black to be Latino/a:' Blackness and Blacks as Foreigners in Latino Studies." *Latino Studies* 1 (2003): 152–59.

Kellogg, Susan. *Law and the Transformation of Aztec Culture, 1500–1700*. Norman: University of Oklahoma Press, 1995.

———. *Weaving the Past: A History of Latin America's Indigenous Women from the Prehispanic Period to the Present*. New York: Oxford University Press, 2005.

Kicza, John E. *Colonial Entrepreneurs: Families and Business in Bourbon Mexico City*. Albuquerque: University of New Mexico Press, 1983.

Klein, Herbert S. *Slavery in the Americas: A Comparative Study of Virginia and Cuba*. Chicago: University of Chicago Press, 1967.

Knight, Alan. "Racism, Revolution and Indigenismo: Mexico, 1910–1940." In *The Idea of Race in Latin America, 1870–1940*, edited by Richard Graham, 71–114. Austin: University of Texas Press, 1990.

Kopytoff, Igor, and Suzanne Meirs. "African Slavery as an Institution of Marginality." In *Slavery in Africa*, edited by Igor Kopytoff and Suzanne Meirs. Madison: University of Wisconsin Press, 1977.

Landers, Jane. *Against the Odds: Free Blacks in the Slave Societies of the Americas*. London and Portland: Frank Cass, 1996.

———. *Black Society in Spanish Florida*. Urbana: University of Illinois Press, 1999.

———. *Slaves, Subjects and Subversives: Blacks in Colonial Latin America*. Albuquerque: University of New Mexico Press, 2006.

Lane, Kris. *Quito 1599: City and Colony in Transition*. Albuquerque: University of New Mexico Press, 2002.

Lewis, Laura A. "Blacks, Black Indians, Afromexicans: The Dynamics of Race, Nation, and Identity in a Mexican Moreno Community (Guerrero)." *American Ethnologist* 27, no. 4 (2000): 898–926.

———. *Hall of Mirrors: Power, Witchcraft, and Caste in Colonial Mexico*. Durham: Duke University Press, 2003.

———. "Home Is Where the Heart Is: North Carolina, Afro-Latino Migration, and Houses on Mexico's Costa Chica." In *The Last Frontier? The Contemporary Configuration of the U.S.-Mexico Border (South Atlantic Quarterly)*, edited by Jane Juffer, 801–29. Durham, NC: Duke University Press, 2006.

———. "Modesty and Modernity: Photography, Blackness and Representation on the Costa Chica (Guerrero)." *Identities: Global Studies in Culture and Power* 11, no. 4 (October–December 2004): 471–99.

———. "Of Ships and Saints: History, Memory and Place in the Making of Moreno Mexican Identity." *Cultural Anthropology* 16, no. 1 (February 2001): 62–82.

Lockhart, James. *The Nahuas After the Conquest: A Social and Cultural History of the Indians of Central Mexico, Sixteenth Through Eighteenth Centuries*. Stanford: Stanford University Press, 1993.

———. "Views of Corporate Self and History in Some Valley of Mexico Towns: Late Seventeenth and Eighteenth Centuries." In *The Inca and Aztec States, 1400–1800*, edited by George Collier et al. New York: Academic Press, 1982.

Love, Edgar F. "Legal Restrictions on Afro-Indian Relations in Colonial Mexico." *The Journal of Negro History* 4, no. 2 (1970): 131–39.

———. "Marriage Patterns of Persons of Africans Descent in a Colonial Mexico City Parish." *Hispanic American Historical Review* LI, no. 1 (1971): 79–91.

———. "Negro Resistance to Spanish Rule in Colonial Mexico." *The Journal of Negro History* LII, no. 2 (1967): 89–103.

Lovejoy, Paul E. "Background to Rebellion: The Origins of Muslim Slaves in Bahia." *Slavery and Abolition* 15 (1995): 151–80.

Lutz, Christopher, and Matthew Restall. "Wolves and Sheep: Black-Maya Relations in Colonial Guatemala and Yucatan." In *Beyond Black and Red*, edited by Matthew Restall, 185–221. Albuquerque: University of New Mexico Press, 2005.

Mahler, Sarah. *American Dreaming: Immigrant Life on the Margins*. Princeton: Princeton University Press, 1999.

Manarelli, Maria Emma. *Hechiceras, Beatas y Expósitas: Mujeres y poder inquisitorial en Lima*. Lima: Ediciones del Congreso de la República del Perú, 1998.

Mancuso, Lara. *Cofradías mineras: religiosidad popular en México y Brasil, siglo XVIII*. Mexico City: El Colegio de México, 2007.

Manzano, María de los Angeles. *Cuajinicuilapa, Guerrero: Historia Oral (1900–1940)*. Mexico City: Ediciones Artesa, 1991.

Marín Bosch, Miguel. *Puebla neocolonial, 1777–1831. Casta, ocupación y matrimonio en la segunda ciudad de Nueva España*. Zapopan, Jalisco: El Colegio de Jalisco, 1999.

Márquez Morfín, Lourdes. "La desigualdad ante la muerte: Epidemias, población y sociedad en la ciudad de México (1800–1850)." Ph.D. diss., El Colegio de México, 1991.

Martin, Cheryl English. *Rural Society in Colonial Morelos*. Albuquerque: University of New Mexico Press, 1985.

Martínez, María Elena. "The Black Blood of New Spain: Limpieza de Sangre, Racial Violence, and Gendered Power in Early Colonial Mexico." *William and Mary Quarterly*, Third Series 61, no. 3 (2004): 479–521.

———. *Genealogical Fictions: Limpieza de Sangre, Religion, and Gender in Colonial Mexico*. Stanford: Stanford University Press, 2008.

———. "The Spanish Concept of Limpieza de Sangre and the Emergence of the 'Race/Caste' System in the viceroyalty of New Spain." Ph.D. diss., University of Chicago, 2002.

McClain, Paul D., Niambi V. Carter, Victoria M. DeFrancesco Soto, Monique L. Lyle, Jeffrey D. Grynaviski, Shayla C. Nunnally, Thomas J. Scotto, J. Alan Kendrick, Gerald F. Lackey, and Kendra Davenport Cotton. "Racial Distancing in a Southern City: Latino Immigrants' Views of Black Americans." *The Journal of Politics* 68, no. 3 (2006): 571–85.

McDowell, John. *Violence and Poetry: The Ballad Tradition of Mexico's Costa Chica*. Urbana: University of Illinois Press, 2000.

Menard, Russell R., and Stuart B. Schwartz. "Why African Slavery? Labor Force Transitions in Brazil, Mexico, and the Carolina Lowcountry." In *Slavery in the Americas*, edited by Wolfgang Binder, 89–114. Würzburg, Germany: Königshausen and Neumann, 1993.

Meza Herrera, Malinali. *Presentación. Jamás fandango al cielo: narrativa afromestiza*. Mexico City: Dirección general de culturas populares, 1993.

Millares Carlo, Agustín, and J. Ignacio Mantecón, eds. *Índice y extractos de los protocolos del Archivo de Notarías de México, D.F.*. 2 vols. Mexico City: El Colegio de México, 1945–1946.

Miño Grijalva, Manuel. "Estructura social y ocupación de la población en la ciudad de México, 1790." In *La población de la ciudad de México en 1790: Estructura social, alimentación y vivienda*, edited by Manuel Miño Grijalva and Sonia Pérez Toledo, 129–71. Mexico City: UAMI, 2004.

———. *La manufactura colonial. La constitución técnica del obraje*. Mexico City: El Colegio de Mexico, 1993.

———. "La población de la ciudad de México en 1790. Variables económicas y demográficas de una controversia." In *La población de la ciudad de México en 1790: Estructura social, alimentación y vivienda*, edited by Manuel Miño Grijalva and Sonia Pérez Toledo, 21–74. Mexico City: UAMI, 2004.

Montiel Martínez, Luz María. "Nuestra tercera raíz." *Nuestra Palabra* 2, no. 11 (November 29, 1991).

———, ed. *Presencia africana en Centroamérica*. Mexico City: Consejo Nacional para la Cultura y las Artes, 1993.

———, ed. *Presencia africana en México*. Mexico City: Consejo Nacional para la Cultura y las Artes, 1993.

Montiel Martinez, Luz María, and Juan Carlos Reyes, eds. *Memoria del III Encuentro Nacional de Afromexicanistas*. Colima: Gobierno del Estado de Colima y Consejo Nacional para la Cultura y las Artes, 1993.

Moreno Hernández, Taurino. *Una historia de poder regional*. Amate: Arte, Cultura, Sociedad de Guerrero 5, September 20–October 4, 1996.

Morin, Claude. *Michoacán en la Nueva España del siglo XVIII: Crecimiento y desigualdad en una economía colonial*. Mexico City: Fondo de Cultura Económica, 1979.

Mörner, Magnus. *La corona española y los foraneos en los pueblos de indios de América*. Stockholm: Almquist & Wiksell, 1970.

Motta Sánchez, J. Arturo. "Tras la heteroidentificación. El 'movimiento negro' costachiquense y la selección marbetes étnicos." *Dimensión Antropológica* 13, no. 38 (September/December, 2006): 115–50.

Murphy, Arthur D., Colleen Blanchard, and Jennifer Hill, eds. *Latino Workers in the Contemporary South*. Athens: University of Georgia Press, 2001.

Murray, John E., and Ruth Wallis Herndon. "Markets for Children in Early America: A Political Economy of Pauper Apprenticeship." *Journal of Economic History* 62, no. 2 (June 2002): 356–82.

Naro, Nancy Priscilla. *Blacks, Coloureds and National Identity in 19th-Century Latin America*. London: London Institute of Latin American Studies, University of London, 2003.

National Public Radio. "Blacks, Latinos and the Immigration Debate," March 31, 2006, available at www.npr.org/templates/story/story.php?storyId=5314491.

Naveda Chávez-Hita, Adriana. "Esclavitud negra en la jurisdicción de Córdoba en el siglo XVIII." Tesís de Maestro en Historia, Universidad Veracruzana, Jalapa, 1977.

———. *Esclavos negros en las haciendas azucareras de Córdoba, Veracruz, 1690–1830*. Xalapa: Universidad Veracruzana, Centro de Investigaciones Históricas, 1987.

———, ed. *Pardos, mulatos y libertos, Sexto encuentro de afromexicanistas*. Xalapa: Universidad Veracruzana, 2001.

Ngou-Mve, Nicolás. *El África bantú en la colonización de México (1595–1640)*. Madrid: Consejo Superior de Investigaciones Científicas-Agencia Española de Cooperación Internacional, 1994.

Ochoa Campos, Moisés. *La chilena guerrerense*. Chilpancingo, México: Gobierno del Estado de Guerrero, 1987.

Ortiz, Fernando. *Hampa afrocubana. Los negros brujos (apuntes para un estudio de etnología criminal*. Madrid: Editorial América, 1917.

Palmer, Colin A. *Slaves of the White God: Blacks in Mexico 1570–1650*. Cambridge: Harvard University Press, 1976.

Pavía Guzmán, Edgar. "Era de los Borbón." In *Historia General de Guerrero: El dominio español*, vol. 4, 235–365. Mexico City: INAH, Gobierno del Estado de Guerrero, JGH Editores, 1998.

Peña, Guillermo de la. "Gonzalo Aguirre Beltrán: Historia y Mestizaje." In *Historiadores de Mexico en el Siglo XX*, edited by Enrique Florescano and Ricardo Pérez Montfort, 192–93. Mexico City, Fondo de Cultura Económica, 1995.

Pérez Rosales, Laura. *Minería y sociedad en Taxco*. Mexico City: Universidad Iberoamericana, 1996.

Pérez Toledo, Sonia. *Los hijos del trabajo. Los artesanos de la ciudad de México, 1780–1853*. Mexico City: El Colegio de México, UAMI, 1996.

Pérez Toledo, Sonia, and Herbert S. Klein. *Población y estructura social de la Ciudad de México, 1790–1842*. Mexico City: Universidad Autónoma Metropolitana Unidad Iztapalapa, 2004.

Pineda, Baron. *Shipwrecked Identities: Navigating Race on Nicaragua's Mosquito Coast*. New Brunswick: Rutgers University Press, 2006.

Powell, Philip. *Soldiers, Indians, and Silver*. Berkeley: University of California Press, 1952.

Proctor, Frank "Trey" III. "African Diasporic Ethnicity and Slave Community Formation in Mexico City to 1650." In *Expanding the Diaspora: Africans in Colonial Latin America*, edited by Sherwin Bryant, Rachel O'Toole, and Ben Vinson III. Champaign: University of Illinois Press, forthcoming.

———. "Afro-Mexican Slave Labor in the Obrajes de Paños of New Spain, Seventeenth and Eighteenth Centuries." *The Americas* 60, no. 1 (2003): 33–58.

———. "Slavery, Identity, and Culture: An Afro-Mexican Counterpoint, 1640–1763." Ph.D. diss., Emory University, 2003.

Querol y Ruso, Luís. *Negros y mulatos de Nueva España, historia de su alzamiento de 1612*. Valencia: Imprenta Hijo F. Vives Mora, 1935.

Quezada, Noemi. *Amor y magia amorosa entre los aztecas: supervivencia en el México colonial*. Mexico City: Universidad Nacional Autónoma de México, Instituto de Investigaciones Antropológicas, 1975.

———. *Sexualidad, Amor y Eroticismo. México Prehispánico y México Colonial*. Mexico City: Universidad Nacional Autónoma de México, Plaza y Valdés, 1996.

Rampersad, Arnold. *The Life of Langston Hughes*, Vol I: 1902–1941, *I, Too, Sing America*. 2 vols. New York: Oxford University Press, 1986.

Reis, João José. "Quilombos e revoltas escravas no Brasil." *Revista USP, São Paulo* 28 (1995–96): 14–39.

Restall, Matthew, ed. *Beyond Black and Red: African-Native Relations in Colonial Latin America*. Albuquerque: University of New Mexico Press, 2005.

———. "Black Conquistadors: Armed Africans in Early Spanish America." *The Americas* 57, no. 2 (2000): 167–205.

———. *The Black Middle: Africans, Mayas, and Spaniards in Colonial Yucatan*. Stanford: Stanford University Press, 2009.

———. "Otredad y ambigüedad: las percepciones que los españoles y los mayas tenían de los africanos en el Yucatán colonial." *Signos históricos* II, *núm.* 4 (2000): 30–31.

Riva Palacio, Vicente. *Los treinta y tres negros*. Mexico City: SEP-Conasupo, 1981.

Riva Palacio, Vicente, Manuel Payno, Juan A. Mateos, and Rafael Martínez de la Torre. *El libro rojo*. Mexico City: Editorial Leyenda, 1946.

Rodney, Walter. *How Europe Underdeveloped Africa*. Dar-Es-Salaam: Bogle-L'Ouverture Publications, London and Tanzanian Publishing House, 1973.

Rodríguez Zepeda, Jesús. "Affirmative Action in Mexico." *México: Voices of Mexico* 71, CISAN-UNAM, June 2005: 15–18.

Romberg, Raquel. *Witchcraft and Welfare: Spiritual Capital and the Business of Magic in Modern Puerto Rico*. Austin: University of Texas Press, 2003.

Romero de Solís, José Miguel. *Breve historia de Colima*. Mexico City: Fondo de Cultura Económica & El Colegio de México, 1994.

Ros, Amparo. *La producción cigarrera a finales de la Colonia. La fábrica en México*. Mexico City: INAH, 1984.

Rout, Leslie B. Jr. *The African Experience in Spanish America: 1502 to the Present Day*. Cambridge and New York, Cambridge University Press, 1976.

Ruiz Rodríguez, Carlos. *Sones de artesa de San Nicolás Tolentino, Guerrero*. Ethnomusicology thesis, Universidad Nacional Autónoma de México, Escuela Nacional de Música, Mexico City, 2001.

———. *Versos: música y baile de Artesa de la Costa Chica: San Nicolás, Guerrero y Ciruelo, Oaxaca*. Mexico City: El Colegio de México, Centro de Estudios Lingüísticos y Literarios, Consejo Nacional para la Cultura y las Artes, Seminario de Tradiciones Culturales, 2004.

Sagás, Ernesto. *Race and Politics in the Dominican Republic*. Gainesville: University of Florida Press, 2001.

Sánchez Díaz, Gerardo. *La Costa de Michoacán. Economía y Sociedad en el Siglo XVI*. Morelia: Universidad Michoacana de San Nicolás de Hidalgo, Instituto de Investigaciones Históricas, Morevallado Editores, 2001.

Scardaville, Michael C. "Trabajadores, grupo doméstico y supervivencia durante el periodo colonial tardío en la ciudad de México, o 'la familia pequeña no vive mejor.'" In *La población de la ciudad de México en 1790: Estructura social, alimentación y vivienda*, edited by Manuel Miño Grijalva and Sonia Pérez Toledo, 227–79. Mexico City: UAMI, 2004.

Schuler, Monica. "Akan Slave Rebellions in the British Caribbean." *Savacou* 1, no. 1 (June 1970): 373–86.

———. "Ethnic Slave Rebellions in the Caribbean and the Guianas." *Journal of Social History* 3 (1970): 274–85.

Schwartz, Rosalie. *Across the Rio to Freedom: U.S. Negroes in Mexico*. Southwestern Studies Monograph 44. El Paso: Texas Western Press, 1975.

Schwartz, Stuart B. "Resistance and Accommodation in Eighteenth-century Brazil: The Slaves' View of Slavery." *Hispanic American Historical Review* 57, no. 1 (1977): 69–81.

Seed, Patricia. *To Love, Honor, and Obey in Colonial Mexico: Conflicts over Marriage Choice, 1574–1821*. Stanford: Stanford University Press, 1988.

———. "The Social Dimensions of Race: Mexico City 1753." *Hispanic American Historical Review* LXII, no. 4 (1982): 569–606.

Sheriff, Robin E. *Dreaming Equality: Color, Race, and Racism in Urban Brazil*. New Brunswick: Rutgers University Press, 2001.

Smythe, William Ellsworth. *History of San Diego, 1542–1908, An Account of the Rise and Progress of the Pioneer Settlement on the West Coast*. San Diego: Kessinger Publishing, 2007.

Socolow, Susan M. "Introduction." In *Cities and Society in Colonial Latin America*, edited by Louisa Schell Hoberman and Susan M. Socolow, 1–18. Albuquerque: University of New Mexico Press, 1986.

Starr, Frederick. *In Indian Mexico*. Chicago: Forbes and Company, 1908.

Stepan, Nancy Leys. *"The Hour of Eugenics": Race, Gender and Nation in Latin America*. Ithaca: Cornell University Press, 1991.

Stern, Steve J. *Peru's Indian Peoples and the Challenge of Spanish Conquest: Huamanga to 1640*. 2nd ed. Madison: University of Wisconsin Press, 1993.

———. *The Secret History of Gender: Women, Men, and Power in Late Colonial Mexico*. Chapel Hill: University of North Carolina Press, 1995.

Sweet, James H. *Recreating Africa: Culture, Kinship, and Religion in the African-Portuguese World, 1441–1770*. Chapel Hill: University of North Carolina Press, 2003.

Tannenbaum, Frank. *Slave and Citizen: The Negro in the Americas*. New York: Vintage Books, 1946; reprint, Boston: Beacon Press, 1992.

Taylor, William B. *Drinking, Homicide, and Rebellion in Colonial Mexican Villages*. Stanford: Stanford University Press, 1979.

———. "The Foundation of Nuestra Señora de Guadalupe de los Morenos de Amapa." *The Americas* 26, no. 4 (1970): 439–46.

———. *Magistrates of the Sacred: Priests and Parishioners in Eighteenth-Century Mexico*. Stanford: Stanford University Press, 1996.

Thompson, Angela T. "To Save the Children: Smallpox Inoculation, Vaccination and Public Health in Guanajuato, Mexico, 1797–1840." *The Americas* 29, no. 4 (1993): 431–55.

Thompson, Richard. *Flash of the Spirit*. New York: Random House, 1984.

Thomson, Guy P. C. *Puebla de los Angeles: Industry and Society in a Mexican City, 1700–1850*. Boulder: Westview Press, 1989.

Thornton, John K. *Africa and Africans in the Making of the Atlantic World*. New York: Cambridge University Press, 1992.

———. "African Dimensions of the Stono Rebellion." *American Historical Review* 96, no. 4 (1991): 1101–13.

Tibón, Gutierre. *Pinotepa Nacional. Mixtecos, negros y triques*. 2nd. ed. Mexico: Editorial Posada, 1981[1961].

Toro, Alfonso. "Influencia de la raza negra en la formación del pueblo mexicano." *Ethnos. Revista para la vulgarización de Estudios Antropológicos sobre México y Centro América* 1, no. 8–12 (1920–1921): 215–18.

Torres, Arlene, and Norman E. Whitten. "General Introduction: To Forge the Future in the Fires of the Past: An Interpretive Essay on Racism, Domination, Resistance and Liberation." In *Blackness in Latin America and the Caribbean*, edited by Arlene Torres and Norman E. Whitten, 3–33. Bloomington: Indiana University Press, 1998.

Tutino, John. *From Insurrection to Revolution in Mexico: Social Bases of Agrarian Violence, 1750–1940*. Princeton: Princeton University Press, 1986.

Vainfas, Ronaldo. *Visões da liberdade: uma história das últimas décadas da escravidão na corte*. São Paulo: Companhia das Letras, 1990.

Valdés, Dennis N. "The Decline of Slavery in Mexico." *The Americas* 44, no. 2 (1987): 167–94.

Valdez, Norberto. *Ethnicity, Class and the Indigenous Struggle for Land in Guerrero, Mexico*. New York: Garland Publishing, 1998.

Valdez Aguilar, Rafael. *Sinaola: Negritud y Olvido*. Culiacán: Talleres Gráficos El Diario de Sinaloa, 1993.

Vargas Lugo, Elisa. *Juan Correa. Su vida y su obra*. 4 vols. Mexico City: UNAM, 1985–1994).

Vasconcelos, José. *La raza cósmica: Misión de la raza iberoamericana*. Paris: Agencia mundial de librería, 1924.

Vaughn, Bobby. "Afro-Mexico: Blacks, Indigenas, Politics, and the Greater Diaspora." In *Neither Enemies nor Friends: Latinos, Blacks and Afro-Latinos*, edited by Anani Dzidzienyo and Suzanne Oboler, 117–36. New York: Palgrave, 2005.

———. "Los Negros, los indígenas y la diáspora. Una perspectiva etnográfica de la Costa Chica." In *Afroméxico*, Ben Vinson III and Bobby Vaughn, 75–96. Mexico City: Fondo de Cultura Económica, 2004.

Vaughn Bobby, and Ben Vinson III. "Unfinished Migrations: From the Mexican South to the American South—Impressions on Afro-Mexican Migration to North Carolina." In *Beyond Slavery: The Multilayered Legacy of Africans in Latin America and the Caribbean*, edited by Darién Davis, 223–45. New York: Rowan and Littlefield, 2007.

Velasco Ávila, Cuauhtémoc. "Los trabajadores mineros en la Nueva España, 1750–1810." In *La Clase Obrera en la Historia de México*, edited by Enrique Florescano, Isabel González Sánchez, Jorge González Angulo, Roberto Sandoval Zarauz, Cuauhtémoc Velasco A., and Alejandra Moreno Toscazo, 291–99. Mexico City: Siglo XXI, 1980.

Velázquez, María Elisa. "Amas de leche, cocineras y vendedoras: Mujeres de origen africano, trabajo y cultura en la ciudad de México durante la época colonial." In *Poblaciónes y culturas de origen africano en México*, edited by María Elisa Velázquez and Ethel Correa, 335–56. Mexico City: Instituto Nacional de Antropología e Historia, 2005.

———. "Juntos y revueltos: Oficios, espacios y comunidades domésticas de origen africano en la capital novohispana según el censo de 1753." In *Pautas de convivencia étnica en la América Latina colonial (Indios, negros, mulatos, pardos y esclavos)*, edited by Juan Manuel de la Serna Herrera, 331–46. Mexico City: UNAM, 2005.

———. *Mujeres de origen africano en la capital novohispana, siglos XVII y XVIII* (Mexico City: INAH, Universidad Nacional Autónoma de México, 2006), 161–228.

Velázquez, María Elisa, and Ethel Correa. *Poblaciones y culturas de origen africano en México*. Mexico City: Instituto Nacional de Antropología e Historia, 2005.

Villa-Flores, Javier. "'To Lose One's Soul': Blasphemy and Slavery in New Spain, 1596–1669." *Hispanic American Historical Review* LXXXII, no. 3 (2002): 435–69.

Vincent, Theodore G. *The Legacy of Vicente Guerrero: Mexico First Black Indian President*. Gainesville: University of Florida Press, 2001.

Vinson, Ben III. "Afro-Mexican History: Trends and Directions in Scholarship." *History Compass* 3, LA 156 (September 2005): 1–14.

———. "Bearing Arms for His Majesty: The Free-Colored Militia in Colonial Mexico." Ph.D. diss., Columbia University, 1998.

———. *Bearing Arms for His Majesty: The Free-Colored Militia in Colonial Mexico*. Stanford: Stanford University Press, 2001.

———. *Flight, The Story of Virgil Richardson, A Tuskegee Airman in Mexico*. New York: Palgrave MacMillan, 2004.

———. "How Memín Sparks Race-Relation Talks Between U.S., Mexico." *Centre Daily Times* (State College), July 25, 2005, A6.

———. "La historia del estudio de los negros en México." In *Afroméxico: El pulso de la población negra en México: Una historia recordada, olvidada y vuelta a recordar*, Ben Vinson III and Bobby Vaughn, translated by Clara García Ayluardo, 19–73. Mexico City: Centro de Investigación y Docencia Económicas and Fondo de Cultura Económica, 2004.

———. "The Racial Profile of a Rural Mexican Province in the 'Costa Chica': Igualapa in 1791." *The Americas* 57, no. 2 (October 2000): 269–82.

———. "'West Side Story' Free-Black Labor in the Mexican Pacific During the Late Colonial Period as Seen Through the Revillagigedo Census." *Journal of Colonialism and Colonial History* 10, no. 3 (2009), available at http://muse.jhu.edu/journals/journal_of_colonialism_and_colonial_history.

Vinson, Ben III, and Stewart R. King. "Introducing the 'New' African Diasporic Military History in Latin America." *Journal of Colonialism and Colonial History* 5, no. 2, Special Issue (2004).

Viqueira Albán, Juan Pedro. *¿Relajados o reprimidos? Diversiones públicas y vida social en la ciudad de México durante el Siglo de las Luces*. Mexico City: Fondo de Cultura Económica, 1987.

von Germeten, Nicole. *Black Blood Brothers: Confraternities and Social Mobility for Afro-Mexicans*. Gainesville: University Press of Florida, 2006.

Von Mentz, Brígida. "Esclavitud en centros mineros y azucareros novohispanos. Algunas propuestas para el estudio de la multietnicidad en el centro de México." In *Poblaciones y culturas de origen africano en México*, edited by María

Elisa Velásquez and Ethel Correa, 259–67. Mexico City: Instituto Nacional de Antropología e Historia, 2005.

———. *Pueblos de indios, mulatos y mestizos, 1770–1870: Los campesinos y las transformaciones protoindustriales en el poniente de Morelos*. Mexico City: Centro de Investigaciones y Estudios Superiores en Antropología Social, 1988.

———. *Trabajo, sujeción y libertad en el centro de la Nueva España. Esclavos, aprendices, campesinos y operarios manufactureros, siglos XVI a XVIII*. Mexico City: CIESAS, 1999.

Wade, Peter. "Afro-Latin Studies: Reflections on the Field." *Latin American and Caribbean Ethnic Studies* 1, no. 1 (April 2006): 105–24.

———. *Race and ethnicity in Latin America*. London; Chicago: Pluto Press, 1997.

Wallerstein, Immanuel. "The Construction of Peoplehood: Racism, Nationalism, Ethnicity." In *The Essentials of Wallerstein*. New York: The New Press, 2000.

Warren, J. Benedict. *The Conquest of Michoacán: The Spanish Domination of the Tarascan Kingdom in Western Mexico, 1521–1530*. Norman: University of Oklahoma Press, 1985.

Weiss, Thomas. "U.S. Labor Force Estimates and Economic Growth." In *American Economic Growth and Standards of Living before the Civil War*, edited by Robert E. Gallman and John Joseph Wallis, 19–78. Chicago: University of Chicago Press, 1992.

Whitten, Norman E., and Rachel Corr. "Imagery of 'Blackness' in Indigenous Myth, Discourse, and Ritual." In *Representations of Blackness and the Performance of Identities*, edited by Jean Muteba Rahier, 213–33. Westport, CT: Bergin & Garvey, 1999.

Widmer, Rolf. *Conquista y despertar de las costas de la Mar del Sur (1521–1684)*. Mexico City: Consejo Nacional para la Cultura y las Artes, 1990.

Williams, Eric. *Capitalism and Slavery*. Chapel Hill: University of North Carolina Press, 1944.

Winfield Capitaine, Fernando. "Población rural en Córdoba, 1788." *La Palabra y el Hombre* 30, no. 2 (1979): 64–72.

Wisch, Barbara. "The Passion of Christ in the Art, Theater and Penitential Rituals of the Roman Confraternity of the Gonfalone." In *Crossing the Boundaries: Christian Piety and the Arts in Italian Medieval and Renaissance Confraternities*, edited by Konrad Eisenbichler, 239–43. Kalamazoo: Medieval Institute Publications, Western Michigan University, 1991.

Wright, Winthrop R. *Café con Leche: Race, Class, and National Image in Venezuela*. Austin: University of Texas Press, 1990.

Wu, Celia. "The Population of the City of Querétaro in 1791." *Journal of Latin American Studies* 16, no. 2 (1984): 277–307.

Zavala, Silvio. *Estudios Indianos*. México: Colegio de México, 1948.

Zeleza, Paul T. "Rewriting the African Diaspora: Beyond the Black Atlantic." *African Affairs* 104, no. 414 (2005): 35–68.

Contributors

JOAN C. BRISTOL is associate professor of history at George Mason University. She is the author of *Christians, Blasphemers, and Witches: Afro-Mexican Ritual Practice in the Seventeenth Century* (2007). Her articles appear in the *Boletín del Archivo General de la Nación* (Mexico) and the *Journal of Colonialism and Colonial History*, as well as in several edited volumes on Africans in Latin America and gender and religion in the Atlantic World. She is currently working on a project on the intersection of ideas about gender and race in colonial Spanish America.

PATRICK J. CARROLL is professor of history at Texas A&M University, Corpus Christi. He is a specialist on race and slavery in colonial Mexico, especially in the area of Veracruz. He is the author of *Blacks in Colonial Veracruz: Race, Ethnicity and Regional Development* (1991, 2001) and *Felix Longoria's Wake: Bereavement, Racism, and the Rise of Mexican American Activism* (2003). He has published widely on the topic of Afro-Mexico, with articles appearing in venues such as *Historia Mexicana* and *Signos Históricos*.

ANDREW B. FISHER is assistant professor of history at Carleton College. He has published on topics related to indigenous collective identity and the interethnic relations among the rural poor in New Spain. He is the co-editor of *Imperial Subjects: Race and Identity in Colonial Latin America* (2009) and is currently working on a book length study of the tierra caliente of Guerrero, Mexico, which spans the late fifteenth through early nineteenth centuries.

NICOLE VON GERMETEN is assistant professor of history at Oregon State University. She is the author of *Black Blood Brothers: Confraternities and Social Mobility for Afromexicans* (2006) and an annotated translation of Alonso de Sandoval's 1627 *De Instauranda Aethiopum Salute* (2008). Her current project explores race, gender, and identity in colonial Cartagena de Indias.

LAURA A. LEWIS is professor of anthropology and coordinator of Latin American Studies at James Madison University. She is the author of the award winning *Hall of Mirrors: Power, Witchcraft and Caste in Colonial Mexico* (2003). She has held fellowships from the National Endowment of the Humanities, the Smithsonian Institution, and the John Simon Guggenheim Memorial Foundation. She is currently finishing an ethnography based on many years of fieldwork in San Nicolás, Guerrero, and Winston-Salem, North Carolina.

JEAN-PHILIBERT MOBWA MOBWA N'DJOLI was born in the Democratic Republic of Congo. He is a Mexican citizen and has lived in Mexico since 1992. He has an MA in Human Rights, specializing in discrimination. His academic training also includes formal work in philosophy and the study of liberation theology. Since 2004, he has worked for Mexico's National Anti-Discrimination Council (CONAPRED). He is a specialist on issues of discrimination against Afro-Mexicans and is the author of *Pueblos Afromexicans y la no discriminación: Retos de identidad, promoción, protección y defensa de sus derechos humanos* (forthcoming).

FRANK "TREY" PROCTOR III is assistant professor of history at Denison University. He is the author of *"Damned Notions of Liberty": Slavery, Culture, and Power in Colonial Mexico, 1640–1769* (forthcoming). His articles include "Gender Manumission of Slaves in New Spain," in the *Hispanic American Historical Review* (2006), and "Afro-Mexican Slave Labor in the Obrajes de Paños of New Spain," published in *The Americas* (2003).

MATTHEW RESTALL is Edwin Erle Sparks Professor of Latin American History at Penn State University. His areas of specialization are colonial Yucatan and Mexico, Maya History, the Spanish Conquest, and Africans in Spanish America. He is editor of Penn State Press's *Latin American Originals* series and co-editor of *Ethnohistory* journal. Since 1995 he has published some forty articles and essays and a dozen books, including *The Maya World* (1997), *Maya Conquistador* (1998), and *Seven Myths of the Spanish Conquest* (2003). His most recent books are an edited volume entitled *Beyond Black and Red* (2005), two coauthored volumes—*Mesoamerican Voices* (2005) and *Invading Guatemala* (2007)—and a history of Afro-Yucatecans, *The Black Middle* (2009).

ALVA MOORE STEVENSON is a native of Los Angeles and received a BA in English and an MA in Afro-American Studies (with a concentration in Latin American Studies) at the University of California, Los Angeles. Her research interests are Afro-Latino history and culture—particularly Afro-Mexicans—and African Americans and African-descended peoples globally. Her thesis, "Afro-Mexican Racial and Ethnic Self-Identity: Three Generations of the Thornton Family in Nogales, Arizona," focused on the racial self-identity of biracial African American/Mexicans. She is program representative, series coordinator and interviewer at the UCLA Center for Oral History Research. The center documents Los Angeles's history, culture, and development with extensive documentation on African Americans.

BOBBY VAUGHN is associate professor of anthropology and director of the Office for Institutional Diversity at Notre Dame de Namur University in Belmont, CA. He is an expert in the history and culture of Mexicans of African descent and has lived more than four years in Mexico over the past fifteen years. His publications include the co-authored book *Afroméxico: El pulso de la población negra en México* (2004) and numerous scholarly articles, including "Afro-Mexico: Blacks, Indígenas, Politics, and the Greater Diaspora."

BEN VINSON III is professor of history and director of the Center for Africana Studies at Johns Hopkins University. He is a specialist on issues of race in colonial Mexico and is the author of *Bearing Arms for His Majesty: The Free-Colored Militia in Colonial Mexico* (2001) and *Flight: The Story of Virgil Richardson, A Tuskegee Airman in Mexico* (2004). His is the co-author of *Afroméxico: El pulso de la población negra en México* (2004) and *African Slavery in Latin America and the Caribbean,* 2nd edition (2007). In addition, he has published numerous articles, book chapters, and special journal editions. His current research is on the colonial Mexican caste system.

Index

The letters *n* or *nn* indicate a note or notes on the page cited. The following number is the note number. The letter *t* indicates a table. A page number in italic type indicates a figure or map on that page.

affirmative action, 227–29
African Diaspora, 186, 209, 210; Afro-Mexican historiography and, 6; Association for the Study of the Worldwide African Diaspora (ASWAD) and, 13; Costa Chica and, 216; literature on, 47n32, 66n4
Afromestizo(s), 90n10, 186, 214–15; museum in Cuajinicuilapa and, 186, 217; San Nicoladenses and, 186. *See also* mestizo(s)
Afro-Mexican historiography: 1940s to 1960s and, 5–7; African Diaspora and, 6, 47n32, 66n4; agency and, 7; case studies and, 6, 16n15; caste versus class and, 5, 6, 8, 16n13; comparative slavery school and, 6; current work and, 8; discourse analysis and, 7; free-black populations and, 8, 18nn21–23; interdisciplinary studies and, 8, 18n20; internationalization and, 5–7, 16n15; postrevolutionary period and, 4–6, 15n6, 15n10; prerevolutionary period and, 3–4, 15n5; religion and magic and, 8, 18n24; rural Afro-Mexicans and, 219n7; social Darwinism and, 4, 15n6; three-track research system and, 6–7
Afro-Mexicans, 183; affirmative action and, 227–29; Catholic Church and, 139; colonial period and, 3, 14n3; confraternities and, 139–52; eighteenth-century population of, 98–99, 101, 126n11; First National Survey on Discrimination and, 224; importance of blackness and, 210–11; inequality and, 99–100;

invisibility of, 224–25; legalized racism and, 138; militias and, 139; as minority ethnic group, 224–25; National Census of Population and, 228; as plebeian class, 3, 15n4; racial labels, self-description and, 139, 184, 186–88; recognition of ethnic groups and, 228; rejection of difference and, 225; slavery and, 99–100; slogan of unity and, 211–12; social inequality in Mexico and, 225–26; Spaniards and, 138; success of, 99–100; in the United States, 221–23

Agrarian Reform, 184, 196

agrarian stress, racism and, 58–61, 72–73

Aguirre Beltrán, Gonzalo, 4–5, 6–7, 30, 75, 90n10, 126n11, 177n16, 226; *La población negra de México*, 5–6

Aguirre Rivero, Ángel Heladio, 229

Álvarez, Catalina, 156, 158

Amapa. *See* Nuestra Señora de Guadalupe de los Negros de Amapa

Amarillas, Marquis de, 79

Amith, Jonathan, 184

Ana, doña, 183

Andrés de Vargas, Francisco, 82

Andrews, George Reid, 187

Arguello, Lucas de, 157–58, 175n3

Association for the Study of the Worldwide African Diaspora (ASWAD), 13n2

Atlantic History Seminar, Harvard, 13n2

Audiencia: Mexico City slave rebellion and, 29; Santa Bárbara de Calderón and, 38–40, 49n50. *See also* Inquisition

Axochitlan, 61–62

Azevedo, Leberina, 97

Bajío region (Guanajuato and Querétaro): Indian population of, 135n77; mining and textiles in, 120–21; mulattos in, 119–20, 135n75; opportunities for free coloreds in, 121–22; population and development of, 119–20, 134n74

balché, 157, 159, 175n2; ritual use of, 159, 162t, 163

Baroque Catholicism, 140, 150–51, 152. *See also* Catholic Church

Basauri, Carlos, 5

Bautista, Juan, 142

Bazán, Pedro, 55

Behar, Ruth, 178n38

Benavides, Alonso de, 24–25

Bennett, Herman, 41, 94n57

black-indigenous relations, 88–89; African slave culture and, 73–74; endogamus marriages and, 95n68; ethnic segregation and, 218n1; explicit historical record and, 74–75, 90n10; implicit historical record and, 75–78; imposition of modern markers and, 90n10; identification as natives and, 81; indigenismo and, 230; intermarriage and, 80; legal actions and, 77–79; love-magic and, 11; Mayans and, 92n25; otherness concept and, 78–81; pardo naturales and, 81–83, 94n62; race versus ethnicity and, 74–75; in San Nicolás, 188; sistema de castas and, 30–31, 83; Spanish colonial system and, 81–84, 86–87; Spanish record-keeping and, 79–81

black naturales, 69n24, 86–87; definitions of, 80; indigenous communities and, 74–75, 77, 80–83, 88–89; Spanish enumeration and, 76, 79, 83, 86–87

blacks: autonomous communities and, 62, 73; bellicosity and, 66, 71n48; in Córdoba, 76–77; definitions of, 66n3; diaspora and, 186, 209, 210; ethnicity and, 230; in indigenous communities, 55–56, 57–64, 66n4, 67n5, 68n14, 73; legal testimony and, 58; magic and, 63–64; as middle men, 11; migration to tierra caliente and, 54–55, 56; native populations and, 9–10, 58–59; occupational status and, 10–11; religious organizations and, 58, 141–43; Spanish colonial system and, 81–84, 86–87, 143. *See also* African Diaspora; identity; palenques

Bonilla, Francisco de, 172–73, 174

Borah, Woodrow, 78–81, 83–84

Bosch, Miguel Marín, 133n62

Bowser, Frederick, 13n2

bozal(es), 74, 87, 147. *See also* negro(s)

Bristol, Joan, 11

Burgos, Juan de, 55

Calles, Elias Plutarco, 221

Carranza, José, 51–52

Carrillo, Manuel, 24

Carroll, Patrick, 9–10, 52

Casa, Juan de, 166–67

Casanova, María de, 155–58, 173–74

Casanova-Maldonado love-magic case, 155–58, 173, 175n3

casta(s), 72, 74–81, 93n47, 159; employment patterns and, 110; magic and, 70n38, 160–61, 169, 173; San Miguel Totolapan and, 60; slavery and, 41. *See also* blacks; sistema de castas

castizo(s), 61, 90n10, 133n61; employment patterns and, 116, 133n62. *See also* mestizo(s)

Castro y Romero, Manuel de, 82–83

Catholic Church: Baroque Catholicism and, 141, 150–51, 152; flagellation and, 141–42; religious piety and, *151*

Cerro de la Esperanza, 211–12

Chabarria, Miguel de, 79

Chimalpahín, 27

Chiquita, Ana María, 37

Coatepeque, 82

Codex Telleriano-Remensis, 142

Cofradía de Nuestra Señora de la Merced, 28

comadres, 183, 201n2

Commission for the Development of Indigenous People (CDI), 228–29

confraternities, 11; Afro-Mexicans and, 139–52; in Bajío, 145–46; blacks and, 58; constitutions of, 143–44; financial arrangements and, 149–50; flagellation and, 141–42; king and queen and, 28, 46n24; low social status, piety and,

147–48; membership patterns and, 149–50; mulatos and, 136–37, 143, 144–45, 146–47; non-Spanish populations and, 140; organization of, 139–40; in Pinzándaro, 149, 150; racial divisions and, 140–41; specific race labels and, 148–49; in Valladolid, 147

Cook, Sherburne, 83–84

Córdoba: blacks in, 76–77; founding of, 26–27

Costa Chica/Costeños, 12, 103, 183–84; Afro-Mexican cultural practices and, 219n8; Afro-Mexican culture discourse and, 217–18; Black Mexicans and, 210; blackness and, 216–17; boundaries and, 210, 218n1; Meetings of Black Villages and, 187; mother and child in, 213; teenager in, 216; woman and child in, 217

Cruz, Victoriano de la, 80

Curtin, Phillip, 6; *Slave Trade*, 6

Danza de los Diablos, 218, 219n8

Danza del Toro de Petate, 219n8

Delgada, Juana, 160, 163

Diáz Cano, Juan, 35

Diego (Mexico City slave), 28

Domingo, don, 183, 186, 208n41

Duarte, Mathias Nicolás, 136–37

Dzidzienyo, Anani, 203

El libro rojo (Riva Palacio), 4

encomenderos, 54–55

Encuentros de Pueblos Negros, 217

Esther, Lydia, 221–22

ethnicity, 90n10; acquisition of, 79–80; blacks, lack of and, 230; versus race and caste, 10, 74–75, 85; United States and, 197

Fernández de Córdoba, Marqués de Guadalacar, Rodrigo, 26–27

Fisher, Andrew, 9–10, 72–73

Fox, Vicente, 7, 17n16

free-colored labor: agriculture and, 101, 126n13; artisans and, 106; big cities and, 107–22; conclusions concerning, 123–24; definition of, 124n5; Guanajuato and, 105; in Mexico City, 108–32; mining and, 105, 127n20; muleteers and, 105–6, 128n23; in the Pacific basin, 127n16; in Puebla, 113–19; sirvientes and operarios and, 103, 105, 127n19; textiles, dress, leatherworking, shoemaking and, 106; transport and service industries and, 105–6; women and, 106–7, 128n25; workforce composition, 101, 102t; workforce mobility and, 101, 103, 127n16

Freyre, Gilberto, 6

Gage, Thomas, 82

Gamio, Manuel, 5

Garcia, Andrés, 29

Garrido, Juan, 54, 57, 222–23

Germeten, Nicole von, 11

González, Ascencio, 35

González de Herrera, Pedro, 25–26, 46n18

Guanajuato, 105. *See also* Bajío region (Guanajuato and Querétaro)

Guelaguetza cultural festival, 219n8
Guerrero, 65–66, 71n48
Gutiérrez Avila, Miguel Angel, 186
Guzmán, José de, 80

Hernández, Marco Polo, 203n13
Herskovits, Melville, 5
Horta Barroso, Antonio de, 155, 178n37
Hughes, James, 223

identity, 1–3; blacks and, 7, 84–85, 88–89, 219n6, 227; confraternities and militias and, 11, 139; Costa Chica/Costeños and, 11–12; culture and ethnicity and, 74–75, 80; definitions of, 220; economic class and, 183; local formation of, 187–90, 206n35; Lockhart on, 84; love-magic and, 173; México Negro movement and, 214–15; modern markers of, 91; mulatos and, 140–50, 152; national unity and, 211; politics and, 91, 219n6; race and, 51–52, 81, 83; sistema de castas and, 86; slaves and, 30–31; Spanish language and, 222. *See also* black-indigenous relations; *specific groups and regions*
indio(s), definitions and usage, 87, 90n10
Inquisition, 64–65; Casanova-Maldonado love-magic case and, 155–58; love-magic and, 160–61, 168, 171, 174, 178n37, 179n55. *See also* Audiencia

Isla, Leonor de, *165*, 171–72
Izazaga, Juan de, 77–78

Jalapa: endogamus marriages in, 95n68; racial categories in, 75–76, 85–86
Jatlazingo, 75
Jemmot, Glyn, 218n3
Joiner, Adeline, 221
Josefa, María, 80

Klein, Herbert S., 130n33
Kopytoff, Igor, 73

labor: black stereotypes and legal restraints and, 97; black unemployment and, 96–97; late eighteenth century and, 98. *See also* free-colored labor; *specific cities*
ladino(s), 74–75, 78–80, 86, 87, 88–89, 90n10
La población negra de México (Aguirre Beltrán), 5–6
Latin America, race in: census categories and, 75; questions concerning, 1–2; study of, 2–3, 12n2
Latin American Studies Association (LASA), 13n2
Latorre, German, 5
Laurencio, Juan, 25
levantamiento de sombra, 219n8
Lewis, Laura A., 11–12, 176n13
Lockhart, James, 84, 88
Los trienta y tres negros (Riva Palacio), 4
love-magic: Afro-Mexicans as intermediaries and, 161, 176n13; black and mulatto social integration and, 174–75; chocolate and, *164*;

fees and, 161, 177n14; goals of, 167–68; Inquisition and, 155–58, 160–61, 168, 171, 174, 178n37, 179n55; interethnicity and, 159–61, 170–71; inversion of existing hierarchy and, 168–71; jonquil and, 173; ligature and, 159; Marta and, 159, 176n8; origins of, 159; peyote and, 163, 177n16; physical materials and, 161–63, 167; prosecution, social status and, 160–61; rituals of, 163, 166–67, 177n23; salamanders and, 165, 173; two Franciscos and, 169–70. *See also* Casanova-Maldonado love-magic case

Luna, Pedro de, 36–37

Macute, 34

Maldonado, Manuel, 156, 160

Maldonado, María, 155–58, 161

Manuel, Fernando, 34, 37–38, 49n50

Marañon, Juan, 97

Mariche, Juana, 211–12

maroon communities, 184, 201n5

marriage, Spanish colonial system and, 87. *See also under specific communities*

Martínez, María Elena, 27

Martínez Montiel, Luz Maria, 186

Matiza, Francisco de la, 26, 30

Mayans, blacks and, 92n25

Medina, Vicente, 97

Meetings of Black Villages, 187, 204nn16–17

Melchor, Pedro, 83

Memín Penguin, 7, 17n17, 203n13

Mérida, 11, 155–58; blacks and mulattoes in, 174. *See also* Casanova-Maldonado love-magic case

Mesa, Nicolas de, 163

mestizo(s), 4, 70n36, 72, 86, 90n10, 187, 218n2; blackness and, 210, 230; castizos and, 133n61; confraternities and, 140; in Costa Chica, 218; mulattos and, 120; Nahuas and, 72, 78; national unity slogan and, 211

Mexico, cities and provinces of, *104*

Mexico City: agregados and, 113, 131n45; artisan trades and, 111–12, 130n41; black population of, 110; cuarteles analyzed and, 108–10, 130n33; household economies and, 113, 131nn43–44; mulatto workers and, 111–12; opportunities for free coloreds in, 111, 131n42; Plaza Major, 22; population and workforce in, 30, 108, *112*, 129n31; Puebla and, 114; slave rebellion of 1611–12 in, 21–22, 27–31, 46n22; tobacco and, 110, 130n37; women workers and, 110–11, 112–13

México Negro movement, 12, 213–15, 218n3, 226, 228, 229; African Americans and, 215–16

Mobwa Mobwa N'djoli, Jean Philibert, 12

Montejo, Michaela, 156, 158, 159

Montserrate, 163

Moreno de Monroy, Luís, 28

moreno(s), 187–88, 192; 201n3, 195; defined, 99, 124n5; Indians and, 195; Margarita and Maximino as,

192–93; population of, 125n9; in San Nicolás, 187–88, 193; in the United States, 190, 194

morisco(s): agregados and, 131n45; definitions and usage, 69n25, 111–12, 113, 124n5, 131n45

Moxica, Miguel, 58

mulato(s): definitions and usage, 56, 137; versus negros bozales esclavos, 147; occupations and, 138; race and class and, 150, 152; relations with Spanish and, 142–43, 152

Muñoz, Juan, 167

Nahua(s): Costa Chica and, 183–84; cultural identity and, 78–81; as indios, 87; language and, 184, 201n3; love-magic and, 158, 163, 174; Spanish colonial systems and, 82–83; Zumpango and, 78

naming patterns, Spanish colonial system and, 87–88

Ñanga, Gaspar, 27

National Commission for the Development of the Indigenous People, 229

National Council for Culture and the Arts (CONACULTA), 226

National Council to Prevent Discrimination (CONAPRED), 228–29

Naveda, Adriana, 27

negro(s), 58, 60, 86, 137, 147, 184, 214–15. See also blacks; bozal(es)

"New Directions in North American Scholarship on Afro-Mexico" (Pennsylvania State University), 8–9

New Spain, *xiv*, 138; free-colored labor in, 101–7; moreno population of, 99, 125n9; slavery in, 23–24, 29–31

Nogales, Arizona, 221–22

Nuestra Señora de Guadalupe de los Negros de Amapa, 22; founding of, 31–34, 47n34; plan of, 32; slavery and, 24

Nuestra Tercera Raíz, 226–29

Ortega, Ana de, 166

Ortiz, Fernando, 6

otherness concept, 78–81

Pacheco, Juana, 157

Palacios, Lucas, 61

Palacios de Mandinga, 31–32

palenques: control of slave population and, 41–43; Costa Chica and, 184; Mandinga, 31–34; Nuestra Señora de Guadalupe de los Negros de Amapa, 22, 32; San Lorenzo de los Negros, 22, 24–27. See also Yanga/Yanguicos

Palmer, Colin, 65, 81

Pánuco, 78

pardo(s): definitions and usage, 75, 94n62, 115, 124n5, 132n54, 137, 139, 147; occupations and, 117, 133n62

Parra, Isabel de la, 172, 179n51

Paugh, Amy, 206n33

Pérez, Benito, 96–97

Pérez, José, 33

Pérez, Pedro, 72

Pérez de Ribas, Andrés, 26
Pérez de Ruíz, Tráncito, 221
phenotypes. *See* sistema de castas; specific phenotypes
Píco, Pío, 223
Pinzándaro, 149, 150
Poliutla, 60
Proctor, Frank, 9
Puc, Catalina, 166
Puebla, 131n45; artisans and, 116; censuses of, 132n53; cobblers in, 119; cocheros in, 117; free-colored labor in, 115–19, 133n56; Mexico City and, 114; middle-tier free-colored workforce in, 118; panaderos in, 117–18; population and development of, 113–14; tailors in, 118–19; tanners in, 115, 133n58; textile and clothing industry in, 116–17, 133n62; tobacco and, 117
Pungarabato, 55, 58

Restall, Matthew, 8, 11, 92n25, 128n23
Revillagigedo census, 98–99, 126n12, 129n31
Reyes, Melchora de los, 160
Riva Palacio, Vicente, 3–4, 15n5; *El libro rojo*, 4; *Los trienta y tres negros*, 4
Rivera, Gaspar Antonio, 76
Rodríguez, Lucio Antonio, 97
Rodríguez Vásquez, Joseph, 79
Rojas, Catalina Antonia de, 160, 166, 179n55
Romero, Antonio, 72–73
Rosales, José, 51–52
Rose of Lima, Saint, 141

Ruano, Pedro, 145–46
Ruíz, Joana, 172–74
Ruiz de Alarcón, Hernando, 63
Ruiz de Castañeda, Manuel, 35

Salazar, Pascual, 63–64, 70n36
Salgado, Joseph Agustín, 59
Salvatierra, town of, 145–46
San Agustín Coahuayutla, 77
San Lorenzo de los Negros, 22; foundation of, 24–27
San Miguel Totolapan, 59–60
San Nicolás/Nicoladenses, 183–208; African Americans and, 194, 206n34, 207n37, 207n39; Afro-Mexican label and, 184, 186; black-indigenous relations and, 188, 195; blackness and, 186–87, 194–95, 203n15; central plaza of, *185*; demographics of, 184; endogamy and, 205n25; La América (Los Apaches), 188, *189*; la cultura and, 198, 208n43; Margarita and Maximino and, 190–95; postmarital residence patterns and, 206n26; redondo in, 186, *211*, 219n8; Saint Nicholas of Tolentino and, 188–89; sones de artesa and, 186; United States and, 190–95, 205nn24–25; whites and, 195–200, 206n28; Winston-Salem and, 184, *185*, 190, *191*, 205n24
San Pablo, 78
San Pedro Churumuco, 77
Santa Bárbara de Calderón: founding of, 35; free black population of, 48n46; great escape from, 35–40; labor conditions in, 36–37; slave population of, 48n44; sugar and, 35

Santa María de la Ascunción de
   Theloloapán, 79
San Thiago de Totutla, 76
Santiago, Pascual de, 60
Santiago Theopantla, 81
Saucedo, Nicolás, 63–64
Simón de Haro, Juan José, 64–65
sistema de castas, 30–31, 83; black
   agency and, 94n57; black identity
   dilemma and, 84–85; cultural
   subcategories and, 86–87;
   Ibero-Catholic church and, 86;
   indigenous population decline and,
   83; indigenous social order and,
   86–88; irrational beings (gente sin
   razón) and, 86–87; in New Spain,
   85; race and, 85; rational beings
   (gente de razón) and, 86–87, 138;
   Spanish phenotypes and, 85–86
Slave and Citizen (Tannenbaum), 6
slavery, 97–98; autonomy and, 100,
   125n10; colonial administration
   and, 41–42, 49n55; decline of,
   rebellions and, 40–41; eighteenth
   century and, 99–100; history
   and legacy of, 226; mining and,
   127–28nn20–21; in New Spain,
   23–24; rebellions, eighteenth
   century, 21–22, 31–34; rebellions,
   seventeenth century, 21, 24–31;
   resistance and rebellions and,
   42–44; Spanish colonial system
   and, 9; sugar production and,
   23, 31; in tierra caliente, 54–55;
   woolen textiles and, 23
Slave Trade (Curtin), 6
social systems, Spanish versus
   indigenous: cultural categories
   and, 86–87, 88; marriage and, 87;
   naming patterns, 87–88

sones de artesa, 186–87, 196, 219n8
Stevenson, Alva Moore, 12
Suarez, Pablo, 82

Tadeo, José, 33
Tannenbaum, Frank, 6; *Slave and
   Citizen*, 6, 41
Taylor, William, 74–75
Tenango del Valle, 80
Tepecoacuilco, 79–80; tributary census
   of, 79–80
Third Root Project, 186
Thomson, Guy P. C., 133n62
Thornton, Daniel, 221
Thornton, James, 220–21
Thornton, John, 73
tierra caliente, 10; agrarian stress and,
   58–61; black population in, 56–57;
   black settlement in, 54–57, 58–59;
   definition of, 52–53; encomenderos
   and, 54–55; free-black survival
   strategies and, 57–64, 65; livestock
   ranches in, 56; popular culture in,
   64–65; racism in, 53–54, 59–60,
   61–62, 66; slavery in, 54–55,
   69n19; social conditions in, 53–54,
   65; Spanish colonial system and, 54
Tlalchiapa, 51–52
Tonameca village, 103
Toro, Alfonso, 4–5
Tracking the Slave Route Project,
   UNESCO, 13n2

Valladolid, 136–38
Vázquez de Espinosa, Antonio, 30
Velasco, Luis de, 24–25, 46n22

Villalva, Juan de, 75–78
Vinson, Ben, III, 10–11, 30–31, 94n57, 138, 139

Wade, Peter, 186
Wallerstein, Immanuel, 85, 90n10
www.afromexico.com, 215

Xtotl, Theresa, 72–73, 89n1

Yanga/Yanguicos, 24–27, 29–30, 32, 34, 39

Zacatecas, 147
Zumpango, 78